PROFESSIONAL ISSUES IN IT

BCS, THE CHARTERED INSTITUTE FOR IT

BCS, The Chartered Institute for IT, is committed to making IT good for society. We use the power of our network to bring about positive, tangible change. We champion the global IT profession and the interests of individuals, engaged in that profession, for the benefit of all.

Exchanging IT expertise and knowledge
The Institute fosters links between experts from industry, academia and business to promote new thinking, education and knowledge sharing.

Supporting practitioners
Through continuing professional development and a series of respected IT qualifications, the Institute seeks to promote professional practice tuned to the demands of business. It provides practical support and information services to its members and volunteer communities around the world.

Setting standards and frameworks
The Institute collaborates with government, industry and relevant bodies to establish good working practices, codes of conduct, skills frameworks and common standards. It also offers a range of consultancy services to employers to help them adopt best practice.

Become a member
Over 70,000 people including students, teachers, professionals and practitioners enjoy the benefits of BCS membership. These include access to an international community, invitations to a roster of local and national events, career development tools and a quarterly thought-leadership magazine. Visit www.bcs.org/membership to find out more.

Further information
BCS, The Chartered Institute for IT,
3 Newbridge Square,
Swindon, SN1 1BY, United Kingdom.
T +44 (0) 1793 417 417
(Monday to Friday, 09:00 to 17:00 UK time)
www.bcs.org/contact
http://shop.bcs.org/

PROFESSIONAL ISSUES IN IT
Third edition

Frank Bott and Neil Taylor

bcs
The
Chartered
Institute
for IT

Published by BCS Learning & Development Ltd, a wholly owned subsidiary of BCS, The Chartered Institute for IT, 3 Newbridge Square, Swindon, SN1 1BY, UK.
www.bcs.org

Paperback ISBN: 978-1-78017-5881
PDF ISBN: 978-1-78017-5898
ePUB ISBN: 978-1-78017-5904

Ebook available

British Cataloguing in Publication Data.
A CIP catalogue record for this book is available at the British Library.

Publisher's acknowledgements
Reviewers: Gillian Arnold, Matt Burton, Rob Burleigh, Paul Martynenko, Susan Singleton and Katie Walsh
Publisher: Ian Borthwick
Commissioning editor: Becky Youé
Production manager: Florence Leroy
Project manager: Hazel Bird
Copy-editor: Hazel Bird
Proofreader: Barbara Eastman
Indexer: Sally Roots
Cover design: Alex Wright
Cover image: iStock/mrbfaust
Typeset by Lapiz Digital Services, Chennai, India.

CONTENTS

LIST OF FIGURES AND TABLES

FIGURES

TABLES

ABOUT THE AUTHORS

Frank Bott studied mathematics at Trinity College, Cambridge, where he was awarded the Yeats Prize. After several years working in the university's Computer Laboratory, he joined SPL International and managed large projects in shipbuilding, the electronics industry and the NHS. He was for two years a visiting professor at the University of Missouri. For 10 years he was the head of the Aberystwyth University Department of Computer Science, and he continued to give lectures after his retirement. He has been an active member of BCS, The Chartered Institute for IT, since 1963, which includes being a long-standing member of its Professional Examinations Board as well as a member of other committees. He is an active member of the Mid-Wales branch. He is a Fellow of BCS, a Chartered IT Professional and a Chartered Engineer.

Frank has published extensively in the field of software engineering and professional issues in IT. He also writes on classical music and is joint author of a biography on the Welsh American composer Joseph Parry.

Neil Taylor studied computer science at the University College of Wales, Aberystwyth, which included a year working at the Ordnance Survey. He has worked on research projects in Aberystwyth in topics such as expert systems, diagnosis and failure mode effects analysis. He worked as a software engineer at Augusta Technology Ltd developing bespoke software applications. He later became the marketing director and company secretary at FirstEarth Ltd, a spin-off company that developed and sold software to the automotive industry based on research from Aberystwyth University. Following the sale of FirstEarth, Neil spent a period as an independent software consultant. He then started work at Aberystwyth University, first as a software engineer and now as a lecturer. He has taught topics in software engineering, web and mobile development, and professional issues.

Neil is an active member of BCS, The Chartered Institute for IT, in its Professional Examinations Board and as a member of the Mid-Wales branch. He is also a Senior Fellow of the Higher Education Academy.

ACKNOWLEDGEMENTS

Frank Bott

Special thanks are due to Professor Mike Tedd, my friend and colleague for more years than either he or I would wish to admit. He it was who, in 1986, first encouraged me to put together a lecture course on professional issues in software engineering; he read the complete draft of the first edition of this book and his wise advice and suggestions proved invaluable. The second edition benefited from the advice of colleagues from BCS, both the mid-Wales branch and the Professional Examinations Board, for which I am most grateful. Over the years, Dr Fred Long has drawn my attention to many reports of incidents relevant to the topics covered here and the fruits of the ensuing discussions can be found throughout the text. The faults that remain are, of course, entirely my responsibility.

Finally, I would like to thank my wife for her patience, forbearance, love and support, not only during the period that this book was being written, but throughout our years together.

Neil Taylor

Special thanks are due to Frank Bott, who kindly asked me to join him in producing this third edition of the book. Frank has encouraged me since I first met him in the Computer Science department at Aberystwyth University. I very much appreciate the guidance and professional advice. I would also like to thank Chris Price, who had the foresight to set up a spin-off company based on research that he led in the university. I learned a lot from working in the company and taking the company through to a sale to another software company. I am most thankful for that opportunity and Chris' support throughout my career. The book has benefited from that experience. My work on this edition has also benefited from working with colleagues in BCS's Professional Examinations Board and Higher Education Qualifications teams, discussions in the Mid-Wales branch and discussions in Aberystwyth University's Computer Science department, for which I am very grateful.

This book would not have been possible without the publishing team at BCS – Ian Borthwick, Becky Youé and Florence Leroy – for their guidance, and including Hazel Bird for detailed editing, spotting possible issues, and asking insightful questions as we edited the text. BCS staff, including Sally Pearce, Sheree Gwilt and Tony Pitchford, helped to clarify issues about areas of BCS's work. The reviewers also helped to check the content and suggest improvements. Thank you to all of them for their valuable support.

I would also like to thank Sarah Todd Taylor for her loving support, cups of tea and encouragement. I hope that I provide similar support as she writes her books.

ABBREVIATIONS

ACAS	Advisory, Conciliation and Arbitration Service
ACM	Association for Computing Machinery
ACS	Australian Computer Society
BCS	BCS, The Chartered Institute for IT
CAN-SPAM Act	Controlling the Assault of Non-solicited Pornography and Marketing Act 2003 (USA)
CEng	Chartered Engineer
CITP	Chartered IT Professional
CMA	Computer Misuse Act 1990
CPD	continuing professional development
DCF	discounted cash flow
DPA 1998	Data Protection Act 1998
DPA 2018	Data Protection Act 2018
EDS	Electronic Data Systems
EEA	European Economic Area
EHRC	Equality and Human Rights Commission
EngTech	Engineering Technician
EPAO	end-point assessment organisation
EPO	European Patent Office
EU	European Union
FMEA	failure mode effects analysis
FOI	freedom of information
FOI Act	Freedom of Information Act 2000
FRC	Financial Reporting Council
GATT	General Agreement on Tariffs and Trade
GDPR	General Data Protection Regulation
HMRC	Her Majesty's Revenue and Customs
HP	Hewlett-Packard
HR	human resources
ICANN	Internet Corporation for Assigned Names and Numbers
ICDL	International Certificate of Digital Literacy

ICO	Information Commissioner's Office
IEEE	Institute of Electrical and Electronics Engineers
IEEE-CS	Institute of Electrical and Electronics Engineers Computer Society
IEEE-USA	Institute of Electrical and Electronics Engineers USA
IEng	Incorporated Engineer
IET	Institution of Engineering and Technology
IRR	internal rate of return
ISP	internet service provider
IT	information technology
IWF	Internet Watch Foundation
KSB	knowledge, skills and behaviours
LLP	limited liability partnership
MBO	management by objectives
NPV	net present value
PAYE	pay as you earn
PECR	Privacy and Electronic Communications (EC Directive) Regulations 2003
PJA	Police and Justice Act 2006
PLC (or plc)	public limited company
PSC	personal service company
RAM	random access memory
RIPA	Regulation of Investigatory Powers Act 2000
RITTech	Registration for IT Technicians
SFIA	Skills Framework for the Information Age
TUPE	Transfer of Undertakings (Protection of Employment)
UDRP	Uniform Domain-Name Dispute-Resolution Policy
UKIPO	UK Intellectual Property Office
URL	uniform resource locator
VAT	value-added tax
W3C	World Wide Web Consortium
WCAG	Web Content Accessibility Guidelines
WIPO	World Intellectual Property Organization

USEFUL WEBSITES

Following are the URLs of many of the websites referred to in the text. In most cases these are the URLs of the home pages, since these are much less likely to change than those of individual pages.

UK government and official bodies

https://www.parliament.uk
This website covers both the House of Commons and the House of Lords. It includes materials placed before Parliament, records of all debates, details of all members and much else.

https://www.legislation.gov.uk
All UK legislation from 1988 to the present can be found on this website, as well as most primary legislation from before that date.

https://www.gov.uk
This general government website includes a great deal of information relating to the law, running a business, the rights of disabled people and many other topics.

https://www.equalityhumanrights.com
The website of the Equality and Human Rights Commission contains much valuable guidance for organisations that need to comply with anti-discrimination legislation.

https://www.ico.org.uk
The website of the Information Commissioner's Office contains useful information relating to data protection and freedom of information, including reports of cases that have been taken to court.

https://www.acas.org.uk
The website of the Advisory, Conciliation and Arbitration Service (ACAS).

https://www.ukri.org/councils/innovate-uk
The website of Innovate UK.

US government sites

https://www.house.gov
The website of the US House of Representatives.

https://www.senate.gov
The website of the US Senate.

Trade associations

https://www.icaew.com/regulation/membership/icaews-guide-to-directors-responsibilities
The Institute of Chartered Accountants in England and Wales has produced a guide to directors' responsibilities.

https://www.sfia-online.org
The website of the SFIA Foundation.

https://www.iwf.org.uk
The website of the Internet Watch Foundation.

https://opensource.org
The website of the Open Source Initiative.

https://www.fsf.org
The website of the Free Software Foundation.

https://www.gnu.org
The website of the Gnu Project.

https://ukbaa.org.uk
The website of the UK Business Angels Association.

https://www.eban.org
The website of the European Business Angels Network.

https://www.wbaforum.org
The website of the World Business Angel Investment Forum.

Professional bodies and international organisations

https://www.bcs.org
The website of BCS, The Chartered Institute for IT.

https://www.theiet.org
The website of the Institution of Engineering and Technology.

https://www.computer.org
The website of the Institute of Electrical and Electronic Engineering Computer Society.

https://www.acm.org
The website of the Association for Computing Machinery.

https://www.ifip.org
The website of the International Federation for Information Processing.

https://www.cepis.org
The website of the Council of European Professional Informatics Societies.

https://www.wipo.int
The website of the World Intellectual Property Organization.

PREFACE

When employers of newly qualified information systems professionals are asked what it is they would most like them to know, the answer is very rarely technical. Much more commonly, the answer is an understanding of the business environment. For this reason, BCS, The Chartered Institute for IT insists that accredited courses contain a significant element of 'professional issues' and, in its own examinations, BCS requires candidates to take a compulsory paper titled Professional Issues in Information Systems Practice. This book has been written as a guide for students taking that paper and it covers the whole syllabus. It is hoped, however, that the book will also prove useful to others, both students on other courses and those who are already embarking on a career in the information systems industry.

It is important for candidates to realise that mere knowledge of the syllabus is not enough, by itself, to pass the paper. Candidates are expected to be able to apply that knowledge to simple scenarios. Failure to do this is one of the commonest reasons for failing the paper. The book includes many such scenarios, some real and some fictitious.

Many of the candidates for the BCS's examinations are from outside the UK. BCS is a British institute and it has to give priority to the situation of the IT professional in the UK. For this reason, the syllabus refers to Acts of the UK Parliament and to the laws of England and Wales (and Scotland where Scottish law differs significantly). However, it is expected that overseas candidates will be concerned with the position in their own countries and, where relevant, this book tries to illustrate how circumstances vary from country to country. (Nowhere is this more evident than when discussing the legal status of professional engineers.) UK candidates should also find it beneficial to learn about the position in other countries.

Despite the existence of some very large and well-known multinational companies, much of the IT industry consists of micro enterprises, with up to nine employees, and small enterprises, with up to 50 employees. Many young entrants to the profession aim to set up such a business of their own. One of the purposes of the Professional Issues module in BCS's diploma examination is therefore to give practical guidance in a range of legal, financial and organisational areas relevant to small IT businesses. This is reflected in many aspects of the book.

A word of warning is needed here. This book tries to explain the central principles and issues in the areas covered, so that you will be aware of areas you need to think about and areas where you need professional advice. The book should give you enough knowledge to talk intelligently to professionals in the fields that it covers. But what the book covers is inevitably introductory and much is omitted. Just as you would not regard an accountant who had read a book on computing and learned to use a spreadsheet and a word processor as competent to design the software for a space shuttle, so you must not regard yourself as a competent lawyer, accountant or other professional on the strength of having studied this book.

The book can be regarded as falling into four main parts:

- Chapters 1 to 4 are concerned with the general context in which professionals work – the law and how it is created, the professions and the nature and structure of commercial organisations.
- Chapters 5 to 8 are concerned very specifically with financial matters – the financing of start-up companies; the nature of financial statements; costing, budgeting and cash flow; and the evaluation of investment proposals.
- Chapters 9 and 10 cover the human aspects of running a company, including human resources and anti-discrimination legislation.
- Chapters 11 to 15 cover more specific legal issues, including software contracts and licences, intellectual property rights, and legislation that affects the way in which computers and the internet are used or misused. Many of these topics are matters of day-to-day concern for most computer users.

There are further reading sections at the end of each chapter. These are intended to:

- enable those who are teaching courses for the examination to deepen and broaden their knowledge so that they can respond to questions and initiate discussion in their classes;
- help students who feel they need to read more in order to get a better understanding of the material;
- provide guidance to readers who need or want to go more deeply into particular topics to satisfy their own professional needs.

Since the first edition of this book, written in 2004, a lot has changed in the industry. There has been the introduction of important new legislation, such as the Equality Act 2010. There have been updates to legislation, such as the Companies Act 2006 and the Investigatory Powers Act 2016.

The UK has left the European Union (EU), in a process widely known as Brexit, leading to the UK creating equivalent legislation that is entirely based on or closely based on EU legislation (e.g. there is now the UK General Data Protection Regulation (GDPR), which is derived from the EU's GDPR). In some cases, the UK has removed some legislation that was created because of the UK's former membership of the EU. This edition updates several chapters with information about the changes that have occurred because of Brexit.

The GDPR (and the UK GDPR) represents a significant update in data protection for EU and UK citizens. The GDPR updates data protection legislation to reflect modern activities on the internet. Chapter 13 discusses the new legislation.

All chapters have been reviewed and updated to reflect the current issues for the IT profession. Other changes include: updated coverage of BCS's activities and how it fulfils its royal charter; coverage of equality, diversity and inclusion and the role they have in improving the provision of IT services; coverage of agency workers and personal service companies; and extended discussion of issues around spam and cookies.

The IT industry and society will continue to change. We hope that this book provides readers with an understanding of the wider issues of the business environment today, and that it helps them to navigate future changes in the delivery of professional IT services.

Frank Bott and Neil Taylor
Aberystwyth
June 2022

1 LAW AND GOVERNMENT

After studying this chapter, you should:

- *understand the nature of the law and the difference between criminal law and civil law;*
- *understand the ways in which law comes into existence;*
- *understand the terms **jurisdiction**, **legislature**, **judiciary** and **executive**, and appreciate the variety of ways in which these concepts are implemented in different countries;*
- *understand why legal issues that cross the boundaries of jurisdictions are complicated.*

1.1 WHAT IS THE LAW?

There are many ways of defining the law. For the purpose of this book, we shall take a very straightforward definition. We shall define law as 'a set of rules that can be enforced in a court'. These rules are different in different countries. The best-known examples of such differences are probably in the rules governing things like divorce or the sale of alcohol. From the point of view of the IT professional, however, differences in the rules governing data protection, the rights of access to information and the misuse of computers are much more significant.

As well as having different laws, different countries have different legal systems – that is, different systems of courts, different rules for court procedure, different procedures for appealing against a court decision and so on. The word **jurisdiction** is used to mean the area covered by a single legal system and set of laws.

Even within a single country, the law and the legal system may be different in different areas. This is most obviously the case in large countries with a federal system of government, where the country is divided into a number of states, each of which can make its own laws in certain areas. Obvious examples are India and the USA.

The term **United Kingdom** (UK), more formally the United Kingdom of Great Britain and Northern Ireland, consists of England, Scotland and Wales (known collectively as Great Britain) together with Northern Ireland. Despite its close connections with the UK, the Isle of Man is not a part of the UK. In some areas the laws of Scotland, Wales and Northern Ireland differ from the laws of England, and Scotland has a different legal system. However, as far as the topics covered in this book are concerned, the laws of the other three countries are, in almost all cases, the same as those of England. When we refer to UK law, we shall be referring to laws that apply across the UK. Sometimes we shall refer to the law of England and Wales, indicating that there are differences elsewhere in the UK. The term **UK law** should never be used in a contract to specify the laws under which the contract should be interpreted. Instead, Scottish law or the laws of England and Wales (or Northern Ireland) should be specified.

1.2 CRIMINAL LAW AND CIVIL LAW

The popular image of the law sees it as the set of mechanisms that tries to punish wrongdoers by fines or imprisonment. This aspect of the law is known as the criminal law. It can be considered to represent society's view of the minimum standard of acceptable behaviour. It defines what constitutes a crime, lays down the mechanisms for deciding whether a person accused of a crime is guilty or innocent, and specifies the range of punishments applicable to different categories of crime.

In general, the police are responsible for discovering who has carried out a specific criminal offence and for collecting evidence that will convince a court that the person in question really did commit the offence. The state, in the form of the Crown Prosecution Service in England and Wales, will then start proceedings by prosecuting the person concerned (who is known as the **accused** or the **defendant**) in a criminal court. The court will decide whether or not the case against the person has been proved and, if it finds the case proved, will sentence the offender to a suitable punishment.

While there are some provisions of the criminal law – those relating to the misuse of computers, for example – that are important in the world of IT and that are dealt with in some detail in this book, we shall be much more occupied with the **civil law**. The purpose of the civil law is to provide rules for settling disputes between people.

Notice that we have referred to disputes between people. Does this mean that the civil law does not apply if one or both sides in a dispute are companies, or organisations of some other kind? It does not mean this, of course, but, in order to overcome the difficulty, we need the idea of a **legal person**. A legal person is an organisation that has gone through a process, called **incorporation**, that gives it the same legal status, so far as the civil law is concerned, as a **natural person** – that is, a human being. There are several different ways in which an organisation can be incorporated. In the UK, an organisation can be incorporated by an Act of Parliament, by registering as a company or by the grant of a royal charter. We shall discuss this process in Chapters 2 and 3.

Court action under the civil law is known as **civil litigation** (so as to distinguish it from criminal litigation). It must be initiated by one of the **parties to the dispute** – that is, by the person, legal or natural, who feels they have been wronged. The person who initiates the court action is known as the **claimant**, although in the USA and some other countries the older term **plaintiff** is still used.

Two important differences between civil law and criminal law in Britain relate to the **standard** of proof and the **burden** of proof.

For a person to be found guilty of a criminal offence, the prosecution must demonstrate that the accused is guilty beyond all reasonable doubt. For claimants to win their case under civil law, they only have to show that their claim is correct on the balance of probabilities. In other words, the standard of proof required in criminal cases is higher than that required in civil cases.

In a criminal case, the burden of proof lies on the prosecution. This means that it is up to the prosecution to prove its case. Defendants do not need to prove their innocence. They are assumed to be innocent until they are proved guilty. In a civil case, on the other hand, both parties present their arguments and must convince the court of their correctness.

1.3 WHERE DOES THE LAW COME FROM?

The two main sources of law in the UK are **common law** and **statute law**. Common law is essentially case law – decisions of judges in the past over the centuries. When deciding the rights and wrongs of a case, a court will look at the way in which similar cases have been decided in the past (by courts of a sufficiently high level); such cases are known as **precedents**.

The common law tradition is shared by many other countries. Almost all the countries of the Commonwealth share the tradition; so, most importantly, does the USA. Although under UK law a judgement of a foreign common law country is not precedent and need not be followed, it is still of persuasive authority and may be considered if the court chooses to do so.

The tradition of common law is not found in the countries of continental Europe, such as France and Germany. Their laws are based entirely on written codes, one for the criminal law and one for the civil law. Those parts of the world that were once colonised by such countries have generally kept such a system of written codes. Confusingly, this system of written codes is often also referred to as civil law. However, in this book, we shall always use the term civil law in the sense described in the previous section – that is, the law used for settling disputes between people.

Statute law is law laid down in Acts of Parliament. It is often referred to as **legislation**. Two hundred years ago, most cases that came to trial would have been tried under the common law. There was comparatively little statute law. Over the past 200 years the position has changed a lot. On the one hand, technical developments and social changes make new laws urgently necessary. Laws to regulate child labour and laws to prevent the misuse of computers are just two examples of Parliament creating new laws for such reasons. On the other hand, in some cases Parliament has passed legislation to bring together the common law in these areas into a single statute. A good example of this is the Theft Act 1968, which consolidated the common law provisions regarding crimes involving stealing. Sometimes common law applies alongside statute law. For example, the common law has traditionally added contractual terms that have not been expressly agreed between the parties when goods are purchased. These terms continue to apply even though there is now sale-of-goods legislation covering the same area.

1.4 THE LEGISLATIVE PROCESS IN THE UK

Like many other democratic countries, the UK has what is known as a **two-chamber** or **bicameral legislature**. This means that the law-making body (the legislature) is made up of two chambers or groups of people.

The UK legislature is known as **Parliament**. One of the chambers is called the **House of Commons**; its members are elected and everyone aged 18 or over has a vote. The country is currently divided into 650 constituencies, each of which elects one Member of Parliament, who is the person who gets the most votes in the election. This is known as the 'first past the post' system.

The other chamber in the UK Parliament is known as the **House of Lords**. At the time of writing (June 2022), the House of Lords has 768 members. Most of these are appointed but 92 of them are chosen, according to some complicated rules, from among the hereditary peers – that is, those who hold inherited titles.

The UK government is made up of members from both the House of Commons and the House of Lords. Members of the House of Lords are never more than a small proportion and the Prime Minister, the Chancellor of the Exchequer, the Foreign Secretary and the Home Secretary are now always members of the House of Commons.

Most new legislation is initiated by the government although it is possible for individual Members of Parliament to initiate legislation in certain circumstances. It is introduced in the form of a **bill**; this is a set of proposals that Parliament is invited to discuss, possibly modify and then approve. The bill is usually introduced first in the House of Commons. It will be discussed and possibly amended there, a process that includes a number of stages. If it is approved by the House of Commons, it is passed to the House of Lords. If the House of Lords approves the bill, it becomes an Act of Parliament. It is then passed to the Queen for her formal approval (**royal assent**), after which it becomes law. (The Queen as a matter of practice does not refuse to give her approval when Parliament has approved a bill.) Acts of Parliament are usually referred to by their title, followed by the year in which they received royal assent (e.g. the Computer Misuse Act 1990).

If the House of Lords rejects a bill or modifies it, the bill is returned to the House of Commons for further consideration. There is a process in both houses involving first, second and third readings of bills, which go back and forth between the House of Commons and House of Lords. The House of Commons has the power to override any changes that have been made by the House of Lords or even to insist that a bill rejected by the House of Lords should, nevertheless, be passed and proceed to receive royal assent. The justification for this is that the House of Commons is democratically elected and so represents the will of the people in a way that the members of the House of Lords, not being elected, cannot do.

In many cases, the government will want to canvass opinion before asking Parliament to approve legislation. It may publish a **green paper**, which typically explains why the government wants to create new laws in a certain area and discusses a number of possible approaches. The green paper will be discussed by Parliament and comments on it will be invited from the public and from bodies that have an interest in the area. Thus, BCS, The Chartered Institute for IT, along with many other bodies, was specifically asked for its views when the question of legislation to address the problem of computer misuse was raised.

Once the government has decided on its general approach, it may publish a **white paper**, which describes the proposed legislation and is used as the basis for discussing and possibly modifying the details of what is proposed. At the end of this process the government will take into account these discussions and produce a bill. In some cases no green and white papers are produced (e.g. this was the case before the Coronavirus Act 2020 was published as a bill in 2020).

Acts of Parliament constitute what is known as **primary legislation**. The complexity of modern society makes it impossible for all laws to be examined in detail by Parliament. To overcome this difficulty, an Act of Parliament will often make provision for **secondary legislation** to be introduced. This means that detailed regulations can be introduced without full discussion in Parliament. Instead, the proposed regulations are placed in the library of the House of Commons so that members of either house can look at them. If no objections are raised within a fixed time period, the regulations become law. An example of secondary legislation in the computer field is the regulations that were produced to apply the Copyright, Designs and Patents Act 1988 to protect the design of semiconductor chips.

In addition to the UK national parliament, there are separate elected assemblies in Scotland, Wales and Northern Ireland. These have considerable powers in some areas but they do not, on the whole, affect the topics covered in this book.

1.5 THE EUROPEAN UNION

The European Union (EU) is a grouping of, currently, 27 European countries that are working towards a high level of economic and social integration involving the harmonisation of many of their laws. The UK joined the EU on 1 January 1973, while a Conservative government was in power. In the general election of October 1974, a Labour government came to power. Many members of the government and many Labour supporters were opposed to the UK's membership of the EU and a national referendum on whether the UK should remain in the EU was held in June 1975. The result was an overwhelming 67.23% of the votes in favour of remaining. A similar referendum in 2016, however, led to a vote of 51.89% in favour of the UK leaving the EU. Lengthy negotiations were necessary to settle the conditions of **Brexit**, the UK's exit from the EU, and the UK finally left the EU on 31 January 2020.

The EU legislature consists of three bodies: the European Parliament, the Council of Ministers (more formally, the Council of the European Union) and the European Commission. EU legislation is initiated by the European Commission but it must be approved first by the Council of Ministers and then by the European Parliament. The European Parliament is directly elected by voters in the member states, using proportional representation. At the time of writing, the European Parliament has 705 members. The Council of Ministers consists of 27 national ministers, one from each member state. Which ministers attend depends on the topic under discussion; thus, for example, when matters relating to agriculture or fishing are to be considered, the

Council of Ministers will consist of the minister with responsibility for this area in each of the 27 countries.

The EU has the legal power to issue **regulations**. These are directly applicable as law in all EU member states. This meant that, so long as the UK remained in the EU, these regulations applied automatically in the UK, without any further action required by the UK Parliament. Such regulations are proposed by the European Commission and must be approved by the European Parliament and the Council of Ministers. An important example of such legislation from the point of view of information systems professionals is the General Data Protection Regulation (GDPR), which was issued in April 2016 and came into force on 26 May 2018. It is discussed in more detail in Chapter 13.

The EU also issues **directives**. These require that member states modify their own legislation, if necessary, to meet a common standard. Like regulations, directives are proposed by the European Commission and must be approved by the European Parliament and the Council of Ministers. For example, the Electronic Commerce Directive, issued in 2000, provides, among many other things, rules governing the liability of internet service providers in respect of material that is transmitted using their services. The directive was implemented in the UK by secondary legislation, namely the Electronic Commerce (EC Directive) Regulations 2002.

When the UK left the EU, all EU directives remained in effect because they were implemented through parliamentary legislation. In addition, the UK issued at least 1,000 new statutory instruments to make it clear, sector by sector, that the existing UK legislation based on EU legislation would continue to apply. The UK Parliament is, of course, now free to amend or repeal this legislation at its leisure. EU regulations, however, have ceased to have any legal standing except (as is commonly the case) where the Brexit statutory instruments say otherwise. An example of such a statutory instrument is the Electronic Commerce (Amendment etc.) (EU Exit) Regulations 2019, which amended electronic commerce law. There were very many such regulations, the bulk of which the UK has kept. Complicated and contentious parliamentary legislation was necessary to handle the situation. For example, the UK has amended the GDPR into an amended version for the UK known as the UK GDPR, which, along with the Data Protection Act 2018, has applied in the UK since 1 January 2021 instead of the GDPR, which applies in the 27 EU member states.

1.6 THE LEGISLATIVE PROCESS IN OTHER COUNTRIES

Although this book is concerned primarily with the UK, the influence and power of the USA in the world of IT is so great that IT professionals need to know something of how government in the USA works.

In the USA, the legislature is known as Congress. It consists of two houses, the Senate and the House of Representatives. Both houses are elected but on very different terms. Members of the House of Representatives are elected for a period of two years. Each member represents a district and each district contains (roughly) the same number of people. The Senate contains two members (senators) for each state; this means that California, with a population of around 40 million, has the same representation in the

Senate as Wyoming, whose population is less than 600,000. Senators are elected for seven years.

Legislation must be approved by both the Senate and the House of Representatives before it can become law; neither chamber can override the other. Furthermore, the president must also give their assent before an Act of Congress becomes law. Unlike the Queen, who cannot withhold her assent to legislation passed by Parliament, the president is allowed to veto legislation passed by Congress and this regularly happens. As in other countries with a written constitution, there is also a Supreme Court, which can strike out legislation approved by Congress and the president on the grounds that it is unconstitutional. As we shall see in Chapter 14, this has happened with legislation concerned with pornography on the internet. This is in contrast to the situation in the UK, where the doctrine of the **sovereignty of Parliament** means that the courts cannot override primary legislation made by Parliament, although they can override secondary legislation.

The members of the government of the USA are not members of Congress. The president is, in practice though not in theory, directly elected by the people. The members of the government are individuals chosen by the president and their appointment must be approved by Congress. The founders of the USA believed that it was very important to separate three functions:

- the **legislature** – that is, Congress, which makes laws;
- the **judiciary** – that is, the judges and other legal officials, who apply and enforce these laws in particular cases;
- the **executive** – that is, the president and the other members of the government, which carry on the actual business of government.

The separation of these functions is recognised in many other countries. Historically, they have not been separated in the UK but recent reforms, embodied in the Constitutional Reform Act 2005, have moved the UK much further in this direction. For example, the UK's highest court, the Appellate Committee of the House of Lords, was replaced in 2009 by the newly named and constituted Supreme Court.

The legislative situation in the USA is made more complicated by the fact that the country is a federation of 50 states. Each state has its own legislature, most of them modelled on the federal legislature, and its own government. On some topics each state can make its own laws but in other areas the law is made at the federal level. For example, as we shall see in the next chapter, each state has its own laws regarding who can call themselves an engineer. The issue of states' rights – that is, the extent to which federal law can override laws made by individual states – has been a live political issue throughout the existence of the USA and remains so today. This has led the federal Supreme Court to declare unconstitutional some laws passed by individual states to regulate use of the internet. This issue of states' rights also arises in other countries with a federal constitution, such as Australia and India.

Smaller countries such as Mauritius, Singapore and Sri Lanka often have a **unicameral** legislature – that is, a parliament that consists of a single chamber. Where there is a historical connection with Britain, much of the legislation may be based on British legislation, as a way of avoiding the expense of law-making on a large scale.

1.7 THE LAW ACROSS BORDERS

What are the geographical limits of the jurisdiction of a country's courts? The immediate reaction is likely to be that a country's courts can only deal with crimes committed within the country's boundaries. This is not in fact true. Most countries would claim that their courts have the power, for example, to deal with a spy who passed on secrets to an enemy country, even if the passing on of the secrets took place on foreign soil. Many countries, including the UK, have legislation intended to combat sex tourism – that is, legislation that enables criminal charges to be brought in their courts against their citizens who have abused children in foreign countries even where it may not be illegal to do so in those countries.

The development of the web and other innovations in the field of telecommunications have, however, created further problems. The very notion of the place where a crime is committed has become hard to ascertain. If a hacker sitting in an apartment in New York hacks into a European air traffic control computer located in the Netherlands so as to cause a mid-air collision over Denmark, where was the crime committed and which country's laws and legal procedures should be used in prosecuting the crime? What happens about an action that is criminal in some of the countries it affects but not in others – publishing obscene material over the internet, for example? The rapid growth of remote working during the Covid-19 pandemic raises more mundane questions: if a programmer resident in India works remotely for a British company, does the programmer require a British work permit and which country's employment laws apply?

Closely related to these questions is the issue of extradition. Under what circumstances can a person be extradited – that is, sent from one country to another in order to face trial for an alleged offence?

Some recent cases have turned these questions into very live issues and we shall have more to say about them in later chapters. However, they are immensely complex questions and anything like a complete answer is well beyond the scope of this book.

Jurisdiction in civil cases that cross borders is also complicated by a few countries having legislation relating to this area but others not. Where a civil claimant has a choice of jurisdiction, where to start the proceedings may depend very much on the circumstances of the case but may well also be influenced by the reputation of a country's courts and how favourable its laws will be to the claimant's case.

FURTHER READING

Until the coming of the World Wide Web in the 1990s, it was difficult to get information about the legislation and the legislative process in countries other than the one in which you were living. It meant going to specialist libraries or to the embassies of the countries concerned. The development of the web has changed all this and, for many countries, such material is easily available on websites, although the quality is variable.

The following website explains how the legislative process works in the UK:
https://www.parliament.uk

The following website contains the texts of all Acts of the UK Parliament that are still current, and of the legislation created by the Scottish Parliament, the Welsh Parliament and the Northern Ireland Assembly:
https://www.legislation.gov.uk

Reports of all parliamentary debates, including transcripts of all speeches, can be found at:
https://hansard.parliament.uk

The following sites explain the functioning of the House of Representatives and the Senate in the USA:
https://www.house.gov
https://www.senate.gov

Most of the individual states have similar sites describing the legislative process in the state and, in many cases, most of the statutes of the state are available on the web.

2 THE COMPUTING PROFESSION

After studying this chapter, you should:

- *understand what is meant by the terms **profession** and **professional**, and be aware of the main professional bodies in the field of IT;*
- *be familiar with the BCS Code of Conduct and understand the obligations that it imposes on members;*
- *understand the concepts of **reservation of title** and **reservation of function** in the context of professional responsibility for public safety.*

2.1 THE CONCEPT OF A PROFESSION

Words like **profession** and **professional** are used in many different ways. Professional footballers are footballers who make their living from the game. Professional employees are employees of a certain status, who are expected, within limits, to put the interests of the organisation they work for above their own convenience. Describing someone as a real professional implies that they can be relied on to carry out their work competently and conscientiously regardless of the circumstances. A professional piece of work means a piece of work that meets established standards of quality. However, the terms can also have negative overtones – for example, professional fouls are fouls committed deliberately by professional footballers who calculate that, on the balance of probabilities, the outcome will be in their favour.

There is no single definition of a profession. The meaning of the word depends on who is using it and what the context is. However, if we look at a range of occupations that would commonly be described as professions – lawyers, doctors, dentists, accountants, veterinary surgeons, architects and so on – we see that there are common characteristics:

- Substantial accredited education and training are required in order to practise the profession.
- The members of the profession themselves decide the nature of this training and, more generally, control entry to the profession.
- The profession is organised into one or more professional bodies.
- Members of the profession are expected to conduct their professional activities in accordance with codes of conduct laid down by the professional bodies and enforced by them.

Many, but by no means all, professions also enjoy a sort of monopoly: the use of a certain title (e.g. architect) or the carrying out of certain functions (e.g. dentistry) – or both – may be restricted by Act of Parliament to members of certain professional bodies. We shall discuss this in more detail later in this chapter (see Section 2.9).

A professional body usually starts by a group of people coming together because of a shared interest in a particular type of activity. There are many professional bodies in the UK and they cover a wide range of professions, including the law, medicine, many different branches of science and engineering, accountancy, architecture and surveying. BCS was set up in 1957 as the British Computer Society by a group of people working in the new and expanding field of computers who wanted the opportunity to exchange ideas. It currently has over 70,000 members. The Institution of Engineering and Technology (IET) is the other main body in the UK that includes information technologists among its members. It was formed in 2006 by a merger of the Institution of Electrical Engineers, which was set up in 1871 by people with an interest in the developing field of electrical engineering, and the Institution of Incorporated Engineers. It covers electrical engineering, electronic engineering and a number of other fields in addition to IT, and has a membership of around 158,000. BCS and the IET have members in approximately 150 countries.

Although the role of professional bodies in the USA is somewhat different from their role in the UK, there are two professional computing bodies based in the USA that are significantly important worldwide. The Institute of Electrical and Electronics Engineers (IEEE) is a professional engineering society based in the USA but with members and activities spread across the world. It was under the aegis of the IEEE that the first professional society in the field of computing was founded in 1946. This was the IEEE Computer Society (IEEE-CS); today it has approximately 373,000 members. This was closely followed by the Association for Computing Machinery, universally known as the ACM. This was founded in 1947 and now has approximately 100,000 members. Like the IEEE-CS, it is primarily a US organisation, but it has members and activities in many countries.

2.2 ROYAL CHARTERS

In the UK, any organisation that believes its main objectives are in the public interest can enter into discussions with the Privy Council with a view to being awarded a **royal charter**. A royal charter is a formal document, written in rather quaint language and signed by the monarch, which establishes the organisation and lays down its purpose and rules of operation. As they grow into mature organisations, many UK professional bodies seek and obtain a royal charter.

BCS was awarded its royal charter in 1984. The Institution of Electrical Engineers was awarded its first charter in 1921 and the IET received its charter in 2008, shortly after the merger.

The charter of BCS sets out very clearly the purpose of the institution:

> to promote the study and practice of Computing and to advance knowledge and education therein for the benefit of the public.

There follows a lengthy list of things that the institution is authorised to do in order to fulfil its purpose. Of interest here, the most important of these can be summarised as follows:

- establishing a code of conduct to regulate the way members of the body behave in their professional lives and a disciplinary procedure to hold members who breach this code to account;
- promoting education in the field of computing;
- setting standards of education and experience that must be met by people wishing to become members of the body;
- establishing mechanisms for disseminating knowledge of good practice and new developments to members, typically through publications and conferences and through the use of the internet;
- promoting and supporting standards and codes of practice;
- advising government and regulatory bodies about matters within its area of expertise.

In the following sections we shall look at the ways that BCS addresses some of these.

2.3 PROFESSIONAL CONDUCT

BCS's Charter specifically requires BCS to 'establish and maintain a sound ethical foundation for the use of computers'. All professional bodies are under a similar obligation; this, indeed, is one of the most important characteristics of a professional body. It is normally done by laying down a **code of conduct** to which members are required to adhere. A code of conduct sets out the standards of behaviour that members of the body are expected to follow in their professional life. Sometimes the code is called a code of ethics. It looks outwards, in the sense that it is concerned with the relationship between members and society as a whole. Although all codes of conduct have much in common, they also have significant differences, if only because the natures of the activities of different professions place different temptations in the paths of their practitioners.

Codes of conduct should not be confused with **codes of practice**, which are concerned with the way in which professional activities should be carried out.

BCS's Code of Conduct is divided into the following sections (please consult the BCS website for the latest version at https://www.bcs.org/media/2211/bcs-code-of-conduct.pdf):

- The Public Interest
- Professional Competence and Integrity
- Duty to Relevant Authority
- Duty to the Profession

2.3.1 The Public Interest

This section requires members to be aware of and comply with aspects of the law and regulations that govern acting in the public interest. For example, members need to safeguard public health, protect the environment, have due regard for privacy and human rights, and avoid discrimination.

Some of these elements can cause problems for members working for clients or companies in countries whose governments practise or encourage systematic discrimination on, for example, the grounds of race, religion or sexual orientation. Information systems developed in such countries may have such discrimination embedded in their design and the effect of this clause is to forbid members of BCS from working on such systems.

The section is also concerned with the rights of third parties as well as copyright and intellectual property. These topics are discussed in detail in Chapter 11.

Finally, the section invites members to promote equal access to the benefits of IT and seek to promote the inclusion of all sectors in society wherever opportunities arise. This could include, for example, helping to ensure that IT systems can be used by disabled people or helping to develop IT skills in groups of people who do not have them.

Although many areas of society rely on IT, there is a portion of UK society that does not have the IT skills or technology to engage with the digital world. This is referred to as the 'digital divide' or 'digital exclusion'. In 2019 the UK's Office for National Statistics produced the report *Exploring the UK's Digital Divide*, which showed that about 10% of UK adults in 2018 did not use the internet or had not used it in the previous three months. This number has declined from approximately 20% in 2011.[1] The continued decrease is encouraging, but this still means that up to 5 million people do not have easy access to digital resources. BCS and its members have the opportunity to help reduce this divide – for example, by members considering initiatives that can help more users access digital services.

2.3.2 Professional Competence and Integrity

Under this section, members are required to keep their professional skills up to date and be familiar with the legislation that is relevant to the professional activities in which they are engaged. Thus, web developers building an e-commerce site for a retail company are required to be conversant with legislation such as the Consumer Contracts (Information, Cancellation and Additional Charges) Regulations 2013 (see Chapter 14). A software engineer working on a railway signalling system would not be expected to be familiar with those regulations but should be familiar with the regulations laid down by the Rail Safety and Standards Board.

There have been instances where companies have claimed to be able to undertake work that they did not have the skills to complete. There is an example from the 1990s

---

1 *Exploring the UK's Digital Divide*, Office for National Statistics (2019), https://www.ons.gov.uk/ peoplepopulationandcommunity/householdcharacteristics/homeinternetandsocialmediausage/articles/ exploringtheuksdigitaldivide/2019-03-04.

involving a failure of the London Ambulance Service's Computer Aided Dispatch System (see Further Reading section). Part of the problem was that a small software company that built the system had claimed expertise that it did not have. It was not deliberate deception, but the company failed to recognise that building the system required skills that it did not have.

This section of the code will help to limit such problems in systems developed today. In addition to undertaking training and showing respect for others, this section of the code requires that members take account of their experience before becoming involved in a system. It is incumbent on members to assess potential issues and to be open about areas where they do not have the skills and experience to create a system.

2.3.3 Duty to Relevant Authority

This section starts by saying that members must:

> carry out your professional duties with due care and diligence in accordance with the Relevant Authority's requirements while exercising your professional judgement at all times.[2]

'Due care and diligence' is what society has the right to demand of any professional. The term **Relevant Authority** means the person or organisation that has authority over what you are doing. If you are employed by an organisation, this is likely to be your employer; if you are an independent consultant, it will be your client; and if you are a student, it will be your school, college or university. In some cases, there may be several relevant authorities; for example, if you are a part-time student who is also employed part time, then the relevant authority as far as your work as a student is concerned will be your school or college but the relevant authority in your employment will be your employer.

According to this section, behaving professionally towards relevant authorities means, in particular, avoiding the following:

- **Conflicts of interest:** These are situations in which there are incentives that might encourage you to do things or take decisions that are not in the best interests of your relevant authority. For example, let's say that you have been asked by your employer to recommend a payroll package for your company. It happens that your sister works in the sales section of a company that supplies a package that you would consider recommending. In such circumstances, you should explain the situation to your employer as it might be better to ask someone else to recommend a suitable package.

- **Disclosing confidential information without permission:** Confidential information may include technical information about a company's products, its financial position, sales leads and so on. (The law relating to confidential information is covered in more detail in Chapter 11.)

---

2 'BCS Code of Conduct' (n.d.), BCS, https://www.bcs.org/media/2211/bcs-code-of-conduct.pdf.

- **Misrepresentation or withholding information:** IT professionals often work with people or sell systems to people who have a limited understanding of the implications of the IT tools and applications. The code requires that professionals do not take advantage of people's inexperience. Therefore, professionals should be careful that they do not misrepresent or withhold information about the performance of systems.

2.3.4 Duty to the Profession

The purpose of this section of the code is to impress on members what is expected of them in order to uphold the reputation and good standing of BCS in particular, and the profession in general.

In this section, there is the duty to support colleagues and help them to develop their skills. In the section Duty to Relevant Authority, there is the need to take responsibility for those that you are managing, which in part is about helping to guide their development.

The code is divided into sections, but it is the code as a whole, with some overlapping items in the sections, that provides the professional guidance for BCS members.

2.3.5 Status of professional codes of conduct

Like most professional bodies, BCS has procedures that allow it to take disciplinary action against members who infringe its code, with expulsion as the ultimate sanction. Where membership of the professional body confers a licence to practise – as in the case of the Law Society, for example – this is a very serious punishment, since expulsion deprives expelled members of the right to earn their living in their chosen profession. Even in the case of BCS, expulsion or other sanctions, although not directly affecting a member's ability to earn a living, could certainly affect their professional standing. A member who has been subject to disciplinary action can thus take the matter to the civil courts, which will expect the disciplinary proceedings to have been conducted in accordance with the rules of natural justice (in essence, the right to defend oneself against an accusation and the knowledge of what the accusation is).

Codes of conduct may contain some very clear rules and some rules that could be open to interpretation. Clause (d) in the Duty to Relevant Authority section of the BCS Code of Conduct is an example of a very clear rule. It states:

You shall ... NOT disclose or authorise to be disclosed, or use for personal gain or to benefit a third party, confidential information except with the permission of your Relevant Authority, or as required by Legislation.

This is quite clear. There is little doubt about what it means and, in any specific case, it should be clear whether a member has complied with this rule. There is no difficulty in taking action against a member who has broken this rule.

The first clause of the Public Interest section, on the other hand, could be open to interpretation. It states:

> You shall ... have due regard for public health, privacy, security and wellbeing of others and the environment.

While no one should quarrel with this, there may not be general agreement as to whether a particular IT development is, or is not, consistent with improvement in public health, safety and the environment. Some people, for example, could interpret that any work carried out for the nuclear industry is detrimental to public health, safety and the environment. Others could argue that the use of nuclear power stations to generate electricity is beneficial to the environment because it avoids carbon dioxide emissions. So it would be unreasonable for BCS to take disciplinary action against members working in the nuclear industry, even though other members might feel passionately that such work is dangerous to health, safety and the environment.

2.4 EDUCATION

BCS promotes education in several ways:

- It runs its own system of professional examinations and grants approval to suitable organisations that provide courses to prepare students for them.
- It accredits degree programmes offered by universities and other institutions of higher education.
- It designs and franchises short courses leading to qualifications in specific areas.
- It provides support for IT apprenticeships by supporting training providers and facilitating assessment of the apprenticeship standards.

2.4.1 Higher education

BCS offers examinations to students in higher education. These consist of three stages: the **Certificate**, the **Diploma** and the **Professional Graduate Diploma**. As well as the normal written examinations, the Diploma and Professional Graduate Diploma levels require the submission of projects. The Professional Graduate Diploma with a project is considered to be the equivalent of an honours degree.

A few other computer societies operate examination schemes. For several years, the Australian Computer Society (ACS) has operated its own system of examinations. These are somewhat comparable with the BCS Certificate and Diploma examinations, without the project, but the ACS course includes a short internship. The IEEE-CS has a Software Professional Certification programme, which provides certification of various development skills. Registration typically requires a previous qualification in an appropriate degree and a number of years of professional experience. The certification is tested through online exams that are somewhat comparable to the BCS Certificate examinations.

2.4.2 Accreditation

The term **accreditation** is used with a confusing variety of related meanings. In the present context, it refers to the process by which a professional body recognises specific academic programmes made by specific institutions of higher education as satisfying, fully or partially, the educational base for registration as a Chartered IT Professional (CITP). Programmes that are recognised in this way are referred to as accredited courses. It is in this sense that the term is used by a range of professional bodies in such fields as medicine, law, engineering and science.

The BCS's accreditation guidelines expect that the degree programmes will be kept up to date with relevant computing content, learning resources and academic guidance provided to the students. External experts, typically from industry, will be involved in the review of programmes in the department. There will be defined quality assurance processes in the department and in the institution, including the involvement of external examiners to inspect the quality processes and assessment of the students. The programme design, review, learning outcomes and quality assurance processes will take account of the appropriate computing benchmark document. It should be possible to show how the programmes help the students to obtain relevant skills that are defined in the appropriate benchmark.

BCS asks course providers to give evidence about how the programmes meet the accreditation guidelines. The evidence is provided to the BCS accreditation panel through a documentary submission. There is also a visit by the panel during which there are meetings with both staff and students. Assuming that the requirements for accreditation are satisfied, accreditation of a course is normally granted for a five-year period.

Part of the CITP application process considers the breadth of knowledge of each candidate. If the accredited award provides full accreditation, the award is used as the evidence for that knowledge. If the accredited award provides partial accreditation, holders of the award will be expected to provide written evidence of their breadth of knowledge. Further, there is an online interview as part of the CITP application process. The interview includes a discussion of the applicant's breadth of knowledge. BCS accreditation may also in suitable cases fully or partially satisfy the educational base for registration as a Chartered or Incorporated Engineer.

2.4.3 Professional certifications

BCS offers a substantial range of qualifications, known as certificates, that are achievable through short courses. The courses are intended as training for staff working in the industry. Typically, they last around 40 hours. BCS designs the syllabus for each course, accredits training organisations that wish to run courses, and sets and marks the examinations.

Courses are available in a wide range of topics, including business analysis, artificial intelligence, agile development, information security, data protection, project and programme management, user experience and software testing.

At the level of the computer user rather than the systems developer, BCS manages and promotes digital literacy qualifications for beginners and those at an intermediate level of knowledge. The Essential Digital Skills Qualification for Work course is free and aimed at helping people to obtain the basic IT skills that are expected by most employers. The International Certificate of Digital Literacy (ICDL) provides intermediate-level skills in a set of common computer applications used in the workplace. BCS also runs the Level 3 Certificate in IT User Skills, which is an advanced level of the ICDL. These courses help people gain IT qualifications that improve their career prospects.

2.4.4 Apprenticeships

BCS provides support for IT apprenticeships, which offer people the ability to work in industry and train at the same time. As well as real work experience, the apprenticeships provide an industry-recognised qualification. Companies can use the apprenticeships as one way to recruit new staff members. Apprenticeships can also be used by organisations to provide training and continuing professional development (CPD) for existing employees.

Companies that decide to recruit apprentices will normally work with a training provider. A training provider can be a further education college or an independent training provider – or, in some situations, the company itself can run the training. The provider can help with the recruitment. It will also work with the company to provide the appropriate training for apprentices.

The provider is responsible for the off-the-job training and development of the apprentice as described by the knowledge, skills and behaviours (often known as KSBs) in the apprenticeship standard. For the remaining 80% of the time, the employer is responsible for supporting the apprentice with their on-the-job training and managing them as they would any other employee. This includes giving the apprentice the opportunity to apply their skills in a variety of settings to enable them to meet the requirements of the standard.

BCS's role is to be an end-point assessment organisation (EPAO), which provides support materials and runs assessments of the apprenticeship standards. These are not BCS qualifications; however, as an EPAO, BCS can run assessments of apprentices' competency. Following an assessment, BCS provides the grade for each candidate and the award is made by the Institute for Apprenticeships and Technical Education. BCS also promotes the use of apprenticeships in industry, focusing on the IT sector.

2.5 THE ADVANCEMENT OF KNOWLEDGE

BCS's royal charter specifically states that one of its objects is to advance knowledge of computing. Many other professional bodies include this among their objectives. In practice, however, much of the research that contributes to the advancement of knowledge takes place in universities and in research establishments, both public and private. As a result, professional bodies tend to be more concerned with the dissemination of knowledge, through their publications, conferences that they organise or sponsor, and various other activities.

One of the first actions of BCS when it was formed (as the British Computer Society) was to establish **The Computer Journal**. The first issue was published in 1958 and the journal has been published regularly ever since. Currently, there are 12 issues a year. The journal carries articles that present the results of research carried out in industry, in research establishments and in universities all over the world. There are four sections: Computer Science Theory, Communications Networks, Computational Intelligence and Security. The IET publishes several journals covering various topics in IT, including **IET Software**, which concentrates on new developments in software engineering, and **IET Networks**.

Most of the articles in *The Computer Journal* and the IET journals are targeted at specialists. For information systems professionals who are not engaged in research and development, the three most useful publications are possibly **Computer** (the flagship publication of the IEEE-CS), **IEEE Software** and **Communications of the ACM**. These contain authoritative articles on new developments and current issues written for practising professionals.

BCS also supports a considerable number of specialist groups. These groups bring together people with interests in specific areas. They cover a wide range of specialist topics, from artificial intelligence to software testing and from human–computer interaction to law. They are particularly effective in spreading knowledge of good practice because they bring together practitioners from different organisations, all working in the same field, who learn from each other. Many specialist groups have gone on to develop an extensive range of resources, from books and reports to special software, to disseminate knowledge about their specialist topic.

This book is an example of another aspect of advancing knowledge. BCS publishes a range of books on current topics in the IT industry (https://shop.bcs.org). The varied list of topics includes project management, business analysis, testing and quality assurance, artificial intelligence, cybersecurity, digital services and legal issues. The books provide a way for BCS to provide detailed content on topics as printed and electronic resources, which can also support BCS's education objective.

2.6 CONTINUING PROFESSIONAL DEVELOPMENT

For many years, little attention was given to how professionals kept their knowledge up to date after qualifying. Thus, it was possible for a doctor, a dentist or a solicitor to practise for 40 years without any formal requirement to update their knowledge. Of course, most professionals were aware of the need to do this and would take whatever opportunities were available. Nevertheless, these opportunities might not have been readily available and the pressures of day-to-day work might have made it difficult for busy professionals to take advantage of them.

The increasing rate at which new knowledge was becoming available and existing knowledge was being used in new ways led, in the 1970s, to increasing concern that professionals should keep their qualifications up to date. This process became known as CPD. It can be defined as the systematic maintenance and improvement of professional knowledge and skills throughout an individual's professional working life. In some professions there is a mandatory requirement to do CPD to maintain a permission to practice. For example, a vet registered through the Royal College of Veterinary Surgeons must report a minimum of 35 hours of CPD per year through an online tool.

2.6.1 CPD services to individual members

In common with other professional bodies, BCS supports CPD both by providing a formal structure through which it can be recorded and assessed, and by providing some means by which it can be achieved. For example, all members of BCS receive a copy of its quarterly publication **ITNOW**, which helps to keep them aware of new developments and current topics of interest to the profession. Additionally, BCS provides its members with many opportunities for CPD through its branches and specialist groups. These provide ways for members to meet to share experiences, talk about common problems and listen to talks about new developments both technical and professional.

Although CPD serves to encourage professionals to keep their expertise up to date, there is a real danger that the knowledge and experience that qualified a member for a professional grade within BCS may atrophy if they are not used. Accordingly, BCS offers a service to allow CITPs to revalidate their skills every five years so that they can demonstrate to employers that they have maintained these skills and are currently competent.

2.6.2 Career development and CPD services to the industry

For many years, employers faced problems managing IT staff. The chronic shortage of qualified and experienced staff together with the rapid pace of change made the problems particularly acute for large user organisations. Such organisations were faced with the problem of where to place IT specialists in their staffing structures. Because of their scarcity, such staff could command high salaries but, elsewhere in the organisation, such salaries would be associated with substantial managerial responsibility. IT staff were different and needed to be treated differently.

BCS started to tackle this problem in the mid-1980s with the development of the Industry Structure Model – now SFIAplus, an enhanced model based on the Skills Framework for the Information Age (SFIA). The SFIA is a common reference model for the identification of IT skills that was developed by the SFIA Foundation. The SFIA Foundation is a not-for-profit organisation set up to manage the development of the SFIA. The SFIA is currently at version 8 and it is typically updated every three years to reflect changes in skills in the industry.

Organisations can use the model in various ways. A common way is to help organisations define roles and the skills for those roles at different levels of responsibility (see the box below). It can be used in other ways, such as identifying skills gaps and training opportunities, and identifying the roles and skills needed during workforce planning. The model saves organisations some of the work in creating relevant descriptions, although there is work needed to decide how to use the model in a particular organisation.

Such a model means that a large employer has a systematic way of structuring IT roles and is therefore in a much better position to address the problems referred to above. BCS also uses the SFIA to highlight skills attained through its professional examinations and skills needed for chartered status.

SFIA responsibilities, attributes and skills

The SFIA has three key elements.

Seven levels of responsibility

Each level is labelled with a word or phrase to summarise the responsibility. These are from Level 7, the highest, to Level 1:

- **Level 7**: Set strategy, inspire and mobilise
- **Level 6**: Initiate, influence
- **Level 5**: Ensure, advise
- **Level 4**: Enable
- **Level 3**: Apply
- **Level 2**: Assist
- **Level 1**: Follow

Five generic attributes

These are Autonomy, Influence, Complexity, Business Skills and Knowledge. For each level of responsibility, there are descriptions of each attribute. For a Level 1 responsibility, a person has little autonomy and works under close supervision. For a Level 7 responsibility, a person has authority over work done and is fully accountable for actions taken.

Over 120 professional skills

There is a wide variety of skills, which represent the range of skills needed in different parts of the IT sector. Example skills are Information Security, Governance, Software Design, Testing, Data Engineering, IT Infrastructure and Sales Support. For each skill, there is (i) a short description of the skill, (ii) some guidance notes that describe typical activities and (iii) a description of the skill for each of the relevant levels of responsibility.

Some skills are practised at most levels of responsibility and other skills are practised at just a few levels of responsibility. For example, Software Design has descriptions for Levels 2 to 6, as it is practised at several levels of responsibility. However, Governance has descriptions for Levels 6 and 7, as it is only practised at the highest levels of responsibility.

The responsibilities, generic attributes and professional skills work together to define a specific competence. For example, a combination of Level 5, Autonomy and a Testing skill would provide a description of what is expected for the skill at the higher-level responsibility, and what that means regarding how much autonomy is expected.

2.7 REPRESENTING THE PROFESSION

Professional bodies are widely regarded as the source of the most authoritative advice on their disciplines. It is normal, therefore, for them to be consulted by the government about changes in the law as it affects the discipline or is affected by it. This consultation may extend over a period of several years, as happened, for example, when BCS was consulted over the European Union Data Protection Directive 1995 and the Data Protection Act 1998. As well as such official consultation, professional bodies are regularly invited to talk to groups of Members of Parliament who are interested in their disciplines.

Professional engineering bodies are also routinely asked by standardisation bodies, such as the American National Standards Institute or the British Standards Institution, to nominate members of committees that will develop standards in the field. Indeed, the IEEE itself runs the standards-making process in the area of local-area networks through its Project 802.

Individual BCS members can influence and shape policy by playing an active part in discussions and contributing to consultations of government and other bodies on a wide range of professional, economic and societal issues.

2.8 MEMBERSHIP GRADES

BCS has three major membership categories: standard grades, professional grades and CITP status. Membership at the professional grades requires a degree-level qualification in IT or an equivalent level of experience. CITP status is available to professional members who demonstrate that they meet additional requirements around skills and experience.

The criteria for membership of the professional and CITP grades are flexible but, for that very reason, they can be complex to understand. Membership at any level requires a commitment to compliance with BCS's Code of Conduct.

The standard grades are for students and apprentices training to enter the industry and associates who are early in their career. There is also an affiliate option for those who are interested in technology but do not have professional experience. The standard grades enable members to engage with the profession and gain career support from BCS.

Also available to membership grades from associate and above is Registration for IT Technicians (RITTech) status. RITTech is the independent competency standard for technical professionals, which recognises their skills and experience through a validation process. Members who pass the validation stage are recorded on the public RITTech register.

There are two professional grades – Member and Fellow – and members are entitled to use the letters MBCS after their name. Fellow is the most senior professional grade. It is open to members who can provide evidence of leadership through their eminence, authority or seniority in the IT profession – for example, if they are an expert in their field, have been recognised for their knowledge and influence, or have held a senior position for a number of years. Fellows may use the letters FBCS after their names.

To achieve CITP status, an individual must be a professional Member or Fellow and must have spent at least three of the past five years working in an IT role carrying significant responsibility and full accountability, and presenting a challenging range of complex work activities. Individuals with this status are entitled to use the letters CITP after their names, along with their membership post-nominal (MBCS or FBCS).

In addition to awarding CITP status, BCS is licensed by the Engineering Council to award Chartered Engineer (CEng) status, Incorporated Engineer (IEng) status and Engineering Technician (EngTech) status.

> The BCS website (https://www.bcs.org) should always be consulted for precise and up-to-date information.

2.9 RESERVATION OF TITLE AND FUNCTION

As mentioned at the beginning of this chapter, in certain cases, where it is considered to be in the public interest, the members of a profession may be granted a sort of legal monopoly. There are two different ways in which this can be done. First, the use of the name of the profession may be restricted to those people who are appropriately qualified. A restriction of this sort is called **reservation of title**. In the UK, for example, the Architects Act 1997 makes it a criminal offence to call yourself an architect unless you are registered with the Architects Registration Board.

Second, the law may state that certain activities are restricted to people with appropriate qualifications or to members of specified professional bodies. This is called **reservation of function**. For example, in England and Wales, only members of the Institute of Chartered Accountants in England and Wales and the Association of Chartered Certified Accountants are allowed to audit the accounts of public companies. Auditing accounts is an example of reservation of function where there is no corresponding reservation of title. Anyone can call themselves an accountant, provided they do not do so for fraudulent purposes.

An example where both reservation of title and reservation of function apply is veterinary surgery. Under the Veterinary Surgeons Act 1966, a person is not allowed to call themselves a veterinary surgeon unless they are registered with the Royal College of Veterinary Surgeons, and in order to be registered they must have the proper qualifications. Additionally, subject to certain limitations, it is a criminal offence to carry out surgical procedures on animals without being registered with the Royal College.

In the USA, title and function are usually reserved not to members of professional bodies but to people whose names are on a register maintained by a state government. In the UK, a somewhat similar provision has been in operation for many years for doctors and dentists. Recent developments have shown a tendency for the UK to move further in the same direction. For example, until the passage of the Architects Act 1997, it was an offence to 'practise or carry on business under any name, style or title containing the word "architect"', unless an individual was a member of the Royal Institute of British Architects. The 1997 Act established the Architects Registration Board, registration with which now replaces membership of the Royal Institute as the requirement for calling oneself an architect.

2.9.1 Possible areas for registration

Whatever the mechanism adopted, there are strong arguments for protecting the public by ensuring that only suitably qualified people are allowed to practise professions in which unqualified people can do serious damage, be it physical or economic. It was a series of civil engineering disasters that led to the introduction of a licensing scheme for engineers in the USA in the 1920s and 1930s. A number of disasters can be traced directly to lack of professional competence on the part of the software engineers who developed the systems. Therac-25 in the USA and the London Ambulance Service's Computer Aided Dispatch System in the UK (see the Further Reading section) are two examples where reports show how the professional incompetence of software developers can lead to avoidable deaths. In both these examples, the developers lacked any professional qualifications in software engineering and were ignorant of such elementary topics as the risks of concurrent access to shared memory and the dangers of dynamic memory allocation, as well as many more advanced topics. While the immediate cause of the failure of these systems was programming error arising from ignorance of elementary topics, these errors occurred in a context that showed a much broader lack of professionalism.

As IT has widespread impacts on people's lives, it is not surprising that some members of the profession have advocated for a legal requirement that all software must be written by registered software engineers, or at least under their supervision. Such a regulation would be impossible to enforce. The number of people qualified to be registered as software engineers is vastly fewer than the number of people developing software. If such a regulation were introduced, the amount of new software that could be developed would be enormously reduced or, more likely, software development would be done secretly. Furthermore, there would be considerable opposition to the regulation. Many software developers would see it as an attempt to establish a monopoly by a small number of people with specific qualifications, with the intention of pushing up their own earnings. The public would share this view and see the move as unnecessary, because most software is not critical.

It would be more realistic and more defensible to require that the design and implementation of all critical systems should be under the control of a registered software engineer; in the UK, this would probably mean a Chartered Engineer or a CITP whose experience and qualifications are in software engineering. By a critical system we mean a system whose failure to operate correctly could result in physical injury or loss of life, or catastrophic economic damage. Society would be justified in demanding that such systems are designed and implemented by properly qualified and experienced engineers.

One difficulty is that the boundary between critical and non-critical systems is not always well defined. While it is clear that an air traffic control system should be considered critical, because a failure can directly result in loss of life, should we consider a medical records system to be critical, because the loss of information concerning, say, a patient's allergy to penicillin could in some circumstances lead to the death of the patient? A second difficulty is that many software engineers have not studied the rather specialised techniques needed for working on critical systems. Nor, for the jobs they are doing, is it necessary that they should.

2.9.2 Differences between countries

In the UK, with a very few exceptions, there is no reservation of function for any sort of engineer, so compulsory reservation of function for software engineers, even for critical systems work, is not a realistic possibility. The UK has shown no inclination to follow the USA in making registration of engineers compulsory and there is little likelihood of this happening. If anything, it is indirect pressures from the Health and Safety Executive or from insurers providing professional indemnity insurance that might increase the emphasis on registration as CEng or CITP. There is reservation of title only to the extent that the use of the titles Chartered Engineer and CITP is restricted to those who have been granted these titles.

In the USA, the certification and registration of software engineers remains a contentious issue because of a lack of unanimity about the definition of software engineering and the extent to which it constitutes a true engineering discipline. Texas is the only state to have introduced compulsory registration for those who wish to describe themselves as software engineers. The National Council of Examiners for Engineering and Surveying began to run examinations in the principles and practice of software engineering in 2013 in association with the IEEE-CS, the IEEE-USA, the National Society of Professional Engineers and the Texas Board of Professional Engineers. The examinations were discontinued in 2019 because of the small numbers of candidates presenting themselves.

Many countries reserve the title 'engineer' to those with approved qualifications or registration, but the question of whether the title includes software engineers is usually not addressed. The state of Queensland in Australia, however, has legislated to reserve both title and function. The Board of Professional Engineers in Queensland is responsible for running the Registered Professional Engineers in Queensland scheme. The scheme's definition of engineering includes 'Informational, Telecommunications and Electronics' and 'IT and Telecommunications'.

A large number of vendor- and product-specific qualifications are now available and further serve to confuse the situation. While such qualifications are useful in demonstrating that individuals have specific expertise, they are of little relevance when it comes to ensuring that critical systems are built by people who know what they are doing.

FURTHER READING

Following are the websites of the main professional bodies referred to in this chapter:
    BCS, The Chartered Institute for IT: https://www.bcs.org
    Institution of Engineering and Technology: https://www.theiet.org
    IEEE Computer Society: https://www.computer.org
    Association for Computing Machinery: https://www.acm.org

All four websites include the organisation's code of conduct or ethics, as well as much information about each organisation and the way it functions. The websites of BCS and the IET also include the full text of their royal charters.

The websites of the two international bodies connected to BCS are:
>International Federation for Information Processing: https://www.ifip.org
>Council of European Professional Informatics Societies: https://www.cepis.org

The website of the SFIA Foundation is:
>https://www.sfia-online.org

The authoritative description of the London Ambulance Service disaster can be accessed (with some related materials) as follows:
>Thames Regional Health Authority (1993) *Report of the Inquiry into the London Ambulance Service*. Communications Directorate, South West Thames Regional Health Authority. http://www0.cs.ucl.ac.uk/staff/A.Finkelstein/las/lascase0.9.pdf.

The Therac-25 disaster is described in a number of books and articles. An updated version of the original *IEEE Computer* article is available on the web:
>Leveson, N. (1995) 'Therac-25 Accidents: An Updated Version of the Original Accident Investigation Paper'. http://sunnyday.mit.edu/therac-25.html.

The website of the Board of Professional Engineers in Queensland is:
>https://bpeq.qld.gov.au

3   WHAT IS AN ORGANISATION?

After studying this chapter, you should know and understand:

- *the different ways in which an organisation can become a legal entity;*
- *the situations for which the different types of legal entity are appropriate;*
- *what a limited company is and why it is the preferred legal form for a commercial organisation;*
- *what is meant by the terms **takeover**, **merger**, **management buyout** and **outsourcing**;*
- *the most important ways in which the law regulates limited companies.*

3.1 THE ROLE OF ORGANISATIONS

An organisation is a group of people working together in a formal way. Our life in a modern society is dominated by our interactions with organisations. We go to school and to college; schools and colleges are organisations. We or our friends and relatives go to hospital; a hospital is an organisation. We have a bank account; a bank is an organisation. We take the examinations of BCS; it is an organisation. And we work for a company or a government department; both of these are organisations. We may even set up a business of our own and thus create an organisation ourselves. However, as mentioned in Chapter 1, organisations need to have a legal existence. In this chapter we shall describe the various ways in which an organisation can acquire a legal existence, concentrating on the idea of a limited company because this is the most important type of commercial organisation.

A very broad distinction can be made between commercial organisations, which are in business to make money, and public organisations and other non-profit-making bodies. This distinction is reflected in the different procedures used to set up the organisations and the different ways in which they are governed. Most of this chapter is concerned with commercial organisations but in Section 3.9 we shall look briefly at non-commercial organisations.

3.2 COMMERCIAL ORGANISATIONS

The law offers several different ways of setting up and operating a commercial organisation. Depending on the circumstances, the business may be operated as a sole trader, a partnership, a co-operative or a limited company.

A **sole trader** is an individual who runs their own business. There are no legal formalities attached to becoming a sole trader; you become a sole trader simply by starting to run a business. If the income of your business is large enough, you will need to register with Her Majesty's Revenue and Customs (HMRC) for value-added tax (VAT) purposes and you may need to negotiate with them about your income tax status, but neither of these is necessary simply in order to become a sole trader.

A sole trader is personally liable for all the debts of the business so that all the trader's assets, including the family home, are at risk if the business fails. For this reason, anyone who is in business in anything other than a very small way should not operate as a sole trader. It is usually better to form a limited company, as discussed later in this chapter.

If a group of people carry on a business with a view to making profits, and the business is not a limited company, then the law will treat them as being in a **partnership**. This will happen whether the people in question intend it to or not. The legal framework governing partnerships was established in the Partnership Act 1890 and has since been changed only in minor ways. The Act has important consequences for people going into business together.

The most important consequence of the Partnership Act is that the liability of the partners is unlimited and that the partners are **jointly and severally** responsible for the partnership's liabilities.

What does this mean in practice? Suppose that you and a friend are working together to write software for a local company. Your friend is doing most of the work and you have agreed that he will get most of the money. Unfortunately, his software doesn't work and the company decides to claim damages for the harm it has suffered because of the defective software. You own a house and a car and have money in the bank; your friend doesn't. The company can sue you for the entire amount of the damages, despite the fact that it was your friend's software that didn't work.

A second problem with partnerships is the difficulty of making changes in the ownership. If one of the partners wishes to leave the partnership, perhaps to retire, how much money are they entitled to receive in return for relinquishing their share of the partnership? And how do the remaining partners raise this money? In the extreme case that one of the partners dies, how much is due to their estate?

Partnerships are mainly used in professions such as the law, medicine and architecture. The bodies that govern these professions have often insisted that their members practise in partnerships because the draconian rules regarding liability are seen to be a way of discouraging recklessness and ensuring the probity of the professionals concerned.

A more recent innovation is the **limited liability partnership** (LLP), which was introduced in the Limited Liability Partnerships Act 2000. Unlike an ordinary partnership, an LLP is a corporate body – that is, it is a legal person and has a continuing existence independent of its members. The members of an LLP have a joint or collective responsibility to the extent that this is agreed when they set up the partnership but they have no responsibility for each other's actions. The LLP structure is commonly used by such professionals as accountants, solicitors and patent attorneys but is increasingly being used by groups of professionals such as management consultants and even web designers.

Co-operatives are another way in which an organisation can acquire a legal existence. They are important in fields such as agriculture and enjoy a special legal status. They are, however, unusual in the information systems industry and we shall say no more about them.

By far the commonest form of commercial organisation is the **company limited by shares**. It is also the most suitable form of organisation for most businesses. Most of the remainder of this chapter will be dedicated to describing this type of organisation. Note, though, that non-profit-making organisations, such as charities and professional bodies, may take the form of a **company limited by guarantee**. This form of organisation is discussed briefly in Section 3.9.2.

3.3 COMPANIES LIMITED BY SHARES

There are three principles that are fundamental to the concept of a company limited by shares:

- The company has a corporate legal identity – that is, it is a legal person, completely separate from the people who work in it and the people who own it.

- The ownership of the company is divided into a number (usually large) of shares. These shares can be bought and sold individually. The people who own these shares are known as the members of the company or shareholders. If the company is profitable, it may decide to distribute some or all of the profit to shareholders, in proportion to the number of shares that each of them holds. Profit distributed to shareholders in this way is known as a **dividend**.

- In the event that the company incurs debts or other legal liabilities, the owners of the company have no obligation to pay these. The most that shareholders stand to lose is the money they paid for their shares.

The UK recognises two main types of company limited by shares: the public limited company (PLC) and the private limited company. The essential difference is that a PLC can, if it so wishes, offer its shares for sale to the public but a private limited company cannot. The name of a private limited company will end with the word Limited or Ltd (e.g. Mann Plumbing and Gas Limited) while the name of a public limited company will end with plc (conventionally lowercase – e.g. Lloyds Banking Group plc).

In return for the privileges, particularly limited liability, that the status of being a limited company confers, a limited liability company has certain obligations. It must provide details about itself to Companies House. This is a government agency that handles the formation and dissolution of UK companies, receives and stores information about companies that is required by law, and makes such information available to the general public. Companies must produce annual accounts (see Chapter 6) and an annual report; these must be submitted to Companies House and will be publicly available. Some of the reporting requirements are eased for small companies, while there are more stringent requirements for companies whose shares are quoted on a stock exchange.

Until the middle of the 19th century, the only way to create a limited company was through an Act of Parliament or the issue of a royal charter – both very slow and expensive routes. The modern idea of the limited company was developed in the UK through a number of Acts of Parliament in the middle of the 19th century and was rapidly taken up in other countries. It has played a very important part in subsequent economic development, which would probably have taken place much more slowly if the convenient mechanism offered by the limited company had not been available.

It can safely be said that the three principles stated at the start of this section hold in any country that recognises the concept of a limited company. Within this framework, however, the details vary widely from country to country (as does the terminology – in particular, the term 'corporation' is commonly used in the USA to denote a large limited company). Several countries (e.g. Australia, Canada and New Zealand) have in recent years enacted legislation that simplifies the law relating to companies.

The UK government carried out a review of company law that was trailed as being a complete overhaul that would greatly simplify the law. It resulted in the Companies Act 2006. This proved to be a **consolidating Act** – that is, an Act that brought together into a single place all the provisions relating to company law, which had previously been distributed throughout many pieces of legislation. This undoubtedly made it easier to understand the existing law and some useful new provisions were introduced. Nevertheless, pressure from those who had a vested interest in the status quo meant that many opportunities for simplification were missed. The Act contains 1,300 sections, making it one of the longest and most complicated pieces of UK legislation.

3.4 SETTING UP A COMPANY

A company limited by shares is created by a group of people who each agree to subscribe a certain amount of money to set up an organisation to pursue some stated goal and to register the organisation as a limited company in accordance with the law. In the UK the process of setting up a limited company is straightforward and it can be done online, quickly and cheaply. It is not necessary to employ a lawyer or an accountant, although this may be advisable if you have little experience of dealing with formal documents.

The commonest way of setting up a company is to buy an **off-the-shelf company**. There are a number of company formation agents that set up companies with a standard constitution; they hold a stock of such companies, which never actually trade, and they sell them to customers wanting a company through which to run their business. Once the customers have bought the company, they can make changes to its constitution, including its name, at their leisure.

The alternative is to create a company specifically to meet the requirements of the business. The process of registering the business is quick and cheap; Companies House offers a same-day service for less than £100. In practice, however, there are decisions to be made and forms to be completed, with the result that the process is likely to be slower and more expensive than buying an off-the-shelf company.

There are only a few countries in which companies can be set up as cheaply and as conveniently as in the UK and the USA. At the other extreme, in some countries it can take up to six months to register a new company and the cost can run into several thousand pounds.

3.5 THE CONSTITUTION OF A COMPANY LIMITED BY SHARES

When a new company limited by shares is incorporated, it is necessary to produce a **memorandum of association** signed by the founding shareholders. This simply states their wish to form a company under the Companies Act 2006 and the agreement of each of them to take at least one share. (Until 2009, the memorandum of association was a longer and more complicated document.) The document must be filed with Companies House.

In order to become incorporated, in addition to the memorandum of association the company requires **articles of association**. These are much more complicated and technical. They relate to such matters as the number of directors, how directors are appointed and removed, what their powers are, what process is required to modify the articles and so on. In order to simplify the setting up of companies, the Companies Act 1948 included a specimen set of articles of association, which have been regularly updated; these were known as **Table A**. Following the Companies Act 2006, these were replaced by a set that are now known as **model articles**. Most new companies adopt these model articles as the basis of their articles of association and specify only the way in which their articles differ from the model ones.

The articles of association specify the **authorised capital** of the company – that is, the maximum number of shares that the company can issue to shareholders, and at what price. The articles also specify the process by which the authorised capital can be changed. Part of the authorised capital can (and frequently does) remain unissued. The part of the authorised capital that has been issued to shareholders is referred to as the **issued share capital** of the company.

Once a company has been registered, the memorandum of association and the articles of association are deposited at Companies House and are public documents, in the sense that anyone may visit Companies House and inspect them. It often happens in private companies that the shareholders wish to conclude a further agreement among themselves. Such an agreement is called a **shareholders' agreement**. It might, for example, say that, if a shareholder wishes to dispose of shares, the recipient of the shares must be a person acceptable to the remaining shareholders. Unlike the memorandum and the articles, a shareholders' agreement is not a public document.

Public limited companies that wish to offer their shares to the public through a stock exchange are subject to regulations imposed by the stock exchange, which are more stringent than those imposed by the Companies Act 2006.

3.6 DIRECTORS

In small companies, it may well be that the shareholders run the company directly, but this is not feasible if there are more than a handful of shareholders; in any case, some shareholders may not wish to be directly involved in the day-to-day operations of the business. The Companies Act 2006 requires a private limited company to have at least one director and a public limited company to have a minimum of two. The law requires that the shareholders appoint directors to take responsibility for running the company on their behalf.

In small companies, the shareholders may actually be directors or at least be in regular contact with them. In large public companies, however, the shareholders have very little opportunity to influence the directors. To compensate for this, the law makes directors subject to certain obligations.

First, the Companies Act 2006 lays down that the overall duty of a director is to promote the success of the company for the benefit of its members as a whole, having regard to the following factors:

- the likely long-term consequences of any decision;
- the interests of the company's employees;
- the need to foster the company's business relationships with suppliers, customers and others;
- the impact of the company's operations on the community and the environment;
- the desirability of the company maintaining a reputation for high standards of business conduct;
- the need to act fairly as between members of a company.

More specifically:

- Directors must act in good faith and for the benefit of the company. Suppose, for example, that you are a director of a small company that writes software and that someone approaches you to have some software written. If you decided that you could do this yourself in your spare time rather than having it written by the company, you would not be considered to have acted in good faith for the benefit of the company, and you could be required to pay the company compensation for the loss of the contract.
- Directors must exercise the skill and care in carrying out their duties that might be expected of someone of their qualifications and experience. This means, for example, that a director with long experience of purchasing computers who signed a contract to buy a computer system that was not suitable for the use the company intended to make of it might be ordered by a court to pay back to the company the cost of the system. Furthermore, directors must take the same care as an ordinary person might be expected to take on their own behalf.
- A director who has an interest in a contract made with the company (e.g. owning an office cleaning company that the company is thinking of employing) must disclose this interest to the board of directors. The model articles stipulate that the director must not be allowed to vote or be counted in the **quorum** (i.e. the minimum number present at a board meeting required to empower the meeting to make decisions) when the matter is discussed but, in the case of a small company, this may well be different.

The obligations listed above can be described as **domestic obligations** – that is, they are obligations owed to the company. In addition, there are certain **external or legal obligations** that the directors must fulfil:

- Directors are required to keep themselves aware of the company's financial position and not allow it to continue to incur debts when they know or should have known that the company will be unable to repay them. If they fail to do this, a court can make them personally liable for the company's debts.

- The directors are responsible for drawing up the company's annual report, including its accounts, and for filing this report with Companies House. We shall explore this in more detail in Chapter 6.

- The directors are responsible for ensuring that the company complies with all relevant provisions of the law. While the company itself, having a legal existence, can be prosecuted for criminal breaches of the law, in some cases directors can be made personally responsible. Thus the Health and Safety at Work etc. Act 1974 provides that, in appropriate circumstances, a director or other senior manager can be criminally liable if a company is found to be in serious breach of the Act.

Many companies have both executive directors and non-executive directors. Executive directors are normally also employees of the company, with specific responsibility for certain areas of its activities. Non-executive directors are directors who act in an advisory capacity only. Typically, they attend monthly board meetings to offer the benefit of their advice and serve on committees concerned with sensitive issues such as the pay of the executive directors and other senior managers. They are usually paid a fee for their services but are not regarded as employees. It is important to realise that, legally, the duties and responsibilities of non-executive directors are precisely the same as those of executive directors.

Every public company must have a company secretary; private companies can choose not to have a secretary. The company secretary is legally responsible for keeping the various records that the company has to maintain and for submitting various statutory returns to Companies House. The secretary will normally also take responsibility for a variety of related matters, and will often be a director. Small companies commonly appoint an outsider, typically a solicitor or accountant, as company secretary, because such people are likely to have the necessary professional expertise.

3.7 TAKEOVERS, MERGERS AND MANAGEMENT BUYOUTS

Limited companies, whether private or public, are, on the whole, short lived. They typically disappear not because they fail – although, of course, some do – or are wound up for other reasons, but because they are taken over by other companies or because they merge with other companies. The pace of change in IT makes this especially true for companies in the IT sector. A related phenomenon occurs when whole IT departments are moved from a user organisation to a specialised IT company.

In cases where the companies involved in takeovers and mergers are public companies whose shares are traded on stock exchanges, the stock exchanges on which the companies' shares are traded impose strict regulations in an attempt to prevent improper exploitation of the situation.

3.7.1 Takeovers

How and why do takeovers, also known as acquisitions, take place? The commonest scenario in the IT industry is of a private company, let's call them SmallGuys, being acquired by a larger company, which we might call BigGuys, probably but not necessarily a public one. The mechanism of such a takeover is that BigGuys acquires all the shares of SmallGuys, paying for them in cash, in its own shares or in a mixture of both. It is likely that the shareholders of SmallGuys will also be its directors and that much of the value of the company will be derived from the skills of these people and their contacts. Accordingly, there may well be an agreement that they will work for BigGuys for, say, the next three years.

Why might the owners of SmallGuys want to sell the company? First, although as the owners of a successful small company they will be quite wealthy on paper, they will probably only be able to pay themselves a comparatively modest salary and they certainly won't feel wealthy. Furthermore, their wealth on paper will be critically dependent on the continued success of the company, which will probably be vulnerable to changes in market conditions. By selling the company, they will be able to convert their paper wealth into real money and, at the same time, protect themselves against fluctuations in the value of the company. A second reason for wanting to sell the company may be the need for further capital investment.

Examples of takeovers

FirstEarth Ltd was a private company that started as a spin-off from research in the Computer Science Department at Aberystwyth University. It was founded in 1997. It had developed software that could automatically carry out failure mode effects analysis (FMEA) on the electrical system of a car – that is, it would predict the result of all the possible ways in which the electrical system could fail. Such an analysis, formerly done by hand, is a requirement before a new model of car can be put on the market. The technical development had been successful but the company did not have the resources to market its software successfully. In 2003 FirstEarth was taken over by Mentor Graphics Inc, a large US-based multinational company that produces electronic design automation tools. FirstEarth's FMEA software complemented Mentor Graphics' electronic design automation software and Mentor Graphics' main motivation in buying the company was to acquire the rights to the FMEA software, along with FirstEarth's highly skilled staff. It bought all the shares in FirstEarth for cash. Mentor Graphics itself was acquired by Siemens AG, a very large German firm, in March 2017, for $4.5 billion. It operated as an independent subsidiary of Siemens until January 2021, when it became a division of Siemens under the name Siemens EDA. As with Mentor Graphics' acquisition of FirstEarth, Siemens' acquisition of Mentor Graphics was motivated by a desire to broaden the coverage of its electronic design software.

A very different type of takeover occurred in 1991, when the British software house SD-Scicon, which specialised in defence and other high-tech systems, was taken over by the American company Electronic Data Systems (EDS). EDS was in the business of providing IT services to large organisations, particularly in the field of health services. It showed no interest in SD-Scicon's traditional markets and rapidly shed the considerable number of highly skilled professional staff who worked for the company. It used the acquisition of SD-Scicon as a means of getting a foothold in the much more profitable market for IT services in the UK but SD-Scicon effectively lost its identity and completely disappeared.

In contrast, when EDS itself was acquired by Hewlett-Packard (HP) for $13.9 billion in 2008, it was initially able to retain its identity, staff and structures. In 2010, it began to trade as HP Enterprise Systems, eventually coming to encompass all HP's software activities. In September 2016, Micro Focus announced that it was merging with HP Enterprise Services. The merger was completed in September 2017. In this instance, HP wanted to enter the large and profitable area of IT services and it chose to do so by acquiring a company that was a major player in the field. To have broken up EDS would have defeated the purpose of the takeover.

Benefits of takeovers
From the point of view of the owners and managers of the acquiring company, the fundamental reasons for taking over another company are to make more money and to get bigger. In more detail, these amount to:

- **Expanding the customer base:** This occurs particularly when the company taken over offers services similar to those of the buying company but in a different geographical area.

- **Expanding its range of offerings:** This occurs when the company taken over offers products or services that are complementary to those of the buying company – for example, when a company offering a human resources (HR) package acquires a company that offers a payroll package.

- **Acquiring new staff:** There has been a shortage of high-quality IT staff for most of the past 50 years and this has prevented many companies expanding as they would have wished. Taking over another company can be a quick way of acquiring additional staff.

- **Acquiring technology that can be used to create new products:** This is very common in the pharmaceutical industry.

- **Economies of scale:** The larger company's HR department, for example, may be able to take on HR responsibilities for the company being taken over, without itself requiring any extra staff. It is frequently claimed that such savings will result from a takeover but the reality is that the savings are usually small and often negligible.

- **Vertical integration:** This refers to bringing different aspects of a business together – for example, when a television company acquires a film production company.

- **Eliminating a competitor:** As, for example, when System Designers acquired SCICON (see below).

Risks arising in takeovers
SD-Scicon had been formed through the acquisition of SCICON by System Designers in 1988. Subsequently, the 1990 accounts of System Designers showed £25 million being set aside for cost overruns on fixed price contracts that had been 'mismanaged

as a result of the merger'.[1] System Designers had not looked sufficiently closely at the financial state of SCICON's fixed price contracts and had therefore failed to appreciate the financial risks that they posed.

The acquisition of EDS by HP, mentioned above, failed to produce the expected benefits because HP did not understand the market into which EDS had been selling. The situation was exacerbated by the takeover, in 2011, of Autonomy, a British software company, by HP. HP paid around $10.2 billion for Autonomy, but just over a year later it announced that it was taking an $8.8 billion accounting charge (i.e. reducing the value of the assets in its balance sheet by $8.8 billion) after claiming 'serious accounting improprieties' and 'outright misrepresentations' at Autonomy.[2] This caused severe financial difficulties and led to extensive and expensive litigation, some of which is still passing through the courts at the time of writing. In January 2022, the UK High Court ruled that Mike Lynch, founder of Autonomy, had fraudulently inflated Autonomy's value by misleading HP about its performance. The same day, the Home Secretary approved Lynch's extradition to the USA to face fraud charges. It is alleged, however, that when it agreed to purchase Autonomy, HP failed to exercise due diligence – in other words, that it did not do enough to satisfy itself that the accounts gave an accurate picture of Autonomy's financial situation. In 2020, the audit firm Deloitte was fined £15 million for the failings in its audit of Autonomy's accounts leading up to the takeover. (See Further Reading for a more detailed account.)

3.7.2 Mergers

In a takeover, one company gains control of another by acquiring a majority, if not all, of its shares. Although the terms takeover and merger are commonly used synonymously, strictly speaking there is a difference. In a merger, the two companies come together on equal terms. A common mechanism is that a new company is set up, and it acquires all the shares of the merging companies in exchange for its own shares; the merging companies themselves cease to exist.

Mergers in this strict sense are comparatively uncommon. A good example, however, was the merger of the two telephone operating companies Bell Atlantic and GTE to form Verizon Communications Inc. This merger, completed in June 2000, was one of the largest in American industrial history. There is a risk that mergers on this scale can have a serious effect on competition and work against the public interest. For this reason, in the UK, they may be subject to examination by the Competition and Markets Authority, a government department responsible for strengthening business competition and preventing and reducing anti-competitive activities. Similar functions are carried out in the European Union by the European Commission's Directorate-General for Competition, and in the USA by the Federal Trade Commission. Investigations into such cases can seriously delay or even prevent mergers or takeovers. For example, it took two years to obtain complete approval of the merger of Bell Atlantic and GTE.

---

1 *SD-Scion 'into the Claws of Eagles'* (1991), System House, https://archivesit.org.uk/wp-content/uploads/2019/01/V2-N11-SEP-1991.pdf.

2 C. Arthur and R. Neate, 'HP Hits Back after Angry Letter from Autonomy Boss', *The Guardian* (2012), https://www.theguardian.com/business/2012/nov/27/autonomy-mike-lynch-letter-hewlett-packard.

3.7.3 Management buyouts

It may happen that some of the senior employees of a company decide to purchase the company from its existing owners. This is known as a management buyout. It will usually require a lot of capital to do this and the purchasers will need to borrow the money. However, the lenders are likely to demand that the purchasers shoulder a significant part of the risk by raising a substantial amount of capital – for example, by mortgaging their homes. At first sight a management buyout looks praiseworthy – the people who are running the company become its owners. In practice, there are many potential conflicts of interest. The management may run the company down over a period before bidding to buy it, thus reducing its apparent value and the sum they have to pay to buy it. Once they have bought it, they can then rapidly build the company up again before selling it at a considerable profit.

3.8 OUTSOURCING

Outsourcing is contracting out activities or processes from one business to another. In the mid-20th century, large companies would employ their own cleaners, their own gardeners to look after their grounds, their own maintenance staff and painters to look after their premises, their own catering staff to run the staff canteen and so on. Nowadays all, or most, of these activities will be outsourced – that is, contracted out to other, specialist companies. More surprisingly, perhaps, the processing of the company's payroll and the maintenance of staff records may be contracted out. Theatres and airlines outsource the sale of tickets. And some organisations outsource the whole of their IT operations.

Outsourcing may take a variety of forms. A local council may outsource its refuse collection activities by contracting out the whole operation to a specialist company. Or it may choose to use its own staff to carry out the collection and disposal of the refuse but contract out the responsibility for supplying and maintaining the vehicles used.

Historically, it has long been common practice for both commercial and public organisations to purchase equipment from outside organisations rather than designing and developing the equipment themselves. Thus, hospitals don't develop their own X-ray machines but buy them from specialist suppliers. The armed forces don't develop their own weapons but contract out their design and production to commercial companies. Oil refineries are typically built by specialist companies that are quite distinct from the companies that operate them.

Outsourcing of operations, as opposed to the development and supply of capital equipment, started to develop in the late 1960s, and it was then that the term **outsourcing** came into use. One of the first business applications of computers was for payroll calculations and associated record keeping. This was a very large market, since all employing organisations were required to process payroll data in accordance with the rules laid down by what is now HMRC. These rules changed frequently. A number of companies developed payroll packages, usually written in COBOL and so easily transferable from machine to machine, which they licensed to organisations that wished to computerise their payroll processing. From here it was an easy step to offer to handle all the payroll processing for customers and, by the early 1970s, such services were widely used.

Historically, outsourcing in the UK was associated particularly with IT and the civil service. It was introduced by the Conservative government that came to power in 1979 under Margaret Thatcher. The Conservative party was committed to the politically popular goal of substantially reducing the number of civil servants. By outsourcing the provision of government IT services, the number of civil servants could be cut dramatically. At the same time, there were good reasons for thinking that this might lead to an improvement in the quality of those services – the civil service had difficulty in recruiting and retaining high-quality IT staff, while specialist outsourcing companies, not being subject to the same staffing restraints as the civil service, had fewer problems.

As a result of this policy – which has been accepted by all succeeding governments, of whatever complexion – much of public sector operational IT is now outsourced. Despite a few spectacular and widely publicised failures, the policy has proved reasonably successful.

Outsourcing is now widely practised by private industry as well as by the public sector. The arguments put forward in favour of outsourcing IT provision can be summed up as follows:

- It frees management to concentrate on the core business of the company.
- It makes the costs of IT more visible and therefore easier to control.
- Specialist companies are able to produce and operate more effective systems because:
  - they have much wider experience of system development than user companies do;
  - they can justify employing highly specialised staff;
  - working in a specialised IT company provides a better career path for IT staff than working for a user organisation;
  - overall, it saves money.

There is an element of truth in each of these points, but there is also a danger that a company that outsources too much of its IT provision may lose control and understanding of its own operations.

Successful outsourcing depends upon very careful specification of what is being outsourced and the obligations of both parties. Outsourcing of such widely differing activities as refuse collection and payroll processing has proved successful, precisely because these are activities in which it is comparatively easy to produce the necessary specifications. In the absence of such specifications, there is a real danger that both sides may feel they are being exploited and the charges by the contracted company can escalate dramatically. A recent and staggering failure of outsourcing, though not in the area of IT, was the attempt, in 2014, to outsource probation services (see Further Reading section).

We shall return to these topics in Section 12.3, while employment issues connected with outsourcing are considered in Section 9.8.4.

Outsourcing is often associated with **off-shoring** – that is, moving activity to other countries. Thus, companies in the UK may outsource software development to companies in India. The reason for doing this is straightforwardly one of cost. Well-qualified and experienced software engineers in India earn much less than they do in the UK and there are plenty of them available.

3.9 NON-COMMERCIAL BODIES

Roughly speaking, about 80% of jobs in the UK are in the private sector and provided, on the whole, by profit-making limited companies. The remaining 20% are non-commercial bodies – that is, bodies that are not intended to make profits. They may be in the public sector – local government, the NHS, education, the police, the armed services and so on – or they may be organisations whose activities are generally seen to be in the public interest and that are not intended to be profit making. Such organisations include professional bodies (such as BCS or the Institute of Physics), political parties, charities (such as Oxfam or Christian Aid) and so on.

There are important differences between the way that commercial bodies are constituted and the way that non-commercial bodies are set up and governed. Some of the more important of these differences are described in this section.

3.9.1 Statutory bodies

It is in the nature of the public sector that it deals with data on a much larger scale than most private sector organisations – very few private companies have as many as a million customers but the Department for Work and Pensions holds records for everyone in the UK over the age of 16 – about 50 million people. Because of the large numbers involved, such public sector bodies make great demands on IT services; they employ many IT staff directly and many more work for private sector companies that provide IT services to the public sector. Large public sector IT projects also have a very poor record of success, precisely because of their size.

Many public sector organisations come into existence by statute – that is, by Act of Parliament. Such organisations are often referred to as statutory bodies. Frequently the organisations themselves are created by secondary legislation. In object-oriented programming terminology, the Act of Parliament defines a class of organisations, specifying their structure, their duties and their powers. Secondary legislation is then used to create objects belonging to that class – that is, specific instances of it (see Section 1.4 for more information). Thus, in the field of local government, the Local Government Act 1992 created the class of unitary authorities together with a body, the Local Government Commission (now replaced by separate commissions for England, Northern Ireland, Scotland and Wales), which would make recommendations for the creation of specific unitary authorities; these authorities would then be created by secondary legislation. The unitary authorities themselves are empowered to create and run schools and certain other public services.

The overall objectives of the directors of a limited company are fairly straightforward even if achieving them is difficult: as we saw in Section 3.6, they have to run the company in order to make as much money for the shareholders as they reasonably can, while having due regard for the interests of the employees and certain other defined considerations. If the shareholders are unhappy, they can either sell their shares or, if enough of them are unhappy, they can vote to replace the directors. If the directors fail to run the company profitably, it will ultimately be forced to close or it will get taken over.

The position in the public sector is very different. The overall objective of a public body is to provide some sort of public service, such as keeping the roads in an area in good condition, providing education for children or administering state pensions. There are no shareholders but everyone has an interest in seeing that the body does its job satisfactorily. But profitability is not a measure of success and the option of closure if the body does not perform satisfactorily is not usually acceptable. There thus needs to be some mechanism for making the management of the body accountable to the general public.

Many different mechanisms have been adopted to achieve accountability in the public sector. At the level of national and local government, accountability is achieved through the ballot box. Members of Parliament and local councillors are elected for limited terms and they take responsibility for the activities of national and local government respectively. However, their role is fundamentally different from that of directors of a company. Company directors – or, more precisely, executive directors – are expected to run a part of the company and are usually selected on the basis of their ability to do this. Members of Parliament and local councillors are elected to represent the public and to contribute to policy making, rather than to carry out policy. The national government and local councils employ professionals – civil servants, engineers, IT staff, social workers, teachers and so on – to carry out their policy. There is often a tension between politicians, who are motivated by policy issues, and the professionals, who are motivated by practical considerations. Too often, councillors feel that the professionals are stick-in-the-muds who are opposed to all change, while the professionals feel that the councillors have their heads in the clouds and don't understand the practicalities. A particular problem that frequently arises concerns timescales. For example, politicians decide that a change to the social security system is required. They fail to realise how long it will take to make and test the necessary changes to the IT systems and insist that the changes are implemented too quickly. The result is that the system fails or causes serious problems for some members of the public. The IT professionals – or, increasingly often, the company to which the development is outsourced – are blamed for the failure. In most such cases, the blame should be shared. On the one hand, those responsible for setting over-ambitious goals and timescales and insisting on them, against professional advice, must take their share of the blame. On the other hand, outsourcing companies are too eager to sign lucrative contracts whose timely fulfilment depends on a lot of very optimistic assumptions.

3.9.2 Other non-profit-making bodies

Non-profit-making organisations outside the public sector usually take the legal form of a company limited by guarantee. In this case, rather than subscribing for shares, the members agree that, in the event that the body has to be wound up, each will pay a small fixed amount (typically £10) to cover liabilities. A company limited by guarantee is not allowed to distribute its profits to its members. It can apply for charitable status and for the grant of a royal charter.

Like most of the larger professional bodies, BCS is a company limited by guarantee and a registered charity, and is established by royal charter. The royal charter states that 'the government and control of the Society and its affairs shall be vested in the Trustee Board'.[3] This means that the Trustee Board performs the functions of the board of directors of a company and of the trustees of a charity. The Trustee Board consists of the president, deputy president and immediate past president, all of whom serve for one year, plus four vice-presidents and five other members. All the members of the Trustee Board are elected by the Council, which consists of the members of the Trustee Board, together with 24 members elected directly by the membership of BCS, and the chief executive, who is the only member who is a paid employee of BCS.

An organisation the size of BCS is much too large to be run solely by its members and so, like most professional bodies, it is run by a combination of full-time employees and volunteers from among its members. The structure described in the previous paragraph seems, on the face of it, to ensure control of BCS rests firmly with its members. In practice, however, the short tenure of the senior elected officers and the limited amount of time that members, who have full-time professional commitments elsewhere, can devote to BCS business inevitably mean that the senior full-time employees have a great deal of influence over BCS's policy and the way it is carried out.

FURTHER READING

The UK government has a website that describes in simple language the duties of a director of a private limited company:
'Running a Limited Company: Your Responsibilities' (n.d.) Gov.uk. https://www.gov.uk/running-a-limited-company.

The Institute of Chartered Accountants in England and Wales has produced a sophisticated guide to directors' responsibilities:
'ICAEW's Guide to Directors' Duties and Responsibilities' (n.d.) Institute of Chartered Accountants in England and Wales. https://www.icaew.com/regulation/membership/icaews-guide-to-directors-responsibilities.

The Companies House website provides detailed information about registering a company, filing a company's annual return, changing a company's details and so on:
'Companies House' (n.d.) Gov.uk. https://www.gov.uk/government/organisations/companies-house.

A detailed, but readable, account of the Autonomy–HP lawsuits can be found at:
Sayer, P. (2022) 'The HP–Autonomy Lawsuit: Timeline of an M&A Disaster'. CIO. https://www.cio.com/article/304397/the-hp-autonomy-lawsuit-timeline-of-an-ma-disaster.html.

A summary of the sorry tale of the outsourcing of probation services can be found at:
Sasse, T. (2019) 'Probation Outsourcing is a Case Study in Failure'. Institute for Government. https://www.instituteforgovernment.org.uk/blog/probation-outsourcing-case-study-failure.

---

3 'Our Royal Charter' (1984), BCS, https://www.bcs.org/about-us/our-royal-charter.

4   STRUCTURE AND MANAGEMENT OF ORGANISATIONS

After studying this chapter you should, in the context of organisations with which you are familiar:

- *be able to recognise how they are structured;*
- *be able to suggest alternative possible structures and identify their advantages and disadvantages;*
- *understand the concept of role or job design;*
- *be aware of the effect that decisions about organisational structure may have on individual employees.*

4.1 ORGANISATIONAL MODELS

As we said at the start of Chapter 3, an organisation is a group of people working together in a formal way to meet shared goals. What this means is that the work that has to be done is shared between these people and that there are rules about who does what. How the work is shared and how tasks and people are grouped together – the structure of the organisation – will vary very much from organisation to organisation. It is surprising, however, that organisational structures have much more in common than might be expected. In this section, we shall describe the most common ways of structuring organisations.

4.1.1 The bureaucratic model

Organisational theory, the study of how organisations are structured and how they work, goes back to end of the 19th century. The founders of the theory were sociologists like Max Weber and Mary Parker Follett, and practical business people like Henri Fayol and Lyndall Urwick. They developed what is known as the bureaucratic model. In a modified form, this model still describes the organisational structures to be found in most large, and many smaller, organisations. (Note that bureaucratic here is simply descriptive; the pejorative sense developed later.)

The ideal bureaucratic organisation was thought to have the following characteristics:

1. All tasks are split up into specialised jobs, in which jobholders become expert; management can thereby hold them responsible for the effective performance of their duties.

2. The performance of each task is governed by precise rules. This means that there should be no variation in the way tasks are carried out and therefore no problems with the co-ordination of different tasks.

3. Each individual (and hence each unit) in the organisation is accountable to one and only one manager.

4. In order to ensure that personalities and personal relationships do not interfere with the organisation's performance, employees are required to relate both to other employees and to clients in an impersonal and formal manner.

5. Recruitment is based on qualifications and employees are protected against arbitrary dismissal. Promotion is based on seniority and achievement. Lifetime employment is envisaged.

These ideas have proved surprisingly long lasting. Remnants even of the fourth were certainly still to be found in banks and local authorities in the 1980s. In the 1970s it was still the case in some companies that if two employees became engaged to be married, one of them would be required to resign.

It is an inevitable consequence of these rules that the organisation will be hierarchical and that its structure can be represented as a tree.

Despite the obvious weaknesses of the approach (at least in this form), it brings many benefits and many companies were run successfully along these lines for many years. Modernised and liberalised versions are still to be found working successfully, particularly in production line industries. Much grief has ensued when companies whose main business is appropriately organised in this way have applied these ideas to software production, for instance by separating the tasks of writing code, compiling it and correcting compilation errors, and testing the code, and assigning them to different groups of specialists.

4.1.2 The organic model

The best-known alternative model is the organic model, particularly associated with Rensis Likert. He expressed the basic assumption of the model in the following (rather verbose) terms:

> An organisation will be effective to the extent that its structure is such as to ensure a maximum probability that in all interactions and in relationships within the organisation, each member, in the light of his background, values, desires, and expectations, will view the experience as supportive and one which builds a sense of personal worth and importance.[1]

This view underlies the organisational structure of most small professional companies – software houses, advertising agencies, even solicitors' and GP practices; it is also common in academic institutions, both schools and universities. The view is not necessarily consciously articulated – nor is this view and the adoption of the structures it suggests sufficient to achieve effectiveness!

---

1 R. Likert, *The Human Organization* (New York: McGraw-Hill, 1967), p. 47.

Proponents of the bureaucratic model claim that it is universally applicable. Proponents of the organic model make similar claims. It says little for common sense that those who hold the obvious view that each has its appropriate place are said to be adherents of the contingency school of organisational design.

4.1.3 Matrix management

It is an essential feature of the bureaucratic model that every individual and every unit in the organisation is responsible to only one manager. This is not realistic in the context of project-based, high-tech companies. Specialists in high-speed communications working for a systems integrator may well find themselves working on two or three projects simultaneously, as well as having a more general responsibility for maintaining the company's expertise in the area. In the past 40 years or so the idea of matrix management has become fashionable as a way of addressing such situations. It accepts that individuals may be responsible to more than one manager and requires rules that will enable possible conflicts to be resolved. In a software company, for example, database specialists may belong to a database group and report to its manager, while at the same time reporting to the project manager of the project they are working on.

4.2 STRUCTURING PRINCIPLES

The bureaucratic model tells us something about the way individuals and groups in an organisation relate to each other. It tells us nothing, however, about how to group together the tasks and activities that have to be carried out. In practice, there are many different ways of doing this and we shall describe some of them in the following sections. It should not be thought that these models are mutually exclusive. In all but the smallest companies, different parts of an organisation are likely to reflect different ways of producing a structure. Furthermore, the structures produced by the different criteria may be combined in a matrix structure.

4.2.1 Structure by function

In almost every organisation, we can identify certain groups of activities that have to be carried out and that fit naturally together.

First of all, there are the activities that are the primary purpose of the organisation. These activities are known as **operations**. The primary purpose of a school is to teach students. The primary purpose of a hospital is to treat sick people. The primary purpose of a software company is to provide software for its customers. In each case, these activities constitute the operations of the organisation concerned. The term **core business** is often used to mean the primary purpose of an organisation.

Second, almost all organisations have to pay their bills and their employees. They will need to ensure that the buildings they use are cleaned regularly. If they charge for their services, they may need to send out bills and ensure that these are paid. They will probably need to hire new employees from time to time. These activities are generally known as **administration**. While operations in different types of organisation will be very different, administration varies much less.

Third, many organisations will need to publicise their services or their products and try to persuade people to use them or buy them. In the business world these activities are usually known as **sales and marketing**. Strictly speaking, marketing means the activities involved in making potential customers aware of the products the business can offer; it also includes planning new products on the basis of what the company might provide and what customers would like. Selling or sales is the activity of persuading individual customers to buy from the company.

It is often thought that sales and marketing are activities restricted to commercial organisations. This is not the case. Health services try to persuade people to go for check-ups and to participate in screening programmes. Publicising these services is a marketing activity; sending out specific invitations to individuals is a sales activity. In Britain, as part of the policy of giving parents a choice of schools for their children, schools are encouraged to compete for pupils. This means schools must produce publicity material, a marketing activity, and must try to persuade parents visiting the school to send their children to it, a sales activity.

Finally, many organisations need to be continually developing new products or services, or developing new ways to deliver them. These activities are known as **research and development**.

A structure based on functions, with an administrative division, an operations division, a sales and marketing division, and possibly a research and development division, is the commonest type of structure to be found in medium-sized companies. It is illustrated in Figure 4.1.

Figure 4.1 A function-based structure

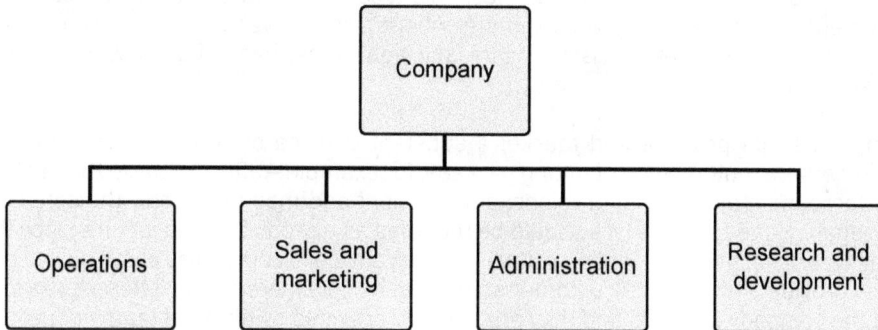

4.2.2 Structure by geography

In many cases it makes sense to group activities together on a geographical basis. Multinational companies – that is, companies that operate in a number of different countries – are usually forced to have some geographical elements in their structure. In most cases, in order to operate effectively in a country, they will need a permanent presence there, and this requires that they have a legal personality, usually in the form of a subsidiary company registered in the country but owned by the parent. The subsidiaries are subject to the laws of the countries in which they are registered – in particular, the laws regarding employment, accounting and taxation. These laws differ markedly from country to country so each subsidiary will need its own administrative capability. Linguistic and cultural factors will usually mean that sales and marketing have to be locally based; certainly this is the case if the company's customers are consumers.

An example of a company that is structured on a geographical basis at the top level is CGI. It is the fifth largest IT services company in the world and is based in Montreal, Canada. It operates in 40 countries and is structured into six geographically based divisions.

Within a single country, geographical factors have become less important as a result of the development of modern communications and, as a result, geographical structures have been replaced by structures based on other factors. British banks, for example, used to operate through local branches that provided all but the very largest customers with all the banking services they required. The local branches themselves were under the control of regional management, based on geographical regions. Now that customers can do much of their banking online over the internet, the role of the local branch and the extent of its manager's authority are steadily declining. Instead, the banks have moved towards a product line structure.

4.2.3 Product line structure

A product line structure is based around the different types of product that an organisation produces. In the above case of banks, different banking services (current accounts, loans, investment advice, etc.) are provided by different divisions of the bank, independent of the local branches. This type of structure is also very common in the engineering industry, for example, where a motor vehicle manufacturer may be structured into three divisions: cars and light vans, heavy goods vehicles, and replacement parts.

Companies that produce and market a substantial piece of software for corporate customers – a multi-user accounting package, for example – often organise themselves into three main operational divisions: development and maintenance of the software, consultancy, and training. This should be regarded as a product line structure since the three types of activity – providing software, giving advice to companies about how to use it and providing training for customer staff – can be considered to be different services that the company provides and they are typically provided by different teams of people.

Large multinational companies almost invariably show a mixture of functional, geographical and product line structures.

4.2.4 Structure by market sector

Structuring by market sector means structuring based on the different market sectors to which a company's customers or prospective customers belong. This approach is very popular within the IT industry. From the sales and marketing point of view, it has the great advantage that each division can fairly readily identify its potential customers.

Moreover, its staff, both sales and technical, are likely to be familiar with customers' problems and to speak a language that the customers will understand.

There are two dangers with this approach. First, there is the risk one division may be unaware of technological expertise that exists in another division. This may lead to inefficient use of resources, through unnecessarily hiring additional specialists or employing consultants, or, worse, failing to learn from mistakes that have been made by other parts of the company.

The second danger with a structure based on market sector is that, by continuing to concentrate on its traditional areas even when these markets are becoming saturated, the company will miss new opportunities and will stagnate.

4.2.5 Structure by technology

A technology-based structure was once a favourite model for software companies. Thus, a company might have divisions specialising in artificial intelligence, communications, web-based systems, databases and real-time systems. There are several problems with this type of structure:

- it usually requires several different technologies to meet a customer's needs;
- there are many applications that cannot be said to require specific technologies;
- there are many competent software engineers whose expertise runs across a number of technologies;
- it is difficult, if not impossible, for sales and marketing staff to predict which potential clients will need which technology.

The last of these is particularly serious and companies that are primarily structured by technology have major problems finding their clients. In marketing jargon they are not sufficiently **customer focused** – they concentrate on selling the technologies that they have, rather than finding out what the customer needs.

4.2.6 Operational structure

The actual operations of a company may be organised on a **project basis** or on a **production basis**, although the line separating the two may be vague.

A project is an activity that has specific objectives that have to be achieved within a fixed time period and with the expenditure of no more than some fixed quantity of resources. Every project is different from every other project. In some companies, nearly all the revenue-earning activities are project based. This is particularly true of companies that produce bespoke software or companies that carry out system integration work.

Project-based activity is not restricted to operations. Most research and development is organised on a project basis and such administrative activities as introducing a new accounting system or transferring a company's head office are also to be regarded as projects, in that they last for a fixed length of time, after which they should be complete.

Projects last a comparatively long time but the team carrying out the work only stays together for the length of the project. Production activities are comparatively short but repeated over and over again so that the team carrying them out stays in existence indefinitely. Classic examples of production activities are motor vehicle manufacturing, oil refining and dairy farming; each of them goes on year after year producing much the same outputs. The central data-processing operations of a company are organised on a production basis. There is a schedule of programs – payroll, accounts payable, accounts receivable and so on – that have to be run regularly on specific dates. It is the job of the operations team to ensure that these activities are completed on schedule. Although the individuals in the team will change from time to time, the team itself will continue to exist.

From the point of view of the employee, the difference between project-based and production structures is very marked. On the whole, if activities are structured on a project basis, employees will find their working environment – their colleagues, their clients and even the job they are doing – changing radically every few weeks or months, as they move from project to project. If they are working in a production environment, change will be slower and more gradual. One environment is not generally preferable to the other; much depends on the personality of the employee.

4.3 DEPTH OF STRUCTURE

The depth of an organisational structure is the number of layers in the structure – or, more precisely, the maximum number of layers, since not all parts of the structure will have the same number of layers. Organisational structures are often described as flat or, in contrast, deep or tall, according to whether the depth is small or large. For a given number of people, the depth of the structure will obviously depend on the number of people reporting directly to each manager; this is sometimes known as the manager's **span of control**.

Figures 4.2 and 4.3 both show 12 people organised in a bureaucratic structure. In Figure 4.2, each manager's span of control is two and there are four layers in the structure. This means that the people at the bottom of the structure, such as H, have to pass through two managers (D and B in the case of H) before reaching the head of the organisation, A. Figure 4.3 shows a flatter structure for the same number of people. Each manager's span of control is six but the number of layers is reduced to three, meaning that people at the bottom of the structure only have to pass through one manager to reach A. It is generally accepted that, in a bureaucratic structure, managers should not be expected to have more than six people reporting to them directly.

Obviously the structure of organisations with large numbers of employees is likely to be deeper than that of smaller organisations. Professional staff generally prefer to work with flatter structures.

4.4 CENTRALISATION

Organisations may be centralised or decentralised. In a centralised company, as much power as possible is kept at the top of the company, with delegation only used

Figure 4.2 Twelve people organised into a four-level structure

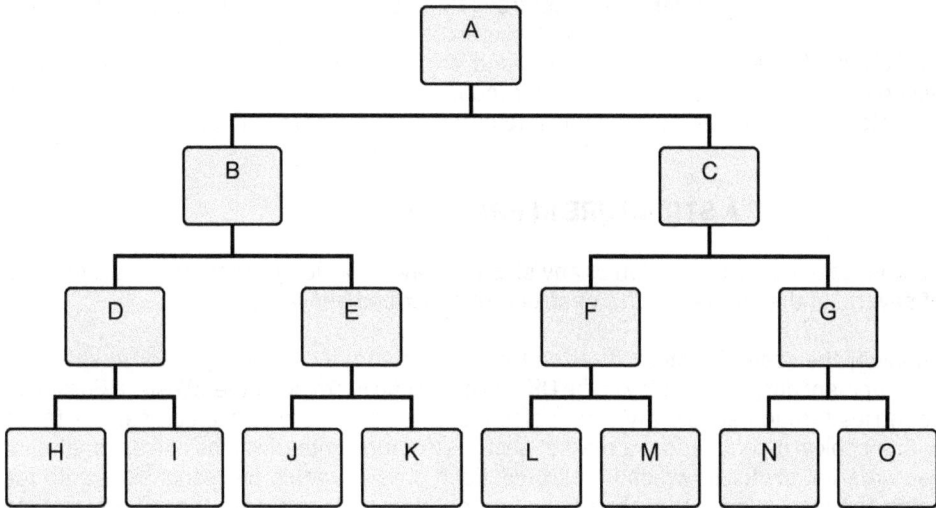

Figure 4.3 Twelve people organised into a three-level structure

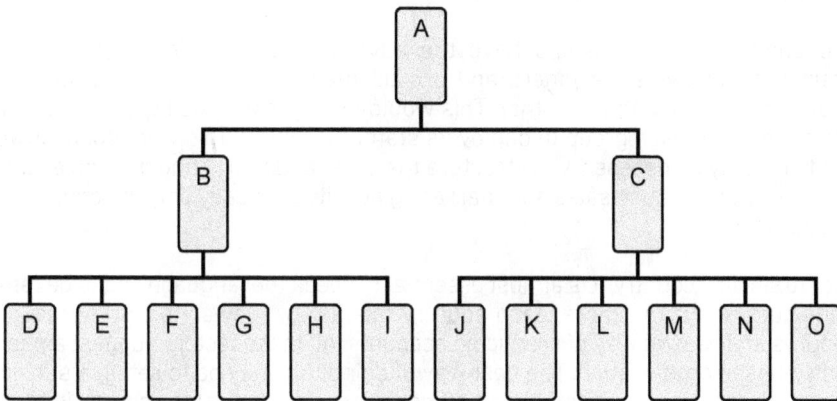

when essential. In a decentralised company, as much power and control as possible is delegated to the lowest level. If we take a software company as an example, centralisation might mean that there were company-wide rules that all projects should use an agile methodology such as Scrum. Such a policy has the obvious advantages that developers can be easily moved from one part of the company to another. On the other hand, it might mean that a project that was much better suited to a waterfall style of development might be forced to use agile methods and tools that were totally unsuitable. Decentralisation would allow the most suitable methods and tools to be chosen for each project but might mean that the staff were very inflexible. It could also lead to a maintenance nightmare in the future, with maintenance staff needing to be familiar with large numbers of obsolete tools.

Finding the correct balance between centralisation and decentralisation is important but difficult. Decentralisation is commonly found in high-tech companies, where there is plenty of talent at lower levels. Centralisation is commoner in large manufacturing companies and other long-established organisations. The ideal might be described as **flexible centralisation**, in which rules and practices are laid down centrally but it is accepted that reasonable arguments for modifying them in specific cases will be readily accepted. Unfortunately, putting this into practice often proves difficult.

4.5 SETTING UP A STRUCTURE IN PRACTICE

In most cases an organisation of any size will have a structure that includes elements of several of the different types of structure described above.

Consider the case of a medium-sized UK-based company providing bespoke software development and consultancy in the UK and operating in several other Western European countries through subsidiary companies there. At the top level, the company is faced with a choice. It could adopt a market sector structure, with divisions corresponding to each market sector in which it operates. Each division would be responsible both for sales and marketing in that sector and for operations – that is, carrying out projects for that sector. Alternatively, it could adopt a functional structure with a sales and marketing department and an operations department. In either case it would seem sensible to have a finance and administration department, probably under the management of the finance director.

The functional structure would have the advantage of bringing together all the programmers, analysts, designers and project managers in one group and all the sales and marketing staff in another. This would offer great flexibility and would likely enable the head of each group to deploy its staff efficiently. If this were done, however, it would probably be necessary to structure the sales and marketing division according to market sector, because sales and marketing activity is usually only effective if aimed at specific sectors.

In order to sell in a country, it is almost essential to speak the language and to be familiar with the culture. Furthermore, each country has its own laws, its own bureaucratic procedures and its own way of producing accounts. All these factors suggest a need for a country-based organisation. The best way of doing this may be to set up a subsidiary company in each country, with a small office responsible for sales and marketing and for administration in that country. The subsidiary would be able to call on the sales and marketing division in the UK for specialist help.

The organisational structure within the operations division presents other difficulties. While a project structure will obviously be used to carry out individual contracts for customers, some higher-level structure is required. Do we group projects by market sector or by technical characteristics? It may be that both are appropriate – that is, projects where the risks and problems are technical are grouped into one or more units, depending on the technology required, while projects where application considerations are more important are grouped into units depending on market sector. Figure 4.4 shows an example of the sort of structure that such a company might adopt.

Figure 4.4 An organisational structure for a bespoke software house

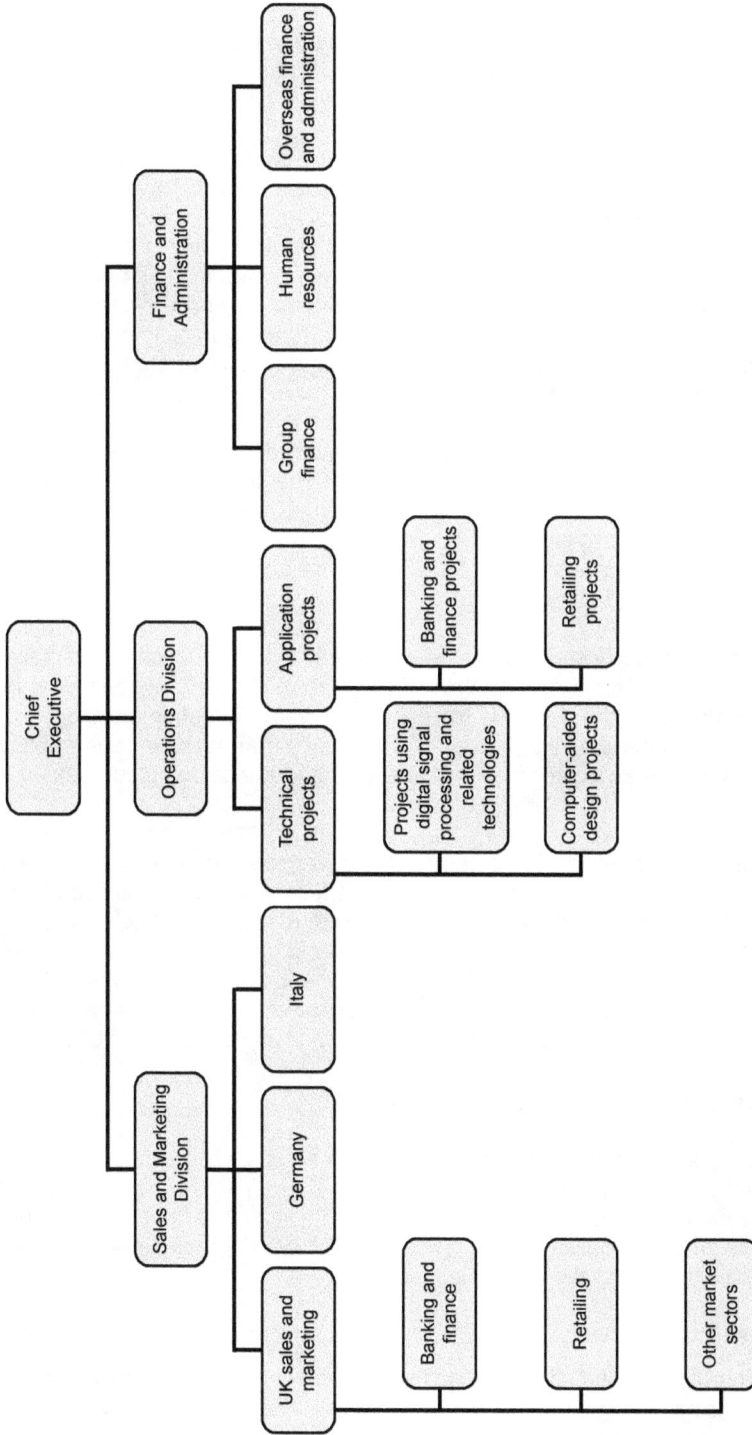

4.6 JOB DESIGN

Setting up an organisational structure implies designing jobs. As soon as a one-person organisation becomes a two-person organisation, it has to decide who does what. In other words, it has to design jobs. In project-based organisations, jobs get designed when the project team is set up and when the project plan is produced. The jobs are ephemeral – they last only as long as the project – and the technical nature of the project determines exactly what tasks the jobs have to cover. Nevertheless, this job design is done within an established framework: a project-based organisation will have (or should have) procedures that lay down the way in which project teams are to operate. Such procedures may mandate the use of agile development frameworks (such as Scrum) or specify the maximum span of control and the responsibilities of team leaders and project quality assurance staff in a hierarchically organised project. The tasks to be carried out will probably be defined by the development methodology that the company uses.

In many large organisations structured along bureaucratic lines, job specialisation leads to very narrow and tightly defined jobs. As a result, the people carrying out those jobs commonly find them dull and unsatisfying. This in turn leads to poor performance and high turnover. In an effort to alleviate this problem, companies have tried three different ways to provide more interesting and satisfying jobs: job rotation, job enlargement and job enrichment (explored below).

Few jobs in the IT industry suffer from the extremes of job specialisation that are found in production line jobs, for example. Nevertheless, managers should bear in mind that a software engineer who is expected to spend a full year on testing a system may well be led to apply for other jobs and that efforts to reduce staff turnover are unlikely to be successful if staff are expected to spend most of their time carrying out tasks that they find dull or distasteful.

The basic ideas of job design becomes of major importance when we are designing information systems. The introduction of the system can have a considerable impact on the jobs of its users. Very often this may involve an element of deskilling – that is, the jobs under the new system demand fewer skills or less knowledge from the people doing them. This tends to reduce job satisfaction. The way in which the system is designed can ameliorate this situation or exacerbate it. Information systems engineers should be concerned with the effect the system they are building will have on the work of its users.

4.6.1 Job rotation

Job rotation – that is, rotating staff through a series of jobs – is the most obvious way of preventing employees from becoming bored with a very narrow and specialised task. Consider the handling of creditors' invoices in a large accounts department with a very specialised regime. An analysis of the process might identify the following tasks, which then might be allocated to the individuals named:

1. Receive incoming invoice and match to purchase order (Freda).

2. Confirm price calculations and dispatch to receiving department for confirmation that goods or services have been received (Gareth).

3. Receive confirmation from department and pass for payment (John).

4. Produce payment (Peter).

5. Handle queries arising at any of the above stages (Julie).

Job rotation could be introduced very simply by arranging that in week one, Freda does task 1, Gareth task 2 and John task 3; in week two, Freda moves to task 2, Gareth to task 3 and John to task 1; in week three, Freda moves to task 3, Gareth to task 1 and John to task 2; and in week four they return to the tasks they carried out in week one. Some extra training would be required but any cost would be more than balanced by the added resilience of the department – that is, by its increased ability to handle absence through sickness or holiday.

However, including tasks 4 and 5 in the cycle would not be so easy. The principle of separation of responsibility as a means of reducing fraud means that the payment function should not be given to anyone who is involved at any point in authorising payment. Task 5 is inherently a more sophisticated task requiring both greater understanding and more experience.

4.6.2 Job enlargement

Job enlargement means redesigning a job so that it includes more tasks at essentially the same level of skill and responsibility. Thus, in the case of the example cited in the previous section, Freda, Gareth and John might each be asked to handle all three of tasks 1, 2 and 3 simultaneously. This might be done by allocating each of them responsibility for invoices from certain suppliers or perhaps for orders from certain departments. In this way, they would see more of the whole process and would be more likely to build up relationships with the departments or suppliers with which they dealt; this, in turn, would be likely to encourage them to take pride in their work.

4.6.3 Job enrichment

Job enrichment means redesigning jobs so that the amount of responsibility, discretion and control required of the employee is increased. In the accounts office example, this might mean encouraging Freda, Gareth and John to try to handle simple queries themselves, rather than refer them all to Julie. Care is necessary here. Some staff may be reluctant to take on extra responsibility, either because they fear that they may not be competent to handle it or because they like a simple and quiet life.

In the context of professional jobs in the IT industry, job enlargement and job enrichment usually turn out to be synonymous. Since almost all tasks involve an element of discretion, judgement and decision making, adding an extra task will always increase the extent of the job holder's discretion. However, whichever term we use, the idea can be an important and valuable one. Software maintenance is a notoriously unpopular task; it is common for an analyst to analyse and specify users' requests for changes while a programmer implements them. The job can be made much more attractive, and also valuable from the point of view of staff development, if it is enlarged so that one individual analyses user requests for changes, specifies the changes and obtains change control board approval, as well as implementing the changes and re-testing the system.

FURTHER READING

There is an enormous literature on organisations and management. At one end of the spectrum are the popular but superficial books to be found on airport bookstalls. The biggest weakness of such books is not that they are wrong nor that that their prescriptions are often imprecise. It is that their authors' experience is usually restricted to one type of company, typically in the retail sector, and that this limitation is reflected in their text. At the other extreme, there are jargon-filled books of great length, usually written by those who have little experience of business or management, which present elaborate theories that are applicable, if at all, only to very large organisations.

Nevertheless, there is a great deal to be learned about the subject from books and this chapter has barely scratched the surface. One author who avoids the two extremes mentioned above and writes in a thought-provoking way about the topics discussed in this chapter is Charles Handy. Two of his books can be strongly recommended, despite their age:

Handy, C. (1995) *Gods of Management: The Changing Work of Organisations* (3rd edition). Oxford University Press, London.

Handy, C. (2005) *Understanding Organisations* (revised 4th edition). Allen Lane, London.

5 FINANCING A START-UP COMPANY

After studying this chapter, you should:

- *understand why start-up companies need capital;*
- *be able to produce a simple business plan;*
- *understand the different ways in which capital can be raised and the advantages and disadvantages of each.*

5.1 WHY CAPITAL IS NEEDED

It is very difficult to start any commercial venture without having some money in hand, because your customers will not be willing to pay you until you have provided them with the service or product they are buying. You, however, have to buy the things you need to make the product or to provide the service, and you have to live while you are making or doing it.

To take a very simple example, suppose that you are setting up in business painting houses. You need to buy paint brushes, paint, ladders and so on. It may take you two weeks to paint a house and during this time you have to live. You will only get paid when you have finished painting your first house. Indeed, you may well find that your customers don't always pay immediately but take another two or three weeks to pay. The amount of money you need may not be very large but you will find yourself in difficulties if you haven't got it.

If you are setting up a company to build websites, you are likely to need much more money. First, because your customers are likely to be other companies, it will take you longer to get paid. In normal commercial practice, invoices for services are issued at the end of a month to cover the work that has been done during the month. A client is unlikely to pay an invoice within one month of receiving it. Two months is more likely with commercial clients and three months is not uncommon; some large companies are notorious for not paying invoices for as much as six or even twelve months. The result is that you need enough cash in hand to be able to live for at least three months. Additional money will be needed for the expenses of starting the company.

If you intend to develop a product, the sum of money needed is likely to be even larger. While the product is being developed, there will be no revenue coming into the company. For this period cash will be needed for:

- salaries, however small, for the founders and for any other staff they may need to employ;
- rent, rates, heating and lighting of the premises used;
- equipment and consumables;
- costs of advertising and marketing the products;
- miscellaneous expenses, ranging from company stationery to travelling expenses for any trips that may be necessary;
- interest on any money borrowed.

While it is often possible to carry out the early stages of development in the founders' spare time, working from their homes, this is not usually satisfactory once commercial sales have started. However successful the development of the package is, it will take some months before sales reach a level sufficient to cover the company's ongoing costs, so, even after development is complete, more cash will be needed.

5.2 THE BUSINESS PLAN

The first step in raising the money is to produce a business plan. This is a document that explains your plans to potential funders and tries to convince them that these plans are well thought out and realistic, and that the venture is likely to be successful. It should contain:

- A description of what the company will be doing, together with information to show that it is technically feasible and that the founders of the company have the necessary expertise.
- A description of the market the company is aiming at, an estimate of its size and an assessment of the competition. It might contain statements like the following: 'The company's target market will be small firms providing repair and maintenance services to householders, within a radius of 15 miles of the centre of Llanafan. So far as can be estimated from the data provided by the Llanafan Chamber of Commerce, there are around 1,200 such firms in the area, only 16 of which have websites. There are two other companies offering website design and hosting services in the area but neither appears interested in this market.'
- Evidence that potential customers will be interested in the product.
- A prediction of the financial performance of the company. This will include budgets, cash flow predictions, and projected balance sheets and profit and loss accounts. These are dealt with in the following chapters.

Armed with the business plan, you are in a position to approach people who might be willing to lend you money, invest money in your company or even give you money as a grant.

It is a mistake to think of a business plan as a prediction of what will happen when and if you succeed in starting your company. It should be seen much more as a scenario that demonstrates that your company has a reasonable chance of success. A business plan should state the assumptions that have been made and analyse the consequences of these assumptions proving to be wrong. Investors will make their own decisions about the credibility of the assumptions. Many of the internet-related companies that failed in the so-called dot-com crash of 2001 did so because their estimates of the size of their markets were hopelessly unrealistic. Any shrewd investor should have seen this from their business plans.

5.3 SOURCES OF FINANCE

Government policy in the UK has, over recent years, strongly encouraged the growth of small companies and, as a result, there are many possible sources of funding. However, they can all be grouped under three headings: grants, loans and sale of equity. Many other countries have similar policies but there are big differences between countries in the way that the policies are implemented, and policy within a single country can swing violently over time.

5.3.1 Grants

A grant is a sum of money given to a company. While the company is obliged to demonstrate that it has been used for the purposes for which it was intended, it is not planned that the grant should ever be paid back to the organisation that gave it. Not surprisingly, grants are only available from government (local or national) or, very occasionally, from charities. Commonly, grants are limited to a certain proportion of the money spent on a particular development and are conditional upon the remainder being raised from other sources.

The availability of grants and other help for new companies depends very much on where the company is located, how many people it expects to employ and government policy at the time. For example, at the time of writing (2022), grants of up to £1,000 are available for companies with fewer than 10 employees starting up in Scarborough and grants of up to £5,000 are available to established companies with fewer than 30 employees planning to move to Scarborough; in either case, the grant is limited to 50% of the costs of what is proposed. The grants are not available to businesses in certain categories, such as estate agents and holiday accommodation.

The Scarborough example is typical of the sorts of grants offered to start-up companies. These are usually:

- intended to assist with capital investment – typically investment in premises and equipment;
- subject to a number of conditions, in particular the raising of capital from other sources;
- limited to a certain proportion of the capital investment that the company can prove it has made.

This means that grants are often of limited usefulness to small software companies, whose investment more usually takes the form of employees' time.

Innovate UK, a government agency, offers grant support to assist in the development of high-tech products. Some of these are very specific programmes aimed at well-defined sectors of industry, such as aerospace or agriculture, while others are available across broader fields.

Very much larger grants than those described above are available to established companies intending to make substantial investments that will lead to the creation of many jobs. The UK government's Automotive Transformation Fund, for example, has provided substantial grants to support investment in electric vehicles and supporting infrastructure.

5.3.2 Loans

While grants are undoubtedly very helpful, their effect on company finance is short term. The major sources of finance are loans and the sale of equity (explored in the next section).

A loan is a sum of money lent to the company. Interest is payable on it, at a rate that may be fixed or variable, and the loan is usually for a fixed period. The company has to pay back the loan eventually and, if it goes into liquidation, the lender is entitled to recover the loan from the sale of the assets of the company. In most cases, security (in this context sometimes known as collateral) for the loan is required. In other words, the company agrees that if it fails to make repayments, the lender is entitled to sell some of the company's assets in order to make up for the shortfall, rather in the same way that, if you borrow money to buy a house and then fail to keep up the repayments, the lender can sell the house to recover the loan.

It often happens that small companies do not have sufficient assets to cover the loan they are looking for. In this case, the lender may ask for personal guarantees from the directors of the company; this may mean that the directors have to use their own homes or other property as security for the loan.

It is usual to divide loans into **overdrafts** and **long-term loans**. An overdraft is the most flexible form of loan. Overdrafts are offered by banks; they allow a company (or an individual) to spend more money than is in its account, up to a specified maximum. Interest is only payable on the amount actually owed and the rate is normally comparatively low; it is usually fixed at a certain number of points above the bank base lending rate, the precise figure depending on the bank's view of the credit-worthiness of the borrower. While overdrafts are the most flexible and usually the cheapest way to borrow, there is a price to be paid. A bank can withdraw overdraft facilities without warning, possibly for reasons of general policy that have nothing to do with the borrower. Many small companies have been forced into liquidation unnecessarily as a result of such action by banks.

In contrast, long-term loans are usually made for a fixed period at a fixed rate of interest. The borrower receives the capital (the amount of the loan) at the start of the period of the loan and is committed to paying interest on that amount throughout the period of the loan. Provided the borrower pays the interest on time, the lender cannot call in the loan. The borrower must repay the capital at the end of the period.

As a result of various government initiatives, a **soft loan** may be available; this is a loan on terms that are less onerous than those that prevail for commercial loans. Soft loans are usually only available to start-up companies; the interest rates may be lower than commercial interest rates and security is not demanded.

Public limited companies can raise loans through stock exchanges by issuing what are known as **corporate bonds**. For private companies, however, loans are usually provided by banks or similar institutions. Even if a soft loan is available as part of a government initiative, it will usually be channelled through a commercial bank. In some instances, start-up companies are able to borrow money from relatives or friends of the founders – or, indeed, the founders may be able to lend the company money themselves. In such cases, it is important that the loan is put on the same sort of formal basis as a commercial loan. If it is not, and things go wrong for the company, there is real danger that confusion will lead to bitter arguments and will end up spoiling personal relationships.

At the time of writing, government-backed start-up loans of £500 to £25,000 are available to those starting up or wishing to grow a small business.

5.3.3 Equity capital

Equity capital is money paid to a company in exchange for a share in its ownership, as described in Section 3.3.

The founders of a new company often find the initial capital from their own resources or from friends and family, but few are able to continue raising capital in this way. If a company looks to have good prospects but needs to raise more capital, it will usually need to resort to business angels or venture capitalists.

Business angels are wealthy individuals who provide equity capital for start-up companies and small firms that are seeking to grow rapidly. They are usually interested in investing in firms operating in areas of which they have some experience and, as well as providing capital, they will usually expect to offer advice on management and other business issues. Business angel networks are organisations that bring business angels together and provide mechanisms to assist small companies to find suitable business angels and vice versa. The networks usually operate at national or regional (i.e. sub-national) levels.

Venture capitalists are companies whose business is investing in small companies with high growth potential. They are usually only interested in fairly substantial investments, from, say, £500,000 upwards.

If the company is already operating, the shares issued to business angels or venture capitalists will usually be new shares, taken from the difference between the issued capital and the authorised capital. The new investors will probably be paying substantially over the par value of the shares.

Both business angels and venture capitalists aim to make money by helping the company to expand and become successful and then selling their shares at a profit. Of course, many of their investments will not be very successful and a significant number may fail completely. They aim to offset these losses by very substantial gains in the most successful cases; often this happens when the company has grown enough to be floated on a stock exchange, so that its shares become publicly traded.

5.3.4 Crowdfunding

Crowdfunding is the practice of funding a project or venture by raising money from a large number of people. It is far from being a new idea. In the 18th and 19th centuries, it was common for the publication of books and music to be funded by inviting members of the public to subscribe – that is, to commit to purchasing a copy of the work when it was published. In recent years, the internet has provided a convenient and effective means of contacting prospective funders.

Crowdfunding is most effective when it is used to fund the development of a specific product that is seen to have some social benefit, particularly when it appears that the development would not take place if it were left to normal commercial sources.

5.4 GEARING

The relationship between loan capital and equity capital in a company is important. It is known as **gearing** or **leverage**. Shareholders are at a much greater risk of getting a poor return on their capital or even losing it completely than are lenders but, in compensation for this, they stand to make a greater profit than lenders if all goes well.

Suppose a company is started with share capital of £100, owned by its two founders, and that it has a fixed-term loan of £100,000 at an interest rate of 10%. If, in its first year, the company makes an operating profit of £10,000, the interest charges will consume all the profit and the shareholders will receive nothing. If the company's operating profit doubles, to £20,000, the lender will still receive £10,000 but, neglecting taxation and assuming that all the profit is distributed to the shareholders, the shareholders will receive £10,000, a very handsome return on an investment of £100. Furthermore, as the profits increase, the value of the company, and hence the value of the shares, increases. If the company is sold, the shareholders will get much more than their original £100 investment, but the lender will still only be entitled to its original £100,000 plus interest. If, on the other hand, the company is unsuccessful and goes into liquidation, the lender will be at the front of the queue of people to whom money is owed, whereas the shareholders will get nothing until everyone else has been paid in full.

Such high levels of gearing are undesirable both from the point of view of the shareholders, because so much of the company's income is committed to interest payments, and from the point of view of the lenders, because shareholders may encourage the company to trade recklessly in the knowledge that they have little to lose and a lot to gain. Most lenders will be reluctant to lend money if a company seems too highly geared.

FURTHER READING

The UK government has a website that includes financial and other advice on setting up a business and gives valuable guidance on producing a business plan. It also provides links to currently active small business support schemes:
>   https://www.gov.uk/browse/business

Information about government-backed start-up loans can be found at:
>   https://www.gov.uk/apply-start-up-loan

Innovate UK (formerly the Technology Strategy Board) is a UK government agency that provides money and support to organisations to make new products and services:
>   https://www.ukri.org/councils/innovate-uk

Information about the UK Business Angels Association can be found on its website:
>   https://ukbaa.org.uk

Additionally, there are a number of regional networks of business angels in different parts of the UK. There is also a European Business Angels Network:
>   https://www.eban.org

There are innumerable books on finance and accounting that will take the reader beyond what is covered in this book; most of them are, however, intended for budding accountants. A good treatment for non-specialists can be found in:
>   Atrill, P. and McLaney, E. (2022) *Accounting and Finance for Non-specialists* (12th edition). Pearson Education, Harlow.

That book covers the material in this chapter and the next three.

6   FINANCIAL ACCOUNTING

After studying this chapter, you should understand the nature and purpose of the three most important financial elements of a company's annual report:

- *the balance sheet;*
- *the profit and loss account;*
- *the cash flow statement.*

You should also be able to interpret them in straightforward cases.

6.1 DISCLOSURE REQUIREMENTS

The proprietors of limited liability companies are privileged, precisely because their liability is limited – they can lose no more than the money they invested in the company. In return for this privilege, the law requires that, every year, the company produces an **annual report**, which must be filed at Companies House. An annual report contains information about a company and its activities during the preceding year. In particular, it contains information about the company's financial health so that those who are considering dealing with the company can judge whether it is likely to meet its obligations.

Precisely what must be included in an annual report depends on the nature of the company. If it is a small company, the requirements are less onerous. If the company is a public one – that is, if its shares are available for purchase by the public through trading on a stock exchange – the stock exchange will impose additional **disclosure requirements**. In other words, it will require the company to make more information public. In recent years, a series of scandals have led to calls for greater openness and more extensive disclosure of companies' activities, which have, in turn, led to the inclusion of further statements and more extensive notes in companies' annual reports. Some of these statements and notes are required by stock markets and some have simply become regarded as good practice. On the whole, but by no means universally, software companies set good examples in this regard.

The financial information in a company's annual report is subject to **audit**. This means that it must be formally checked and verified by registered auditors. In the UK, registered auditors must be members of one of the following bodies:

- Association of Authorised Public Accountants;

- Association of Chartered Certified Accountants;
- Institute of Chartered Accountants in England and Wales;
- Institute of Chartered Accountants of Scotland.

6.2 THE BALANCE SHEET

The purpose of the balance sheet is to show what the company owns – its **assets** – and what it owes – its **liabilities**. It is a snapshot of the state of the company at a particular point in time, normally at the end of the last day of the company's financial year.

6.2.1 Balance sheet for a student

Perhaps the easiest way to get to understand the idea of a balance sheet is to look at the balance sheet not of a company but of an individual. We take an imaginary student called Jemima Puddleduck and, as is usual, we show her present position side by side with her position a year ago, so that it is easy to make a comparison. Notice also the common accounting convention of putting a number in parentheses to indicate that it is negative, rather than using a negative sign as is normal in science or mathematics. Jemima's balance sheet is shown in Table 6.1.

Table 6.1 Balance sheet for a student

Jemima Puddleduck Balance sheet As at 31 October 2021	2021	2020
ASSETS		
Cash in hand	25	40
Cash at bank	361	240
Pre-paid accommodation	1,300	1,180
Debts owed by friends	18	0
Computer	240	360
Guitar	160	180
Personal effects	200	200
Total assets	2,304	2,200
LIABILITIES		
Credit card bill	174	64
Student loans	4,800	1,900
Total liabilities	4,974	1,964
Net worth	(2,670)	236

Jemima's most obvious asset is money. She has £25 in cash in her purse and another £361 in her bank account. The next two items are less obvious. The accommodation item refers to the fact that Jemima has paid a term's fees to the hall of residence in advance; since the balance sheet refers to the position on 31 October, some 60% (six weeks out of ten) of this accommodation has not been used. Depending on the regulations of the hall, if the accommodation is no longer required, Jemima may be able to get a refund on the unused period or sell it to another student; in other words, she has paid for the right to live in hall for a further six weeks and this right could be converted into cash and is therefore an asset. In a similar way, the debt of £18 owed by friends could be turned into cash and is also therefore an asset.

The next two items are more complex because they represent capital items – that is, things that Jemima will continue to own and use for a fairly long period. She owns a computer, which cost £480 including the software when her parents bought it for her two years ago. She also owns a guitar, which she bought for £200 in 2019. Standard accounting practice is to reduce the value of fixed assets each year to reflect the likely lifetime of each asset; the fall in the value of the asset from one year to the next is called **depreciation**. Thus, Jemima will probably keep her computer for four years before it becomes obsolete and she has to replace it with a new one. The simplest and commonest way of calculating the depreciation is to assume that it falls in value uniformly – that is, that it loses value at a rate of £120 per year. Hence after one year, it is worth £360, after two years £240, after three years £120 and at the end of the fourth year it no longer has any value. Musical instruments typically have a longer life than computers. We have assumed that the guitar will have a life of 10 years, so that its value drops by £20 each year.

The figure given for personal effects covers the many personal items that everyone owns, including clothes and books. We simply take an approximate figure for these, because the calculations involved in dealing with them precisely would be far more extensive than the value of the items justifies.

The valuation of assets can be a contentious issue. For the moment we shall simply accept the figures given in the balance sheet but we shall have more to say on this topic when we come to look at a commercial balance sheet.

Jemima's liabilities are more straightforward. She owes money on her credit card and she has a student loan. The credit card debt is an example of a short-term debt; she is expected to repay it fairly quickly, although she may increase the debt by making further purchases. The student loan is a long-term debt that does not need to be repaid until she graduates and is earning a reasonable salary.

As its name suggests, a balance sheet must balance: the total assets and total liabilities should be equal. To achieve this we need to include a **balancing item** on one side or the other; it is often labelled 'excess of assets over liabilities' but in this case we have chosen to call it 'net worth' because it represents the amount of cash that Jemima would have if all her assets were sold and all her debts were paid off – in other words, how much, in financial terms, she is 'worth'. The net worth plus the liabilities together equal her total assets. In her case, as with many students, her net worth is negative.

6.2.2 Commercial balance sheets: Assets

Commercial balance sheets are prepared on precisely the same basis as we have just described but the assets and liabilities are grouped into various categories and a single figure is given for each category. There will be several notes to the balance sheet describing the basis of the accounts and giving more detail about certain items; such items will cross-reference the notes. Table 6.2 is an example of such a balance sheet for an imaginary software services company.

Table 6.2 Balance sheet for a services company

XYZ Software Ltd Balance sheet As at 31 October 2021	2021 £'000	2020 £'000
FIXED ASSETS		
Intangible assets	475	–
Tangible assets	960	770
Investments	50	82
Total fixed assets	1,485	852
CURRENT ASSETS		
Work in progress	550	621
Debtors	3,400	2,580
Cash in hand and at bank	2,491	1,770
Total current assets	6,441	4,971
CREDITORS: AMOUNTS FALLING DUE WITHIN ONE YEAR	(3,210)	(2,601)
Net current assets	3,231	2,370
Total assets less current liabilities	4,716	3,222
CREDITORS: AMOUNTS FALLING DUE AFTER ONE YEAR		
Borrowings	(154)	(61)
Provisions for liabilities and charges	(7)	(16)
Net assets	4,555	3,145
CAPITAL AND RESERVES		
Called-up share capital	318	308
Share premium reserve	350	145
Profit and loss account	3,887	2,692
Shareholders' funds – equity	4,555	3,145

Assets are classified as **current assets** and **fixed assets**. The essential difference between the two is that fixed assets contribute to the company's productive capacity and are held primarily for the purpose of creating wealth, while current assets are items which are bought and sold in the course of its day-to-day trading activities. The fixed assets are further subdivided into investments (e.g. shares in other companies), **tangible** assets (assets which have some physical existence) and **intangible** assets (assets such as copyright in software or ownership of brand names, which have no physical existence).

In most cases the difference between fixed assets and current assets is easily perceived. A new file server bought to support program development facilities in a software house and a machine tool used to produce satellite dishes are clearly examples of fixed assets; a stock of paper for the laser printer is equally clearly a current asset. It should be borne in mind, however, that the treatment of the same item may vary from organisation to organisation or even within the same organisation. Thus, if a company buys a car to enable one of its sales staff to operate more effectively, this is a fixed asset; however, if a car dealer buys a car in order to resell it as part of the business, this is a current asset. If the software house buys a computer on which it will implement special software before delivering the whole system to a client, the computer is a current asset, not a fixed one.

The rules of accounting state that current assets are shown on the balance sheet with a value that is the lower of what they cost and what it is expected they could be sold for. Suppose a company has a stock of 1,000 user manuals for a piece of software that it sells. The manuals sell at £10 each but cost £2 each to produce. Then they will appear on the balance sheet as worth £2,000, the cost price, rather than £10,000, the resale price. On the other hand, a stock of printer paper that cost £5,000 would only be saleable for a lower figure, say £2,000. It would therefore appear on the balance sheet at the resale price, because this is lower.

In contrast to current assets, fixed assets are not expected to be sold in normal trading operations and their resale value is irrelevant; what is needed is a measure of their value to the company. In practice, this is done by reducing their value each year in accordance with the company's depreciation policy. Much the commonest way of doing this is the so-called straight-line method we described in connection with Jemima's computer. We first decide how many years the asset will continue to be useful for. We then divide its initial cost by that number to get the annual depreciation. Each year, we reduce (or **write down**) the value of the asset by the amount of the annual depreciation until the value of the asset reaches zero. Suppose a company buys a large database server costing £100,000 and expects to use it for five years. Then the annual depreciation will be £20,000 (£100,000 / 5) and the values shown in the balance sheet will be £80,000 at the end of year one, £60,000 at the end of year two, £40,000 at the end of year three, £20,000 at the end of year four and zero at the end of year five. It is customary to depreciate all items of the same type over the same period and this will be stated in the notes to the accounts, which might include statements such as 'it is the company's policy to write off all computer equipment over a period of three years and office furniture over a period of ten years'.

Assets are generally valued on the basis of historical cost – that is, their original monetary cost. In times of high inflation, this can be seriously misleading. The value of certain types of fixed assets, in particular land and buildings, may increase rather than decrease. Some companies therefore arrange to have their property revalued from time to time and include this valuation in the balance sheet.

Tangible fixed assets must be recorded in the company's fixed asset register and, from time to time, their presence will be physically checked by the auditors. Each year, depreciation must be calculated and, if a fixed asset is sold for a sum higher than its depreciated value, the company must show the difference as income. Because of these complicated procedures, it is usual to treat all purchases of less than, say, £1,000 as expenses in the year in which they are incurred.

There are some items that are difficult to classify. Software is one example. Consider a payroll package. A company buys a licence to use such a package because it will help the company to carry out part of its day-to-day operations more efficiently. The licence will be bought with the intention of using it for some time, at least five years and probably ten or fifteen. Logically, the package should be treated in the same way as a piece of machinery – that is, as a fixed asset – and the initial cost should be depreciated over its useful lifetime. The rules of accounting allow this to be done. But, because software is intangible, many companies treat the cost of buying it as current expenditure.

The treatment of research and development is a particular problem. Logically, resources spent on developing new products should be regarded as an investment that will produce a fixed asset – that is, something that will allow the company to operate more effectively. However, the results of research and development are always uncertain and often prove to be worth very little. To treat all the costs as investment would be misleading. In practice, most software companies in the UK treat expenditure on research and development as current expenditure rather than as investment, although the accounting rules allow for more flexible treatment. In the USA, there are strict rules regarding the capitalisation of software that is developed for sale; these rules are based on a rather unrealistic model of the product life cycle.

Intangible fixed assets are the source of much discussion in the accounting profession. Software is generally regarded as an intangible asset but it is more tangible than many items (e.g. brand names, which are often shown as intangible assets). An item that frequently appears under intangible assets on the balance sheets of software product companies is **goodwill**. This might arise, for example, if XYZ Ltd purchased another company, PQR Ltd, that owned the rights in a profitable package. If, as is likely, the package was not shown as an asset on PQR's balance sheet, XYZ would probably have paid much more to buy PQR than the value of its net assets. The difference between the price paid for PQR and the value of its net assets would represent XYZ's estimate of the value of the rights in that package (and, possibly, other things such as the value of PQR's name). This would need to be shown on XYZ's balance sheet. While it would be preferable for the value of the package to be shown explicitly, this is not normal practice and the whole of the difference between the purchase price and the value of PQR's net assets would normally be shown under the heading of goodwill. It would then, of course, need to be depreciated over a fixed period. The notes to a company's accounts will normally itemise any acquisitions and give details of the goodwill arising from each one. When internet companies change hands, a similar situation occurs, but, in this case, the intangible assets may be much more difficult to identify; they are certainly less tangible than the rights to a package.

Readers who are football fans may be interested to know that football clubs that are organised as public companies – Manchester United, for example – include among their intangible assets the rights to the services of players whom they have bought.

6.2.3 Commercial balance sheets: Liabilities and owners' equity

The entry in Table 6.2 under 'creditors: amounts falling due within one year' refers to debts that the company has and is committed to repaying within one year. These will include trade creditors – that is, outstanding invoices that the company has received but has not yet paid – in just the same way that the 'debtors' item refers to invoices that the company has issued but that have not yet been paid. They will also include any bank overdraft, as opposed to a long-term loan.

The figure obtained by subtracting the current liabilities (i.e. 'creditors: amounts falling due within one year') from the current assets, referred to as 'net current assets' in the example, is also known as the **working capital**. It represents the amount of money invested in the day-to-day operations of the company, as opposed to its infrastructure.

'Creditors: amounts falling due after one year' refers to long-term debts. These may be long-term borrowings or they may be other sums that the company expects to have to pay at some time in the future – for example, payment of compensation arising from the company's failure to fulfil a contract.

When the total liabilities are subtracted from the total assets, we arrive at a figure called the 'net assets'. These are balanced by items under the heading of 'capital and reserves'. There are a number of ways in which the capital and reserves may be listed. First, there is the item labelled 'called-up share capital'. This is the amount raised from the par value of the shares that the company has issued. When a successful company decides to issue more shares, these are often sold at more than their par value. The extra is known as the share premium and the money raised from this is shown under the next heading, as the 'share premium reserve'. In our example, the remainder is labelled as 'profit and loss account', indicating that it results from the accumulated surplus on the profit and loss account over the life of the company.

The total under the heading of 'capital and reserves' is often known by names such as shareholders' equity, owners' equity or owners' claim. It notionally represents the value of the company to its shareholders.

6.3 THE PROFIT AND LOSS ACCOUNT

The profit and loss account shows how much money has been received and how much has been spent in a given period – usually the organisation's financial year. In the USA it is usually known as an income statement and in the case of non-profit-making organisations it is usually called an income and expenditure account.

6.3.1 Profit and loss account for a student

Table 6.3 shows a profit and loss account (which can also be called an income and expenditure account) for our imaginary student. It does not include money borrowed or received from the sale of equity, nor does it include expenditure on acquiring fixed assets.

Table 6.3 Income and expenditure account for a student

Jemima Puddleduck Income and expenditure account Year ended 31 October 2021	2021	2020
INCOME		
Contribution from parents	1,500	1,300
Income from summer job (net)	1,840	1,682
Total income	3,340	2,982
EXPENDITURE		
Course fees	1,050	1,025
Hall fees	2,100	1,980
Books	30	25
Clothes and personal items	179	120
Transport	134	112
Food	1,400	1,247
Entertainment	1,303	840
Depreciation	140	140
Total expenditure	6,336	5,489
Excess of income over expenditure	(2,996)	(2,507)

It is important to observe that the excess of expenditure over income – that is, the amount that Jemima has overspent – is the same as the difference in her net worth between 2020 and 2021. This will usually be the case in simple situations where there has been no capital investment. In more complicated cases, particularly with commercial organisations, other items enter into the relationship.

Just as in the balance sheet, there is a certain arbitrariness about the way in which items have been aggregated. We could, for example, have lumped together 'food' and 'entertainment' under the heading 'living expenses' or have split 'transport' into 'road' and 'rail'. We have chosen to show the income from the summer job net (i.e. the take-home pay) rather than show it gross (i.e. before deductions) with tax and National Insurance on the expenditure side.

Some explanation of the depreciation item is required. The net figure at the bottom of the profit and loss account should reflect the extent to which the organisation – or, in this case, the individual – is better or worse off at the end of the year than at the beginning. Clearly, a fall in the value of the assets tends to make the organisation or individual worse off. Depreciation, although it is not an expenditure in the sense that cash is paid out, reflects this decline and is therefore shown as an expenditure. The figure of £140 arises from the depreciation of the computer and the guitar.

6.3.2 Profit and loss account for a company

A commercial profit and loss account looks very different from Jemima's income and expenditure account, even though precisely the same ideas underlie it. Table 6.4 shows an example for a fictitious computer services company. Just as with the balance sheet, we see that items have been aggregated into very broad categories; the notes to the accounts will usually provide more detail. A package company, for example, might show in the notes how much of its income came from sales of packages, how much from training and consultancy, and how much from maintenance contracts.

Table 6.4 Profit and loss account for a services company

XYZ Software Ltd Profit and loss account Year ending 31 October 2021	2021 £'000	2020 £'000
TURNOVER		
Continuing operations	14,311	11,001
Acquisitions	407	–
Total turnover	14,718	11,001
COST OF SALES	(11,604)	(8,699)
Gross profit	3,114	2,302
OTHER OPERATING EXPENSES	(1,177)	(805)
Operating profit	1,937	1,497
INTEREST PAYABLE	(23)	(27)
Profit on ordinary activities before taxation	1,914	1,470
TAX ON PROFIT ON ORDINARY ACTIVITIES	(719)	(480)
Retained profit for the year	1,195	990

A number of points about this statement need to be explained. First, the turnover for a company acquired during the year is shown separately from the turnover from continuing operations – that is, operations that were carried on in 2020 and 2021. This is to facilitate the comparison between the two years. In the same way, if part of XYZ had been disposed of in 2020, its turnover would have been shown under the heading 'discontinued operations'.

A second point is the distinction between 'cost of sales' and 'other operating expenses'. This distinction is an uncertain one and some companies do not show the items separately. However, for a package software company, there is a real difference between, on the one hand, expenditure on selling, printing documentation, installing software and so on (all of which are the costs of sales) and expenditure on the development of new versions of existing packages or on new products (which would come under the heading of 'other operating expenses').

The bottom line shows the retained profit – that is, the profit not paid out in tax or dividends to shareholders. This is added to the retained profit in the previous year's balance sheet to give the value of the retained profit that is shown in the new balance sheet.

The profit and loss account itself gives very little information about where the company's revenue during the year has come from or how it has spent its money. Such information is normally given in the notes to the accounts. The notes to the accounts in the 2021 annual report of Sage Group plc (see the Further Reading section), for example, give a breakdown of turnover by both geographical area and market sector (Sage is a UK company that is one of the largest suppliers of accounting software in the world). It shows numbers of staff and expenditure on wages and salaries, social security costs, and pension costs – and other costs are also broken down into a number of categories. Package companies will often also show a breakdown of revenue into licence fees, maintenance charges and consultancy fees. On the whole, software companies are fairly open in revealing information in the notes to their accounts but the level of detail provided in other sectors varies enormously from company to company.

6.4 THE CASH FLOW STATEMENT

As we have already pointed out, the income and expenditure account does not show expenditure on capital items, only their depreciation; capital expenditure affects the balance sheet but the balance sheet does not give sufficient information to deduce how much this expenditure amounts to and how it was funded. The link that ties the balance sheet and the profit and loss account to the capital expenditure is the cash flow statement.

6.4.1 Cash flow statement for a student

A moment's examination of our student's financial statements will reveal that, because there is no cash flow statement, there is no explanation of where the money to purchase her guitar came from.

FRS 102 (the Financial Reporting Standard; see Further Reading section) defines cash as 'cash at bank and in hand and cash equivalents less bank overdrafts and other borrowings repayable within one year of the accounting date'. In Jemima's case, this means £361 (the money in her bank account) plus £25 (the notes and coins in her possession) less £174 (her credit card debt) – that is, £212. The previous year the figure was £240 + £40 – £64 = £216. One function of the cash flow statement is to explain this difference of £4.

The most obvious source of a change in the amount of cash Jemima holds is her profit and loss account. She appears to have spent £2,996 more than she received. This is her major cash outflow. In fact, not all of this sum is a cash outflow. The item of £140 for depreciation corresponds to a reduction in the value of her capital assets but not to any outflow of cash. To take this into account, we add the depreciation back in as a cash inflow. The only other cash outflow is the £18 that she has lent to a friend. This is not expenditure because it is repayable. Nevertheless, it represents cash that has been paid out. If Jemima had bought her guitar during the year, its cost would also have appeared as a cash outflow.

We see from her balance sheet that Jemima's student loan increased by £2,900 from 2020 to 2021. This means that she received £2,900 in cash from that source. While it is an inflow of cash, it is not income, because it will have to be repaid; hence it does not appear as income on the income and expenditure account.

These changes are summarised in Table 6.5, which shows Jemima's cash flow statement.

Table 6.5 Cash flow statement for a student

Jemima Puddleduck Cash flow statement Year ended 31 October 2021	2021	2020
CASH INFLOW		
Addition to student loan	2,900	1,900
Add back depreciation	140	140
Total cash inflow	3,040	2,040
CASH OUTFLOW		
From income and expenditure account	2,996	2,507
Loans made to friends	18	0
Total cash outflow	3,014	2,507
Increase/(decrease) in cash over the year	26	(467)

Jemima Puddleduck's cash flow statement tells us very little more than we could deduce from her other financial statements. In the case of a company, however, the cash flow statement has much more to tell us, because there are many more sources of cash flows.

6.4.2 Cash flow statement for a company

Figure 6.1 shows the cash flows that are captured in the cash flow statement of a typical company. The arrows show the *normal* direction of the flow in a profitable company but it is always possible for the flows to be in the opposite direction. Table 6.6 shows the cash flow statement for our example company.

The first source of cash is the operating profit before tax generated during the year. This needs to be adjusted for certain items that may appear in the profit and loss account but do not involve the movement of money in or out of the company. The most obvious of

Figure 6.1 Sources and destinations of cash flows

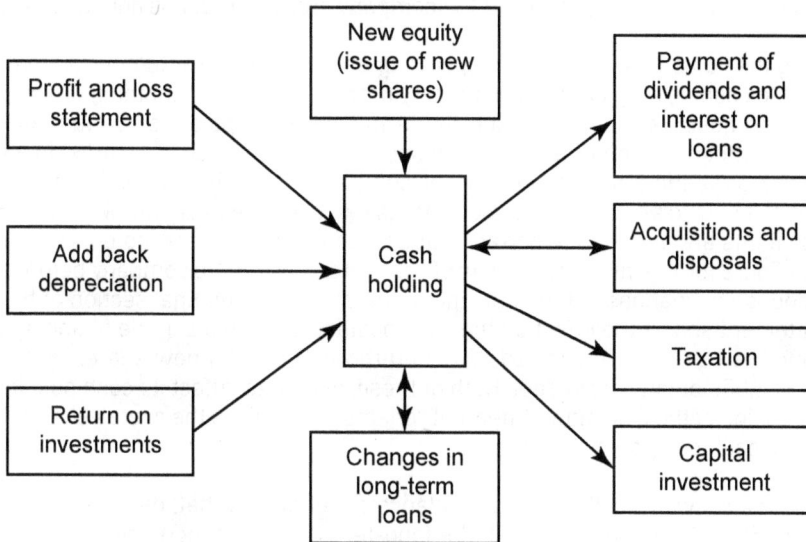

Table 6.6 Cash flow statement for a software company

XYZ Software Ltd Cash flow statement Year ending 31 October 2021	2021 £'000	2020 £'000
Net cash inflow from operating activities	2,105	1,620
Returns on investments and servicing of finance	(23)	(27)
Capital expenditure and financial investment	(220)	(265)
Taxation	(719)	(480)
Acquisitions and disposals	(380)	
Equity dividends paid		
Cash outflow before financing	(1,342)	(772)
Net cash inflow before financing	763	848
FINANCING		
Issue of share capital	215	100
Repayment of long-term loan	(50)	
Net cash inflow from financing	165	100
Increase in cash in the year	928	948

these is depreciation. This was entered in the profit and loss account to reflect the extent to which the life of the fixed assets was consumed during the year; in no way did it reflect the movement of money out of the company and so it must be added to the profit.

Following the adjusted figure for the operating profit, there are a number of items that may lead to cash flowing out of the company for reasons that are nothing directly to do with its operations. Taxation, interest payable and dividends paid are obvious examples. Capital investment in equipment or premises is another reason cash may flow out of a company, as is the purchase of another company. In some circumstances (e.g. the disposal of a subsidiary company), these items can give rise to an inflow of cash. When all these items are added together and subtracted from the operating profit, we arrive at a total figure for the inflow or outflow of cash into or out of the company before taking into account any changes in the financing of the company. The final section of the cash flow statement shows the effect on the cash position of changes in the financing of the company. The company has raised £215,000 through issuing new shares; it has also paid off £50,000 of long-term debt. Both of these, of course, affect its cash position and the bottom line of the cash flow statement reflects this; it gives the overall change in the company's cash position over the year.

The alert reader will recall that XYZ's balance sheet shows that, despite the fact that a loan of £50,000 has been paid off, the long-term debt has increased from £61,000 to £154,000 and that there is nothing in the cash flow statement to account for this. It almost certainly arises from the acquisition of another company. The statement shows that £380,000 was spent on acquisitions; the likelihood is that the company brought substantial debts that were taken over by XYZ as part of the deal. This would be explained in the notes to the accounts.

At this point we should make clear that the financial statement of XYZ Software Ltd shows a vigorous company growing very rapidly in an expanding market. It is typical of some young and successful IT services companies but not typical of many other industries.

6.5 THE OVERALL PICTURE

The balance sheet, the profit and loss account, and the cash flow statement can none of them be understood or interpreted in isolation. Their relationship to each other needs to be understood and they need to be looked at together when assessing the financial state of a company.

The balance sheet shows a snapshot of the financial position of a company at the end of an accounting period (usually the company's financial year), while the profit and loss account and the cash flow statement describe what has happened during the accounting period and thus explain the relationship between successive balance sheets. This is illustrated in Figure 6.2. The profit and loss account explains the relationship between the owners' equity in the two balance sheets, while the cash flow statement explains the relationship between the cash items shown in the two balance sheets. This is illustrated in Figure 6.3.

Figure 6.2 The relationships between the three financial statements

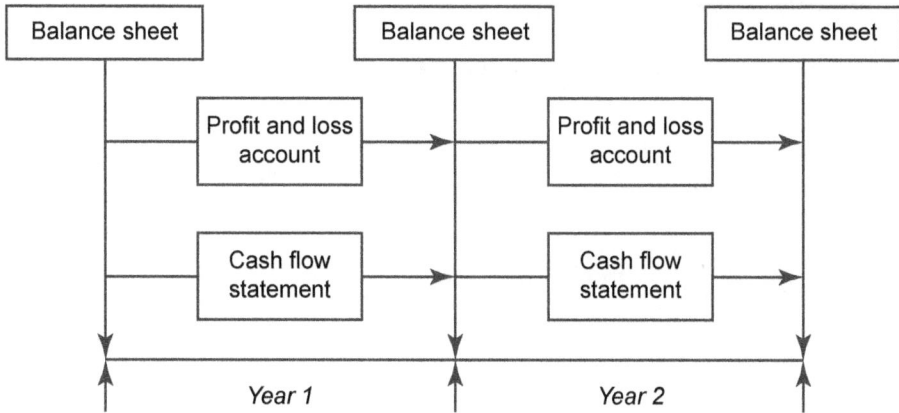

Figure 6.3 How the cash flow statement and the profit and loss account affect the items in the balance sheet

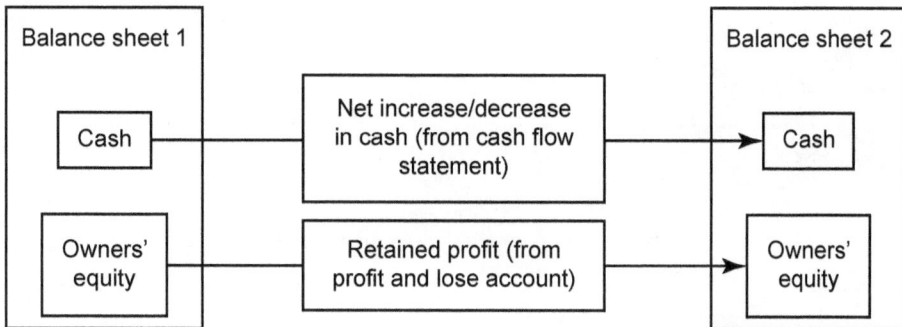

FURTHER READING

The book by Atrill and McLaney recommended at the end of Chapter 5 also covers the material in this chapter.

The Financial Reporting Council (FRC) is the body responsible for regulating accountants, auditors and actuaries in the UK by setting standards for corporate governance, financial reporting and audit. The standards for financial reporting that apply to most commercial organisations are laid down in FRS 102 (The Financial Reporting Standard), which is applicable in the UK and the Republic of Ireland. The latest version of this document can be found on the FRC's website:
      https://www.frc.org.uk

It is a lengthy, detailed and complicated document and is not for the faint hearted!

The annual report of the Sage Group for 2021 can be found at:
'Download and Browse Our FY21 Annual Report and Accounts' (n.d.) Sage. https://www.sage.com/investors/financial-information/annual-report.

The accounts and the notes to them start on page 178.

7   MANAGEMENT ACCOUNTING

After studying this chapter, you should:

- *understand how to produce a budget and a cash flow forecast, and know how to monitor them;*
- *be able to calculate the unit cost of labour;*
- *understand the concept of overheads and the different ways in which they may be distributed;*
- *be able to determine how much it costs to produce a particular product or provide a specific service.*

7.1 PLANNING AND MANAGEMENT INFORMATION

The previous chapter was concerned with financial accounting – that is, with reports about the financial state of a company as a whole. Such reports are public and are required to meet standards set by the law and by stock exchanges. The information they contain is intended primarily for potential investors and trading partners. It is historical – that is, it is concerned with what happened in the past.

The reports produced by financial accounting are not very useful in the day-to-day running of a company. Managers need plans and accounting information that will help them to make good business decisions. This means, above all, up-to-date information about costs and sales, so that the company's actual progress can be monitored against the plans included in its budget and its cash flow forecast. It is these documents that are the main subject of this chapter.

The need for up-to-date and accurate financial information implies a need for a well-planned financial system based on suitable software. Unless a company has suitable experience within its staff, it is advisable to seek professional advice in this area.

7.2 BUDGETS AND OVERHEADS

A budget is a financial plan showing the expected income and expenditure of an organisation over a specific period, typically one year. In order to produce a budget for a company, we have to make some assumptions about what it will be doing. We shall illustrate the idea of a budget by considering a small company that sells desktop computers that it assembles from bought-in components and basic software. We will suppose the owner runs the company and that it employs three technicians and a part-time administrative assistant. It owns a van that it uses for delivering computers to customers.

The company makes three models of computer: the Basic, the Advanced and the Professional. Table 7.1 shows the costs of the components for each model, the number of hours of technician time it takes to build each one and the expected sales of each model over the next year.

Table 7.1 Direct costs and expected sales

Model	Cost of components	Technician time	Expected sales
Basic	£200	10 hours	250
Advanced	£300	12 hours	100
Professional	£400	15 hours	50

A possible budget for the company is shown in Table 7.2. It contains an estimate of the company's costs and income over the next year of operations.

Table 7.2 An example budget

OVERHEAD EXPENDITURE	
Owner's payroll costs	42,000
Admin assistant's payroll costs (part time)	8,000
Costs of van (including depreciation)	3,500
Internet connection, telephone, postage, etc.	1,000
Advertising	2,000
Premises (heating and lighting, rent, rates, etc)	4,500
Professional fees	1,000
Insurance	500
Total overheads	62,500
OPERATING COSTS	
Technicians' payroll costs	101,160
Bought-in components	100,000
Total operating costs	201,160
Total costs	263,660

(Continued)

Table 7.2 (Continued)

SALES INCOME	
Basic model (250 @ £595)	148,750
Advanced model (100 @ £795)	79,500
Professional model (50 @ £895)	44,750
Total income	273,000
Profit	9,340

The costs under the heading 'overhead expenditure' are ones that the company will have to pay regardless of how many computers it sells. For this reason, they are often known as **fixed costs**. Most of these costs are obvious enough but three items may require some explanation. We have said that the company is run by its owner. For many reasons, to do particularly with taxation and National Insurance (social security), the owner should be treated as an employee and pay themselves a salary, rather than attempt to live on the company's profits. This accounts for the item labelled 'owner's payroll costs'. Unless the owner is an experienced accountant, the services of an accountant will be necessary to help prepare the annual accounts and possibly to give advice from time to time. The advice of a lawyer may also be necessary on occasion. These items are covered under the heading 'professional fees'. Finally, employers are legally required to have insurance to cover any claim against them for injuries suffered by employees during the course of their employment. Other insurance, against theft from the company's premises, for example, may also be necessary. This explains the heading 'insurance'.

The total figure of £62,500 for overheads is money that the company has to pay out and that it therefore needs to recover from its sales.

Unlike the overheads, the figures under the heading 'operating costs' depend on the number of computers the company sells. For this reason, they are known as **variable costs**. The cost of components is directly connected to the number of computers sold, while the cost of the technicians can also be adjusted to match the sales volumes, though less easily, by recruiting another technician or making a technician redundant.

The sales income is based on the company's best estimate of how many computers it can sell and at what prices. We note that the prices are not directly related to the costs (by whatever method of calculation).

Once a budget has been agreed, it should be used to monitor the company's financial progress. The first step is to break it down to show monthly income and expenditure – a budget broken down in this way is sometimes called a **profiled budget**. At the end of each month, the management then compares what has actually happened during the month with what was planned in the budget. Where income or expenditure differ significantly from what was planned, the management will investigate the reasons for the exceptions and decide what action, if any, to take. If, for example, sales income is 30% lower than predicted, managers might decide to mount a further advertising campaign or they might decide to cut costs by reducing staff. The point is that they will be made aware of the problem as soon as it appears and can take appropriate action quickly.

7.3 COST OF LABOUR

The cost of employing someone is more than just the cost of their salary. In most countries, employers are required to pay a tax for every employee. This tax usually goes by a name such as Employers' National Insurance Contribution (the UK name) or social security contribution; it is proportional to the employee's salary. In some countries, this contribution may be as large as 60% of salary while in others it is very much smaller. We discuss the situation in the UK further below.

There may be other costs associated with an employee, depending on the law and the practices of the individual country. We discuss pension schemes below. Additionally, the company may pay for medical insurance for its employees. Senior employees may be provided with a car or other benefits. The total cost of employing a person – that is, the salary plus employers' social security contributions plus any other costs directly associated with the employee – is sometimes known as the employee's **payroll cost** or **direct cost**.

Consider one of the technicians who is employed to assemble the computers and suppose that they are paid an annual salary of £30,000. To calculate the cost of the time the technician spends assembling a computer, the annual payroll cost is not very helpful. What we need to know is the cost per hour. This is harder to calculate than we might expect. First, we need to calculate how many days we can expect the technician to work. There are 52 weeks in a year. Assuming the company works a five-day week, there will be 260 weekdays. However, the company will be closed for public holidays and the technician will not be working. The number of public holidays varies from country to country and even within a country. In England and Wales there are normally eight public holidays a year. There are also eight in Scotland but they are different. In Northern Ireland there are normally ten. In 2022, however, there was an extra public holiday throughout the UK to celebrate the 70th anniversary of Elizabeth II becoming queen. Elsewhere, there are 10 public holidays in the USA and in Pakistan, 12 in Singapore, 17 in Mauritius and 22 in Sri Lanka.

In addition to public holidays, employees are generally entitled to a certain amount of paid leave. In the UK, most employees are, by law, entitled to 28 days of paid annual leave; public holidays are counted towards these. (This is generous by international standards. Indeed, in many countries there is no requirement to grant paid annual leave.)

In addition to their annual leave, employees may miss some working days because of sickness. While we cannot predict accurately how much time will be lost in this way, it is usual to guess at a reasonable average of, say, five days per employee. Finally, it may well be that there are some days in the year when, because of scheduling difficulties, there will be no revenue-earning work available for the employee. Finally, we assume that employees work for seven hours per day. Table 7.3 shows how all these factors can be taken into account to obtain a figure for the number of revenue-earning working hours that can be expected from an employee over the period of one year.

Table 7.3 Calculation of the number of revenue-earning hours in a year

Total number of weekdays (1)	260
Public holidays (2)	10
Annual leave (3)	28
Sick leave (4)	5
Unproductive time (5)	15
Total non-revenue-earning time (6) Calculated as: (2) + (3) + (4) + (5)	58
Total number of revenue-earning days (7) Calculated as: (1) – (6)	202
Total number of hours available Calculated as: (7) × 7	1,414

In the UK, the law requires employers to make a contribution to a pension scheme. The details are complicated but we shall assume here that the employer's contribution is equal to 3% of an employee's salary. The employer also has to pay what is called the Employer's National Insurance Contribution. At the time of writing, this is 13.8% of salary above £9,564 per year. Table 7.4 shows how the cost per hour is worked out.

Table 7.4 Calculation of the hourly cost of labour

Annual salary		£30,000
Employer's pension contribution	3% of £30,000	£900
Employer's National Insurance Contribution	13.8% of £(30,000–9,564)	£2,820
Total annual cost		£33,720
Hourly direct cost	£33,720 / 1,414	£23.85

The direct annual cost of employing the technician will thus be £30,000 plus the 3% pension contribution and the Employer's National Insurance Contribution, which is 13.8% of (£30,000 – £9,564). This leads to an annual direct cost of £33,720, so that the direct cost of an hour of a technician's time is £33,720 / 1,414 = £23.85. The budget makes provision for three technicians at a salary of £30,000 each.

7.4 ALLOCATION OF OVERHEADS

In a large business, there are many ways in which overheads can be spread over the different activities the business performs; there is no single 'right' way of doing this.

One way or another, the company has to recover the overhead costs of £62,500. The only way it can do this is collect it from the income it gets from sales. However, there are many different ways in which this can be done. We shall describe three of the most common ways of doing this.

The simplest way is to allocate the same fixed overhead to each computer sold, regardless of the cost of the components or the amount of labour involved. Since we expect to sell 400 units, this means £156.25 per computer. The Basic model would then cost

$$£156.25 + £200 + 10 \times £23.85 = £594.75$$

The Advanced model would cost

$$£156.25 + £300 + 12 \times £23.85 = £742.45$$

and the Professional model would cost

$$£156.25 + £400 + 15 \times £23.85 = £914.00$$

The second way of allocating the overhead is to make it proportional to the number of hours of labour involved. This means adding an overhead component to the cost of an hour of a technician's time. Since we have three technicians, each supplying 1,414 hours of productive labour per year, we need to add

$$£62,500 / (3 \times 1,414) = £14.73$$

to the cost of an hour's labour, making it up to £23.85 + £14.73 = £38.58. Now the cost of the three models comes out at

$$£200 + 10 \times £38.58 = £585.80 \text{ (Basic)}$$
$$£300 + 12 \times £38.58 = £762.96 \text{ (Advanced)}$$
$$£400 + 15 \times £38.58 = £978.70 \text{ (Professional)}$$

Finally, we can distribute the overhead in proportion to the total cost – that is, taking into account the cost of components as well as the cost of labour. The direct cost (components and labour) of each model are

$$£(200 + 10 \times 23.85) = £438.50 \text{ (Basic)}$$
$$£(300 + 12 \times 23.85) = £586.20 \text{ (Advanced)}$$
$$£(400 + 15 \times 23.85) = £757.75 \text{ (Professional)}$$

The total direct cost is therefore

$$£(250 \times 438.50 + 100 \times 586.20 + 50 \times 757.75) = £206,132.50$$

This means that we take this direct cost (components and labour) and add on a fixed proportion to generate an extra £62,500 of income. To calculate this proportion, we divide the total overhead by the total direct cost of all the units we expect to sell – that is, we divide 62,500 by 206,132.5, which gives 0.30. This means the costs are £(438.50 × 1.30) = £570.05 for the Basic model £762.06 for the Advanced model and £985.08 for the Professional model.

Table 7.5 summarises the cost (to the nearest pound) of the three different models according to the three different ways of distributing the overheads.

Table 7.5 Effects of different overhead calculations

	Fixed overhead	Overhead proportional to labour content	Overhead proportional to total direct cost
Basic	595	586	570
Advanced	742	763	762
Professional	914	979	985

The costs calculated in this way can form the basis for pricing the computers. Certainly, computers should not normally be sold at prices that are lower than the costs. More commonly, the prices will be set on the basis of 'what the market will bear', that is, how much customers will be willing to pay, and this depends very much on the competition. The cost calculations will, however, show us where our costs lie and how to go about reducing them so that we can sell our products more cheaply.

7.5 CASH FLOW FORECAST

A company may be very profitable but unable to pay its bills. For that reason, it may be forced into receivership. This apparent paradox typically arises because bills have to be met – in particular, staff have to be paid – before the income the staff generate is received. In order to avoid this difficulty, businesses need to prepare cash flow forecasts – that is, estimates of the amount of cash that will flow into and out of the company each month.

Table 7.6 shows a cash flow forecast for our example company's operations. In order to keep the overall picture clear, we have only shown a six-month forecast. In practice companies normally try to forecast twelve months ahead. We have also made the rather unrealistic assumption that the company is launching into its operations at full stretch from day 1. Finally, because sales and energy costs are both seasonal, we have assumed that the company is starting operations on 1 January.

The figures in each cell show the amount of cash entering or leaving the company during that month, under the heading given at the left-hand end of each row. Thus, the figure of £500 given in the January column and the 'insurance' row means that an insurance premium of £500 will be paid sometime in January. The figure of £7,000 in the March column and the 'income from trade sales' row means that £7,000 will enter the company's bank account in March as a result of trade customers paying invoices.

The timing of the payments is important and it depends on commercial practice. Thus, rents are normally paid quarterly, in advance. Hence the rent payment will be made at the beginning of January and the beginning of April. Components will probably be

Table 7.6 A six-month cash flow prediction

	Jan	Feb	March	April	May	June
CASH OUTFLOW						
Rent and property taxes	500			500		
Energy costs		400	400	300	200	200
Payroll costs	9,666	9,666	9,666	9,666	9,666	9,666
Communications		83	83	83	83	83
Insurance	500					
Components		4,000	7,000	10,000	10,000	10,000
Advertising		1,100		250		500
Road tax and insurance on van	700					
Professional fees			300			
Van operating costs	100	100	100	100	100	100
Monthly cash outflow	11,466	15,349	17,549	20,899	20,049	20,549
CASH INFLOW						
Income from retail sales	5,000	5,000	5,000	5,000	5,000	5,000
Income from trade sales		5,000	7,000	10,000	15,000	18,000
Monthly cash inflow	5,000	10,000	12,000	15,000	20,000	23,000
Net monthly cash flow	(6,466)	(5,349)	(5,549)	(5,899)	(49)	2,451
Cumulative cash flow	(6,466)	(11,815)	(17,364)	(23,263)	(23,312)	(20,861)

bought against credit accounts with one or more suppliers. Under such arrangements, invoices for components delivered in one month will be issued at the end of that month and customers will be expected to pay the invoice within 28 days of its being issued. Similar arrangements will probably apply to energy costs but these will reduce as we move from the cold winter months into the warmer seasons.

We have assumed that retail sales – that is, sales to individuals – are paid for immediately and that these run at a steady level of £5,000 per month throughout the period. Trade sales – that is, sales to businesses – are typically paid for in the month following delivery. We expect these sales to increase steadily during the period. The total cash received for the six-month period is estimated to be £85,000. Since trade sales made in June will not appear in this figure, it looks as though the sales for the period are estimated to be around £105,000. The budget (Table 7.2) is based on total sales of £273,000, leaving £168,000 to be earned in the second six months. This is not unreasonable; demand both from consumers and from businesses is traditionally at its highest in September, October and November in many industries.

Assuming that the estimates are realistic, this forecast shows that at no time during the period will the cash received come close to balancing the cash paid out. At the worst point, at the end of May, the cash paid out will be £23,312 more than the cash received. This has nothing to do with the company's profitability; it could well be that the company is on track to meet the budget in Table 7.2 and make a respectable profit. Nevertheless, the company will need to have at least £23,312 available in cash if it is to keep operating through this period. Prudence suggests that it should plan on requiring £30,000 to allow for things going wrong.

The amount of cash required to allow the company to continue to operate over a period is known as its **cash requirement**. It is also often referred to as **working capital**, although, as we saw in Section 6.2.3, this term is more correctly used to refer to the difference between current assets and current liabilities. The two concepts are related but they are not identical. The traditional way of funding a company's cash requirement is through a bank overdraft but banks are not always eager to lend to small companies and loans from other sources may be necessary.

An initial cash flow forecast is an essential part of a business plan but a well-run company will maintain a rolling twelve-month cash flow forecast. That is, each month it will produce a new cash flow forecast for the next twelve months, the first eleven months of which will be an updated version of the figures in the previous month's forecast. Such forecasts will provide early warning of any prospective cash shortage and banks will generally respond well to a request for an increase in overdraft facilities that is made well in advance and based on detailed cash flow predictions.

At first sight, cash flow forecasts and budgets seem very much the same thing. It is important to understand the difference. Cash flow forecasts deal with the flow of cash or its equivalents in and out of the company. Budgets deal with income and expenditure. If our company delivers computers worth £100,000 to a large corporate customer today and sends it an invoice, this will immediately appear as income when we are monitoring the budget. However, many large companies are very slow to pay their bills and it may be three or four months before the invoice is paid and the corresponding sum appears as cash. The difference can be crucial.

FURTHER READING

The book by Atrill and McLaney recommended at the end of Chapter 5 also covers the material in this chapter.

8 INVESTMENT APPRAISAL

After studying this chapter, you should:

- *understand what is meant by the time value of money;*
- *be able to carry out a discounted cash flow analysis to assess the viability of a proposed investment proposal;*
- *be able to interpret a discounted cash flow analysis in commercial terms.*

8.1 INVESTMENT PROPOSALS

Successful companies are always looking at ways in which they can change and develop. The senior management will be faced with a number of different proposals, ranging perhaps from the development of a new product to establishing a company presence in a new part of the world. The company will only have a limited amount of money of its own available, and lenders and investors will only be prepared to offer limited amounts. The management is therefore faced with the need to decide which of the proposals to support.

There is no single way of assessing and comparing the different proposals; factors that must be taken into consideration include:

- the extent to which the proposals are consistent with the company's long-term plans;
- the risk attached to the proposals;
- the availability of the necessary resources even if the money is available.

One important criterion, however, is the financial one: which of the proposals will give the best return on the investment? The usual way of determining this is to use the method known as **discounted cash flow** (DCF). This is what we shall describe in this chapter.

It is important to realise that DCF is a tool that is used for many different purposes, for example:

- by investors on the stock market to assess whether the share price of a company accurately reflects its financial prospects;
- to assess whether it is better to purchase capital equipment or to lease it;
- to decide which of several possible projects is the most financially appealing;
- to decide whether a proposed capital project will be worthwhile.

In this book, however, we are concerned almost exclusively with the third and fourth of these.

8.2 THE TIME VALUE OF MONEY

Advertisements for cars often make offers like the following:

Wolseley Hornet
£8,995 or
only £500 down and £400 per month for 24 months

Suppose that you have £8,995 available so that you could pay cash if you decided to. Would you be better off at the end of two years paying cash at the beginning or taking the easy payment terms? We shall show how to answer this question a little later. For the moment, we consider a simpler situation.

Suppose that you have £100. You can choose to deposit it with a bank or some other savings organisation. If the rate of interest is 3%, then in a year's time you will have £103. In other words, the promise of £103 in a year's time is worth the same as £100 now. This simple example illustrates what is known as the **time value of money**. It forms the basis of DCF analysis.

In general, if the interest rate is r (expressed as a fraction, such as 0.03, not a percentage), then the present value of a sum of money (X) due in t years' time is:

$$\frac{X}{(1 + r)^t}$$

The quantity $1/(1 + r)^t$ is known as the **discount factor**. Table 8.1 shows the discount factors for periods up to five years for a range of interest rates.

Table 8.1 Discount factors for periods up to five years

Interest rate	Year 1	Year 2	Year 3	Year 4	Year 5
3%	0.9709	0.9426	0.9151	0.8885	0.8626
4%	0.9615	0.9246	0.8890	0.8548	0.8219
5%	0.9524	0.9070	0.8638	0.8227	0.7835
6%	0.9434	0.8900	0.8396	0.7921	0.7473
7%	0.9346	0.8734	0.8163	0.7629	0.7130
8%	0.9259	0.8573	0.7938	0.7350	0.6806
9%	0.9174	0.8417	0.7722	0.7084	0.6499
10%	0.9091	0.8264	0.7513	0.6830	0.6209
15%	0.8696	0.7561	0.6575	0.5718	0.4972
20%	0.8333	0.6944	0.5787	0.4823	0.4019

To use this table, we look for the cell in the row corresponding to the discount (interest) rate and the column corresponding to the time period. The value in this cell gives the discount factor. Thus, the discount factor for an interest rate of 8% over a period of four years is 0.7350. This means that, if the interest rate is 8%, the present value of a sum of £1,000 payable in four years' time is £1,000 × 0.7350 = £735.

We are now in a position to tackle the question of buying the car. The easy terms on the offer mean we pay £500 now, £400 at the end of the first month, another £400 at the end of the second month and so on until the end of the 24th month. Using the idea of discount factors, we can calculate the present value of each of those monthly payments. If we add the present value of all those payments to the £500 that we have to pay immediately, we will obtain the present value of the total of the payments we have to make. If this is more than £8,995, we will be better off buying the car outright immediately.

The discount rate that we need to use in doing our calculations is the rate of interest that we would receive on our £8,995 if we left it in our savings account. Let us assume that this is around 3% per year. We, however, need the equivalent monthly rate and this is 0.2466% per month. The equivalent monthly rate is not simply 1/12th of the annual rate because the interest is compounded. The monthly equivalent of a rate of r (as a fraction) is $(1 + r)^{1/12} - 1$. With this discount rate, the discount factors at the end of months one to three are 0.9975, 0.9951 and 0.9926. The present values of the first three £400 payments are thus £400 × 0.9975 = £399.00, £400 × 0.9951 = £398.04 and £400 × 0.9926 = £397.04. The necessary calculations are tedious but, fortunately, spreadsheets such as Excel have a built-in function for calculating the net present value (NPV) of a series of payments at a given discount rate. The result of applying this function to a sequence of 24 payments of £400 with a discount rate of 0.2466% is an NPV of £9,310.30. To this we must add the £500 down payment. This shows that the NPV of the payments on easy terms is £9,810.30. Clearly we will be much better off buying the car outright for £8,995 if we have the money available.

8.3 APPLYING DISCOUNTED CASH FLOW TO A SIMPLE INVESTMENT PROJECT

The essence of investment is that money is spent now so as to produce benefits in the future; assuming those benefits can be quantified in monetary terms, we need to ask what is their present value. To do this, we calculate the net cash flows that the project will generate over each year of its life and convert these to a present-day value. Then we add these up to get the NPV of the project as a whole.

As an example of simple DCF analysis, consider a small computer maintenance company. The company has one van that it uses for transporting computers that cannot be repaired on site to and from its workshop. When things are busy, the one van is not enough and the company often has to rent a second van. It is considering whether it is worthwhile to buy a second van.

A new van will cost £20,000. There will be annual costs of £1,000 for insurance and £275 for road tax. The cost of maintenance is estimated to be £400 in each of the first two years, £500 in year three, £600 in year four and £700 in year five. At the end of the fifth year, it is expected that the van will be sold for around £4,000. The interest rate that the company pays on its borrowings is 10%. Tax and insurance are subject to inflation, which is judged to be around 5% over the period, but the resale value of the van is the cash figure expected at the time. Van hire costs £60 per day and this is expected to increase by 5% per year. The company hires a van for about 100 days a year.

Table 8.2 shows the cash flows in the two cases. Most of the figures are in brackets, indicating negative cash flows, because the flows of cash are out of the company.

Table 8.2 Discounted cash flow analysis of van purchase versus renting

	Year 0	Year 1	Year 2	Year 3	Year 4
BUYING A VAN					
Van purchase/sale	(20,000)				4,000
Tax and insurance	(1,275)	(1,339)	(1,406)	(1,476)	(1,550)
Maintenance	(400)	(400)	(500)	(600)	(700)
Annual cash flow	(21,675)	(1,739)	(1,906)	(2,076)	1,750
NPV of annual flow	(21,675)	(1,581)	(1,575)	(1,560)	1,195
Total NPV	(25,196)				
CONTINUING TO RENT					
Annual costs	(6,000)	(6,300)	(6,615)	(6,946)	(7,293)
NPV of annual costs	(6,000)	(5,727)	(5,467)	(5,218)	(4,981)
Total NPV	(27,393)				
Discount factor		0.9091	0.8264	0.7513	0.6830

The NPV of the cost of continuing to rent is £27,393, while the NPV of the cost of buying a van is £25,195. We conclude that the company will be better off by buying a van, although the difference between the two options is not great. This conclusion depends, of course, on the validity of the assumptions. The main uncertainty is in the number of days for which a van would have to be rented. If the company's business expanded so that it would have to rent a van more often, the cost of the rental option would increase so that buying would have more of an advantage. If, however, business declined or the company were able to use the existing van more efficiently, the cost of the rental option would decrease and the advantage of buying would be reduced or even disappear.

8.3.1 Timing of the cash flows

The analysis assumes that the cash flows take place at the start of each period, so that the discount factor for year 0 is 1. In other words, the first payments are at the start of project so that their NPV is their actual monetary value. This is realistic for the costs involved in buying the van; the cost of the van itself is due when it is bought, which is effectively the start of the project, while the insurance and the road tax are both due at that point and on the same date in succeeding years. Only the comparatively small maintenance costs occur at different points during the year.

This assumption about the timing of the cash flows is not, however, valid for the rental option. The maintenance company is likely to have an account with the rental company so that it receives monthly invoices for the rentals in the previous month, so that the cash flows are distributed throughout the year. If we assume that on average the rental costs are paid half way through the year, we can correct for the result of assuming that the cash flows take place at the beginning of the period by applying a further six-month discount factor to the NPV. This factor is the square root of the annual discount factor, 0.9091 – that is, 0.9535. The resulting NPV is £26,118. The advantage of buying the van is thus slightly less than in the original calculation but is still significant.

8.3.2 Cost of capital

We said that the company pays 10% interest on its borrowings and we assumed that it would have to borrow the money to buy the van. This is an over-simplification.

Even if the company has the cash available to buy the van outright, there is still a cost because the company will lose the income it could have received by investing the money somewhere else – in a suitable interest-bearing account, for example. Such a cost is known as an **opportunity cost**. If the company is able to pay cash for the van, this is the interest rate it would be appropriate to use in the DCF analysis.

As we saw in Chapter 5, large companies raise money by taking loans, the rate of interest on which may be fixed or variable; by the issuing of shares, on which dividends may be paid; or by retaining profits. When a large company invests in new projects, the money required is likely to come from a combination of these. The company's financial director is expected to carry out arcane calculations to balance the cost of money from these different sources and come out with a single figure for the cost of capital, which the company will use in appraising all investment proposals.

8.3.3 Handling inflation

Inflation in a financial context means the fall in the value of money over time. It is usually expressed as an annual percentage. Thus, for example, an inflation rate of 5% means that in a year's time goods that today cost £100 will cost £105. In two years' time, they will cost £100 × 1.05 × 1.05 = £110.25. The inflation rate can vary very much from time to time and from country to country. Typically, in countries with a stable economy it will be under 5%, while in countries where the economy is disintegrating and out of control it can rise to several thousand per cent.

The presence of inflation means that the **monetary rate of interest** – that is, the rate that is normally quoted – is something of a delusion. For example, £100 invested at a quoted interest rate of 10% will be worth £110 in money in a year's time. However, if the rate of inflation is 5%, this £110 will only buy as much as £110 / 1.05 = £104.76 would buy today. Thus, the **real rate of interest** is only 4.76%.

In the example, we initially estimated all costs in today's pounds sterling. We then assumed an inflation rate of 5% and adjusted the cash flows for future years to take this into account. We used the monetary rate of interest rather than the real rate. In normal economic conditions this is the simplest way to carry out a DCF analysis. It is perfectly possible, however, to carry out a DCF analysis ignoring inflation and using the real rate of interest as the discount factor.

8.3.4 Financial cash flows

It is not necessary to include the cash flows associated with borrowing the money to buy the van – that is, the cash inflow when the bank loan is received and the interest payments are made to the bank. The DCF analysis automatically takes these into account so that the same result is obtained whether or not they are included.

8.4 ASSESSMENT OF A SOFTWARE PRODUCT PROPOSAL

As a more sophisticated example, we consider a company that is assessing a proposal for the development of a software product. It is estimated that three people will be required for development in year zero and a further person and a half in year one; suitable staff cost £35,000 per year, including the employer's pension and National Insurance costs. The product will be released in year one. After year one, maintenance is expected to require one person, full time. Sales and marketing costs are estimated to be £20,000 in the first year, rising to £30,000 for each of the next four years. The product itself is fairly high value but specialised. It is expected that about 100 copies will be sold over this period, at around £5,000 a copy. Table 8.3 shows the DCF analysis of the project over a five-year period, using 10% as the (monetary) cost of capital.

Table 8.3 Discounted cash flow analysis of a proposed software package development

	Year 0	Year 1	Year 2	Year 3	Year 4
COSTS					
Development cost	(105,000)	(55,125)			
Maintenance			(38,588)	(40,517)	(42,543)
Sales and marketing	(10,000)	(21,000)	(22,050)	(23,153)	(24,310)
INCOME					
Number of sales		10	20	40	30
Revenue		50,000	100,000	200,000	150,000
Net cash flow	(115,000)	(26,125)	39,362	136,330	83,147
Discount factor	1	0.9091	0.8264	0.7513	0.6830
Present value	(115,000)	(23,750)	32,529	102,425	56,789
Cumulative present value	(115,000)	(138,750)	(106,221)	(3,796)	52,993

In this table, we have shown additional entries for the **cumulative present value**. This is the NPV at the end of the first year, the NPV at the end of the second year (i.e. the present value of the cash flows for the first two years) and so on. The NPV of the project over its five-year life is the cumulative present value at the end of year four, shown in the bottom right-hand entry (£52,993), but there are other measures of a project's attractiveness that can be deduced from this table. One is the **pay-back period**; this is the time required for the project to achieve a positive net cash flow. For the project in the table, this is a little over four years, since the cumulative cash flow at the end of year three (£3,796) is close to zero and the cumulative cash flow is firmly positive by the end of year four. (The term **simple pay-back period** is sometimes used to refer to the pay-back period calculated without taking into account the time value of money.)

The pay-back period is important in a project like this one because predicting the sales of a software product three or four years ahead is a very uncertain activity. A project that promises pay-back within two years will therefore usually be preferred to one whose pay-back period is four or five years. The same thing would not necessarily be true of a project in a more stable industry, such as electricity generation, where it is quite normal to look 20 years ahead and to accept projects whose pay-back periods are 10 years.

It is also possible to calculate the **internal rate of return** (IRR) of a project. This is the cost of capital that would lead to the NPV being precisely zero. The calculation involves some difficult mathematics but, fortunately, most spreadsheets provide a function to calculate it. The IRR is the maximum cost of capital at which the project would be viable. For the figures in Table 8.3, it is 23%. The term **accounting rate of return** (or **simple return on investment**) is used to denote the average annual benefit as a percentage of the average investment.

There are times when interest rates can fluctuate quite violently, even in basically stable economies. This happened, for example, in the UK in the mid-1970s and again in the late 1980s. The IRR is a useful guide to the viability of a project in such an environment. An IRR of 23% at a time when a company's cost of capital is 10% means that the viability of the project will not be affected by any likely increase in interest rates.

A proposal will normally be rejected out of hand if its NPV is not positive, if its pay-back period is greater than some pre-set threshold or if its IRR is less than the current cost of capital. If there still remain projects between which a choice must be made, the organisation should probably choose those that have the highest positive NPV. This, however, usually reflects a long-term view and other pressures may cause companies to accept the projects with the highest IRRs or the shortest pay-back periods.

8.5 PITFALLS OF DISCOUNTED CASH FLOW

Because of its apparently precise nature, there is a tendency to put too much trust in DCF analysis. However precise the calculations, the cash flow predictions are inherently uncertain. An example of a case where uncertainty is comparatively low is the replacement of plant or equipment in the manufacturing or process industries. If the new plant is installed and functioning correctly by the scheduled date and if market conditions do not change dramatically, the cash flow predictions should be reasonably accurate and the major source of uncertainty will be the cost of capital. There will, of course, be occasions when the assumptions about installation of the plant and market conditions will prove false but this is likely to be the exception rather than the rule.

If we use DCF analysis to assess a proposal for developing a software product, as we have done above, then the sources of uncertainty are very much greater. Although a NPV of £52,993 and an IRR of 23% look attractive, we must take into account that:

- most software projects take more effort than expected;
- most software doesn't work very well when it is first released;
- we may not manage to sell as many copies as we expect;
- there is a considerable risk that a competitor will launch a similar product before ours is ready.

We need to assess how sensitive the project is to such risks. The way to do this is to carry out a series of DCF analyses with different estimates of the cash flows and the discount rate and see how the results change. If the project remains attractive under the different sets of assumptions, it is comparatively low risk; if it becomes unattractive under small changes, then it is high risk and should probably be rethought. In the example given, if the sales in year three dropped from 40 to 20, the cash flow would never become positive. Predicting sales this far ahead is very uncertain, so the project should be regarded as high risk. On the other hand, if the price were increased to £6,000, the NPV would rise to £117,420 and the pay-back period would fall to two years. This sensitivity to changes in sales volumes and selling price is characteristic of software product developments.

FURTHER READING

The following book is highly recommended. It contains a lot of more detailed material specifically concerned with the assessment of IT investment proposals, as well as some material covering other aspects of finance and accounting:

Blackstaff, M. (2012) *Finance for IT Decision Makers: A Practical Handbook* (3rd edition). BCS, London.

The book by Atrill and McLaney recommended at the end of Chapter 5 also covers the material in this chapter.

Much of the other literature on DCF is aimed at investors on the stock market or in other financial markets. It is not therefore directly relevant to the appraisal of alternative investment proposals within a company.

9   HUMAN RESOURCES ISSUES

The purpose of this chapter is to explain some of the most important human resources issues that affect companies in the IT sector. After studying it, you should:

- *appreciate the complexity of the law in this area;*
- *understand the constraints under which management and human resources staff act;*
- *understand why and to what extent managers need to be aware of general human resources issues.*

9.1 INTRODUCTION

The term human resources (HR) emphasises the fact that the people who work for an organisation are an indispensable part of its resources. Very often, the people are the most important part. For this reason, the organisation will try to ensure that it always has available the appropriately skilled, qualified and experienced staff that it needs in order to exploit its other assets. This must be done without wasteful over-staffing and within the constraints of what is lawful. The cost of recruiting new staff is high and the loss of continuity when staff leave can also be very expensive. Accordingly, the organisation will want to keep staff turnover low. Many organisations (though by no means all) want to behave as 'good' employers and will therefore try to follow the best of current employment practice.

Any organisation that employs staff will be faced with the need to handle administrative issues relating to their employment. When the number of employees grows to, say, a dozen, one person will have to devote a significant proportion of their time to this. By the time the number of employees reaches around 30, a full-time personnel officer or HR manager will be required. It is important that managers and HR staff can work together to meet the needs of the organisation and its staff, as well as meeting the legal requirements.

9.2 THE LEGAL CONTEXT

HR management is practised in an environment beset by legislation. The legislation is primarily designed to protect the rights of employees, because employers often have more power in their relationship with their employees.

Employment is an area in which it is often difficult to legislate clearly. The practical effect of much of the legislation can only be assessed in the context of subsequent decisions by the courts and by tribunals. To make the situation worse, it is a political battleground so that changes in the legislation occur frequently – there were four Acts relating to employment and three relating to trade unions between 1980 and 1993, for example. There was a consolidating Act – the Employment Rights Act 1996 – that was intended to bring all the employment legislation together but there have since been further substantial changes. Examples of more recent legislation include the Enterprise and Regulatory Reform Act 2013, the Small Business, Enterprise and Employment Act 2015 and the Trade Union Act 2016. Therefore, anything on the subject is in danger of being out of date, which makes this very much a field for experts.

During the 20th century, up to the end of the 1970s, industrial relations in Britain were based on collective bargaining and were conceived very much in terms of relations between **trade unions** and employers. In particular, the rights of trade unions received much more prominence than the rights of individual employees. There were times when industrial disputes about employment issues led to strikes, with notable instances in the 1970s and early 1980s. **Secondary action** was common, so that companies that had nothing to do with a dispute could find themselves subject to strike action.

There were attempts at some reforms in the 1960s under a Labour government, but they failed because of the strength of the opposition from trade unions. It was the 1980s when successive Conservative governments changed the law relating to industrial relations and trade unions. The changes were aided by economic conditions that led to the decline of the heavy industries, which had been the stronghold of trade union power. While trade unions do not have the same power as during most of the 20th century, they still play an active role in the UK. The unions represent and support the employment rights of their members, particularly in the civil service, the NHS, education and local government.

The erosion of the collective power of employees through the limitations on the rights of trade unions has been balanced by a significant increase in the rights of individual employees. This started in the 1960s with legislation to ensure equal pay for women. This is an example of **anti-discrimination legislation**; this topic is so important we shall deal with it in a chapter of its own (Chapter 10). **Employment tribunals**, sometimes known as **industrial tribunals**, were introduced in 1964. These are special courts designed to handle cases concerning employment rights and related matters. They provide a cheap and comparatively speedy way for employees to take action if they consider that their rights have been breached. The concept of **unfair dismissal** was introduced in the Industrial Relations Act 1971. There has been a steady stream of legislation outlawing discrimination of various kinds, which was brought together in the Equality Act 2010.

Responsibilities of the HR department

The greater attention paid to the rights of individual employees and the need to comply with anti-discrimination legislation have very considerably increased the workload of HR departments in the UK. The following list is a summary of the responsibilities they are expected to take on within the overall aim of ensuring that the organisation has the workforce that it needs:

- ensuring that recruitment, selection and promotion procedures comply with anti-discrimination legislation;
- overseeing staff training and development;
- setting up and monitoring remuneration policy;
- setting up and monitoring appraisal procedures;
- administering dismissal and redundancy procedures;
- handling contracts of employment;
- engaging in workforce planning;
- designing and administering grievance procedures;
- being aware of new legislation affecting employment rights and advising management of what the organisation must do to comply with it;
- overseeing health and safety;
- administering consultative committees.

The need to comply with so much new legislation has forced HR departments to adopt formal, bureaucratic procedures. The procedures aim to help organisations meet their legal obligations so that there is a reduced risk of legal action. The procedures deal with some sensitive areas such as recruitment and grievance procedures, where delays and mistakes can have an impact on people's lives and the organisation. Unfortunately, the procedures are sometimes felt to be burdensome and unwelcome by those staff who see themselves as carrying out an organisation's core functions. At the same time, comparatively junior staff in HR may find themselves having authority over some decisions that more senior staff elsewhere in the organisation regard as their prerogative. Effective management of HR issues requires early action and patience from staff throughout an organisation, to successfully deal with the complexity in employment law.

9.3 RECRUITMENT AND SELECTION

HR managers often make a distinction between the terms **recruitment** and **selection**, using recruitment to mean soliciting applications and selection to mean selecting the applicants to whom offers will be made. The two can be seen as separate activities, and recruitment, particularly at a professional level, may be outsourced to specialised agencies. Such agencies handle the advertising and, often, carry out initial screening of applicants, before presenting their clients with a shortlist of suitable applicants. They charge a fee that is normally based on the salary of the person appointed, typically something like 25% of the first year's salary.

The best of these agencies are thoroughly professional and offer an excellent service. Unfortunately, some recruitment agencies indulge in very questionable practices that might discourage people from considering the jobs. Taking time to select an agency with a good reputation will help the recruitment process.

9.3.1 Recruitment

Before you employ a recruitment agency, you need a description of the job to be filled and the type of qualifications or experience you expect in the successful applicant; a good agency can help draw this up. Note that there are two clearly different situations: it may be that you need to fill a specific post, such as Manager of Feline Rodent Elimination Agents, or it may be that you are looking for as many good staff with experience of programming in Python as you can find. In the latter case, the job description is likely to be much less precise, specifying simply a range of activities that people appointed may be expected to carry out.

Some organisations may encourage their employees to promote job opportunities to their contacts. There may be financial rewards for the employee if one of their contacts is selected through the usual process and stays with the organisation. This happens sometimes where recent graduates provide a connection to other graduates with similar skills from the same university.

9.3.2 Selection

Selection is kept in the hands of the employer, although a member of the recruitment agency staff may sometimes be invited to advise. A wide range of selection techniques are available and are used in making professional appointments. Some of these follow. Note, though, that the methods below apply to professional appointments. Selection of, say, bar staff or cleaners is likely to be done using a single interview backed up by references.

One-to-one interviews
A series of one-to-one interviews with senior management and senior technical staff can be a very reliable method of selection, particularly if records are kept so that you can look back and see how effective each individual's judgement has been. Unfortunately, this approach does not make it easy to demonstrate that anti-discrimination legislation has been complied with.

Interview by a panel
Despite extensive research evidence demonstrating its unreliability, this technique is widely used, particularly in the public sector. It tends to favour applicants who are smooth talkers. The composition of the panel can determine how successful it will be. If the panel contains a majority of people who are neither professionally experienced in the area of the appointment nor operationally involved in the work that the appointee will be doing, they might not make the best decision. For example, the interview panel for the post of head of physics in a high school might be made up of the head teacher of the school, the chair of the governors plus two other governors, the head of mathematics and a representative of the local education authority, none of whom are physicists. Including independent members is thought to help prevent issues such as nepotism, discrimination and bias, but these issues are still possible.

Organisations can make interviews by a panel more effective. Ways to do this include carefully selecting a diverse set of panel members that includes people with relevant experience in the area of the appointment and a person to monitor and advise on the process. You can also provide training to the panel, including on issues such as bias, so that they understand their obligations and need for a fair process.

Assessment of references
In appointments in the public service, great importance is usually attached to references, especially for academic posts. In contrast, commercial employers usually pay little heed to them and use them only as a final check that candidates are who they say they are. Legislation in many countries is making it possible for job applicants to demand to see references written about them and even to sue for damages if they consider the reference unfair. Employers, or others, who feel that they have been misled by a reference can also sue if they can show that the reference was written without proper care. Because of these legal dangers, references are being used less and less.

Psychometric tests
These are of three types. **Ability tests** measure an individual's ability in a general area, such as verbal or numerical skills. **Aptitude tests** measure a person's potential to learn the skills needed for a job. Such tests can be effective, provided that the ability they are assessing is well correlated with the ability you are looking for. In the past, these were widely used for recruiting trainee programmers. However, results can be spoiled if the candidates have had the opportunity to practise, and this is usually the case nowadays. It is difficult to design satisfactory tests for higher-level skills. **Personality tests** attempt to assess the characteristics of a person that significantly affect how they behave in their relationships with other people. Unfortunately, there are several competing theories of personality and, although the tests are widely used, their value is far from clear.

Situational assessment
This is much used in selecting military officers and by prestigious multinational companies when recruiting new graduates. The shortlisted applicants are brought together and put into a variety of situations where their performance is observed and assessed by the other participants in the situations. It is expensive and is only suitable for use when several candidates for jobs can be brought together. However, the use of situational questions in interviews is valuable. The interviewer describes a scenario to the candidate and asks them what they would do in such circumstances.

Task assessment
Candidates are asked to carry out some of the tasks that they would be required to do in the job (e.g. asking them to write a program). This works very well, provided that the tasks the successful candidate will be expected to undertake lend themselves to being assessed in this way. The trouble is that, where a job involves some skills that can be assessed in this way and some that can't, the former will tend to be over-emphasised. Thus the ability to write a short program can be easily assessed in this way but the ability to write a 2,000-statement program cannot – it would take too long. Unfortunately, there are many people who can write short programs but not long ones.

Relationships and acquaintances
Another method of staff selection is one that focuses on relationships and acquaintances and not on the skills necessary for the job. For example, this could be any selection that

chooses family members or friends or former colleagues. From one perspective, if a person has worked with someone in the past and seen that they are effective in the role that needs to be filled, then offering them the job is a low-risk way of filling it. However, when the decision is more concerned with who they are and not whether they have relevant skills for the available job, then such selection can be unfair or ineffective.

As described in the next chapter, it is very important to comply with anti-discrimination legislation and with codes of good practice associated with it. In a large organisation, the HR department is likely to spend a good deal of effort in ensuring this compliance.

9.4 STAFF TRAINING AND DEVELOPMENT

Compared to companies in some other countries, UK companies have not always invested in staff training and there can be a lack of concern around qualifications to help staff to advance their careers. In the USA, for example, employers commonly encourage staff to undertake part-time masters degrees by paying the fees and buying the books needed for the course – and, most importantly, by not promoting people who do not have masters degrees. Such behaviour has been rare in the UK.

Successive UK governments have been well aware of this problem and there are a number of initiatives that provide positive encouragement and support to firms to invest in staff training. Some of these, such as the Apprenticeships programme run by the Education and Skills Funding Agency, are intended to give employees the opportunity to acquire skills and obtain qualifications. It usually falls to the HR department to establish and administer a policy for staff training and development, particularly if support is to be received through a government programme.

In general, government programmes are not aimed primarily at professional staff although there is no reason in principle why they should not be used to support CPD. The introduction of apprenticeship standards in 2015 meant that training could be available to existing employees as well as new apprentices.

Furthermore, concerning IT professionals, unless the company specialises in IT, internally organised courses are more likely to cover general business issues (e.g. being on a recruitment panel) than technical issues (e.g. via courses that will contribute to the CPD of a information systems engineer). For this reason, it may be up to individuals themselves, and their managers, to identify specific needs and seek out conferences or external courses through which these needs can be addressed. In this context, it is worth noting that the Code of Conduct of BCS not only requires members to maintain their own professional knowledge but also to encourage their subordinates to do so. This means that managers are expected to take some responsibility for the CPD of their staff.

Staff training and development are of particular importance in high-tech companies, where failure in this respect can threaten the company's raison d'être. It is unfortunate that training is often the first thing to be cut when money is tight.

9.5 REMUNERATION POLICIES AND JOB EVALUATION

One of the major sources of discord and staff dissatisfaction in organisations both large and small is perceived disparities in remuneration. (We use the term **remuneration** rather than **salary** to indicate that other things, such as private health insurance or a company car, may be included.) It is the difficult task of HR management to provide a framework for fixing remuneration that will avoid giving rise to such disparities.

In the public services, this is achieved by using fixed scales that employees move up by annual increments. The financial effect of a promotion is that an employee is moved to another, higher scale. Regular negotiation with trade unions leads to the scales as a whole being increased from time to time. These increases might reflect inflation, increases in the aspirations of the employees involved, or changes in the esteem in which the public or the government hold them. Some systems also include provision for allowances for specific responsibilities (e.g. being dean of a college or being in charge of keeping school premises tidy). By and large, as might be expected, any discord that arises under such systems stems from the allocation of jobs to grades. This is now often done by bureaucratic job evaluation schemes; these require the preparation of elaborate job descriptions that are then carefully compared against sets of criteria for each grade.

The trouble with such systems is that they have difficulty in coping with market conditions. Thus, the civil service has always had difficulty in recruiting and retaining good software staff because the grading system always ends up paying them much less than they could get in private industry.

Formal bureaucratic systems of this type are also employed in some of the larger companies, albeit with, in most cases, much more flexibility to cope with market conditions. However, automatic annual progression up a fixed scale is uncommon. In professional environments it is more usual to fix salaries individually, within broad guidelines. Ensuring that these guidelines are adhered to is always difficult.

We know of a case where someone threatened to leave, whereupon his annual salary was increased from £25,000 to £40,000. Either he was underpaid before or he was overpaid afterwards; in any case it is very likely that this increase breached whatever guidelines the HR department was trying to maintain.

Job evaluation is a technique that is often used to compare the relative worth of jobs and allocate jobs to specific grades. Job evaluation must always involve an element of individual judgement but the aim is to be as objective as possible.

Anti-discrimination legislation has led to the need for organisations to be able to demonstrate that they comply with the doctrine of 'equal pay for work of equal value'. Job evaluation has a valuable role to play here. In the private sector, mergers and acquisitions of one company by another also lead to a need to harmonise remuneration policy, and job evaluation is a valuable tool in these circumstances. It also has a place in younger, rapidly growing companies, where it is used to underpin the reward system to provide clarity and consistency, while flexibility is maintained.

Many organisations are now using job evaluation as the basis for flatter, broad-banded pay structures. Having extended pay ranges means that the emphasis moves away from promotion as the only way of progressing. Instead, employees can gain new responsibilities or move laterally between roles without needing to be formally promoted. It has often been the case in the IT industry that the only way in which highly competent designers could be rewarded adequately was by promoting them to managerial positions for which they were potentially unsuitable. Broad-banded pay structures allow the salaries of such staff to be increased, possibly at the same time as their existing role is adapted.

To further facilitate career management, some companies have established generic role profiles that include the elements measured during a job evaluation exercise (see the box below). This allows roles to be compared across the organisation. Some companies seek to strengthen the links between job evaluation and other HR activities by using competency frameworks as a unifying factor.

Job evaluation schemes

Job evaluation schemes may be **analytical** or **non-analytical**. Non-analytical schemes involve comparing whole jobs without considering the individual elements and skills that go to make up the job. There are a number of fairly simple non-analytical techniques in use. One technique that has been widely used in the public sector is known as **job classification**. Using this technique, the number of grades is decided first and descriptions of the characteristics of jobs in each grade are then produced.

Analytical job evaluation schemes assess each job on the basis of the different elements that are involved. Such elements might include financial responsibility, supervisory responsibility, degree of autonomy, decision-making powers, IT skills, linguistic skills and so on. Each of these elements is given a weight to reflect its importance relative to the others. Each job is then assessed for each of the elements on a scale, typically from 0 to 4, with the criteria for each level specified as objectively as possible. Thus, for linguistic skills, an employer might ask which of the statements in Table 9.1 most accurately describes the job and award the score shown.

Table 9.1 Example scale for assessing the linguistic skills required for a job

There is no requirement or opportunity to speak a language other than English.	0
Situations occasionally occur when it is helpful that the holder can speak a second language.	1
The holder of the post regularly has to use a second language in informal situations and the ability to do this is a requirement of the job.	2
The holder of the post is required to speak and read a second language fluently.	3
The holder of the post is required to be completely fluent in a second language, including being able to write it correctly and to act as an interpreter when required.	4

A score for the job is then calculated by adding together the scores for each element, with the score for each element multiplied by the weight assigned to it.

Analytical job evaluation is usually preferred because its (spurious) objectivity is considered to make it more likely to be successful against a claim for 'equal pay for work of equal value'.

It is always stated that job evaluation schemes are intended to evaluate the job and not the person currently doing the job. This is reasonable when there are a large number of people doing a more or less identical job. It does not make sense in an organisation where every individual is doing a different job and where individuals are valued for their own individual contribution.

When job evaluation schemes are first introduced, it is usual to ask each employee covered by the scheme to complete a fairly lengthy form describing their job. The questions on the form are often worded in ways that are open to more than one interpretation, which isn't useful. Thus, a person whose job includes looking after petty cash may reply 'No' to the question 'Does your job carry any financial responsibility?' on the grounds that they make no decisions about what the money is spent on, or 'Yes' because it is their job to make sure that all petty cash is correctly accounted for. The cumulative effect of such misinterpretations can be very great and lead to significant differences in remuneration between people doing identical jobs in different parts of the organisation.

9.6 AGENCY WORKERS, PERSONAL SERVICE COMPANIES AND IR35

An issue related to remuneration is that of pay and benefits for agency workers. An agency worker is employed by a temporary work agency, which we will refer to as Company A. The person is hired out to work temporarily for another company, which we will refer to as Company B. During the period of work, the person works under the direction of Company B. This is different from Company B subcontracting some work to another company or to someone who is self-employed.

The Agency Workers Regulations 2010 were introduced to provide equal treatment of agency workers compared with workers who are employed directly by the other company (Company B in the example above). There are some basic elements of equality applied from the day that an agency worker starts at the other company, including access to canteens and other facilities. At 12 weeks, agency workers become entitled to equal pay to those who do the same job but are employed directly by the other company. There are also other rights around pensions and paid leave. There are rules on how the 12 weeks are counted and whether any extended breaks may affect that calculation. For example, if an agency worker transfers to a different workplace, a return to the original workplace will mean that the count of 12 weeks will start again. Also, considerations such as maternity and paternity leave do not cause a break in the 12-week period.

This may be relevant to IT in an organisation, where agency workers may be used to fill short-term gaps in IT skills. The HR department will need procedures to monitor the use of agency workers so that regulations are complied with.

Some IT staff do not use an agency and are not employees. Instead, they may work under contract by way of a personal service company (PSC), which is a limited company that they own, or they may work as a sole trader contracting directly with the various customers to which they provide their IT services. Her Majesty's Revenue and Customs (HMRC) has to determine in each case which of the following applies:

- The person is working for a company in a way that means they should really be a pay as you earn (PAYE) employee with tax and National Insurance contributions taken off their pay at source in the usual way.

- The person is working as a consultancy that usually provides IT services to many different companies at one time and is genuinely a self-employed sole trader or genuinely providing services through their PSC.

For example, suppose that a person says that they are a contractor but works for one company only. The company expects the person to attend its premises full time. The company does not allow the person to engage in work for any other company, pays all of their expenses, and provides holiday and sick pay. This person is effectively an employee.

As another example, suppose that a person says that they are a contractor and their work involves advising several clients a day. The person works from their own premises, controls their own flow of work and pays their own expenses. They could also choose to hire other people who can be a substitute for them for some or all of the work. It is clear that this person is not an employee of any one of their clients.

Some cases, however, are in the middle ground, where it is less clear whether a person is an employee of a company or not.

There are tax laws concerning off-payroll working; these are more commonly referred to as **IR35**. They can apply if 'a worker provides services to a client through an intermediary', such as a PSC.[1] IR35 does not apply to sole traders. IR35 aims to stop people using an intermediary to claim that they are not employed by their client. If a person would be considered to be an employee, then IR35 is about making them pay similar income tax and National Insurance to other employees of the client.

Changes in 2017 mean that public sector organisations now need to decide whether the IR35 rules apply to anyone whom they contract through the person's own intermediary. In 2021, medium and large companies in the private sector also became responsible for these decisions. The rules are complex. HMRC provides the Check Employment Status for Tax service on its website, which can help you to understand whether off-payroll working rules apply to a person's situation (see Further Reading).

---

1 'Private Sector Off-Payroll Working for Intermediaries and Contractors' (2021), HM Revenue and Customs, https://www.gov.uk/guidance/ir35-what-to-do-if-it-applies.

The 2021 changes were so substantial that some buyers of IT services decided that all agency staff and contractors that were involved with providing IT services would be changed to be PAYE employees. Some organisations did this for sole traders too, even though IR35 does not apply to sole traders. Each employer should take its own legal advice on these matters. In 2021 many individuals in the IT sector found their effective net pay reduced substantially due to the newly amended IR35 rules and how employers were interpreting them.

9.7 APPRAISAL SCHEMES

It is astonishing and contrary to all common sense that people should be able to spend 30 years in a professional job without anyone, colleague or superior, giving them any indication of how well they are doing the job or how they might improve. Yet, for many years this was commonly the case for school teachers, university lecturers, many civil servants, and not a few managers in commercial and industrial organisations. To be more precise, there are or have been organisations where no procedures or regulations ensured that there was any such feedback. In practice, many senior practitioners in these fields would try to keep an eye on new entrants to the profession and help and advise them; equally, the newcomers would commonly seek such help from their more senior colleagues. Nevertheless, there was no requirement that this should happen and very often it did not. Even when it did happen, it would probably cease by the time the practitioner reached the age of, say, 35, and they would continue to practise for the next 30 years with no feedback, unless they were disastrously incompetent.

It falls to HR management to design procedures to avoid this undesirable situation. Appraisal schemes are the usual formal way of doing this. They derive from the idea of management by objectives (MBO). This idea was developed by Peter Drucker in his book *The Practice of Management* (1954). Drucker was one of the most distinguished management theorists in the 1970s. MBO rapidly became popular in industry and was adopted by the UK government in the 1980s.

The essence of MBO is that managers and their subordinates agree on a set of objectives for the subordinate to achieve over the next period, typically six months. These objectives should be precise, objectively verifiable and, ideally, quantifiable. In other words, objectives such as 'increase the turnover of your division by 10% while maintaining its present level of profitability' are preferable to objectives such as 'improve the public image of your products'. At the end of the period, manager and subordinate meet and discuss the extent to which these objectives have been achieved. If the objectives have not been achieved, they will discuss the obstacles that have prevented them from being achieved and how these might be overcome. They then agree a revised set of objectives for the next period. The process filters down from the highest level of management, where the overall objectives of the organisation are set. At each level, managers take their objectives and break these down into more specific goals. From these goals, they delegate tasks by negotiating goals for their subordinates.

The strength of MBO is that it makes managers and others aware of what the organisation's objectives are and how they are expected to contribute towards achieving them. Its main weaknesses are as follows:

- Not all legitimate objectives can be easily specified in precise and quantifiable terms. Such objectives are often therefore ignored when MBO is used. For example, it is a legitimate objective when developing software that the software should be easily maintainable. However, software maintainability is difficult to measure until the software has been running for some time. Standards for development processes and techniques such as testing could be good indicators that a team is following good practice. However, measuring the degree of compliance with standards is difficult and a high degree of compliance does not guarantee that the software is easily maintainable.

- The insistence on quantifiable objectives can distort behaviour. For example, setting specific targets for cutting the length of waiting lists in the NHS can lead to doctors choosing patients for treatment based on the effect on the waiting list rather than on the patient's clinical needs.

- MBO tends to emphasise short-term objectives at the expense of long-term strategic objectives. In one instance, the manager responsible for the sales and marketing of a widely used software package was set the objective of increasing the revenue generated by 20% over the next year. He succeeded in meeting this objective simply by increasing the annual licence charge for the package by 20%. Moving to another package would have been time consuming, so existing clients had little choice in the short term but to pay up. However, in the following year, sales of the package dropped by 50% as disgruntled customers moved to other products.

Modern management practice has moved away from the idea of setting rigid, formal objectives, while maintaining the general principles of MBO. Some companies will emphasise **empowerment** – that is, telling employees at all levels what is expected of them but then leaving it to them to decide how to achieve this.

Appraisal schemes usually involve an appraiser and an appraisee meeting regularly (every six months, every year or even every two years) to discuss the employee's performance and career development under several headings. The result is a report signed by both parties; if they cannot agree on certain points, this will be recorded in the report. There is an obvious similarity to MBO because many schemes seek to identify objectives to be achieved by the time of the next appraisal interview.

There is no doubt that such schemes are useful. Professional staff (in the widest sense) are usually willing to listen to ways in which they can improve their performance and will usually accept that someone else can throw new light on the way they do their job; they also provide a good opportunity to review career plans and ambitions and to assess training needs. A good appraiser will do all these things. (From an employee's point of view, it is worth noting that appraisal reports, assuming they are favourable, can provide valuable ammunition in unfair dismissal cases.)

However, the process has many weaknesses. It often seems artificial and appraisal interviews can be rather uncomfortable affairs. Appraisals are supposed to be non-judgemental but this may be difficult to achieve when the appraisee is not felt to be performing satisfactorily. Without adequate training, appraisers may prove unable to perform satisfactorily in the role. There is the difficult question of whether appraisals should have any link with promotion or salary increases. Too close a link may mean that they are not conducted with the openness and frankness that is essential if the participants are to get the best out of them; if there is no link – and perhaps the appraiser has no influence on the promotion procedure – then appraisees may regard the process as a farce: if your appraisals for the past five years have said that you are ready to become a project manager but you have never been given that opportunity, you can be forgiven for doubting the usefulness of the appraisal system.

A good appraisal process will succeed in motivating employees to see how their work contributes to the success of the organisation. The process can also help to identify areas for improvement and growth by the employee, which can be achieved through CPD. By defining an appropriate process, training appraisers to conduct effective reviews and making the reviews part of the organisation's culture, the HR department can have a positive impact on the development of the organisation.

9.8 REDUNDANCY, DISMISSAL AND GRIEVANCE PROCEDURES

It normally falls to the HR department to ensure that, when staff are made redundant or are dismissed, the proper procedures are followed. Failure to follow the proper procedures can lead to the organisation facing the embarrassment of actions for unfair dismissal in an employment tribunal. This is expensive in terms of staff time as well as money and is bad for an organisation's image. Unless the dismissal or redundancies are seen to be fair as well as lawful, the effect on the morale of the remaining staff will be bad.

9.8.1 Unfair dismissal

For a dismissal to be fair, the reason for the dismissal must also be fair and the dismissal procedure itself must have been carried out fairly. If either of these conditions is not satisfied, an employee can take action in an employment tribunal alleging unfair dismissal. If the tribunal finds in favour of the employee, it will usually order the employer to pay compensation to the employee who has been unfairly dismissed. The amount of compensation awarded depends very much on the circumstances of the particular case; the Enterprise and Regulatory Reform Act 2013 imposes a limit of annual salary or £93,878 (for the 2022/23 year), whichever is lower.

A tribunal can also order reinstatement of the employee – that is, order the employer to take the employee back. In practice, tribunals are reluctant to do this. If the issue reaches a tribunal, there has been a significant disagreement between the employee and the employer and it is unlikely, but not impossible, that they will want to work together in future. Employees can only claim unfair dismissal if they have been working for their employer for two years or more. (This restriction does not apply if the dismissal is for reasons of political belief or affiliation.) Claims must be brought within three months of dismissal.

The Employment Rights Act 1996 accepts a wide variety of reasons as justifying dismissal. Specifically, it accepts:

- lack of capability;
- misconduct;

- breach of the law – not by the employee (that would be covered by misconduct) but by the employer if it would be in breach of the law if it continued to employ the employee (e.g. because the employee was a foreign worker whose work permit had expired);

- redundancy (see next section).

Furthermore, it allows for 'some other substantial reason' that would need to be justified. However, there are many reasons that cannot be used to justify a dismissal. These include anything excluded by anti-discrimination legislation (see next chapter), taking legal action against an employer to enforce employment rights and taking part in trade union activities.

> Dismissals are **automatically considered to be unfair** unless the statutory dismissal procedure has been followed. In other words, no matter what the employee has or has not done, if the employer has not followed the statutory procedure in dismissing them, an employment tribunal will judge them to have been unfairly dismissed and will award them compensation.

The statutory dismissal procedure is not, on the face of it, unreasonable. It requires the employer to give the employee a written statement of why dismissal is being considered; the employer must then arrange a meeting at which both sides can state their case. Following that meeting, the employer must inform the employee of the decision. If it is decided to go ahead and dismiss the employee, then the employee must be given the opportunity to appeal, with the appeal being considered by a more senior manager where this is practicable.

Tribunals determine whether employees' claims for unfair dismissal are successful. Possible claims include:

- The statement of why dismissal was being considered did not provide enough detail or was not provided far enough in advance of the meeting for the employee to properly consider their response.

- The employer was too slow in following the procedures.

- The meeting was conducted in such a way that the employee did not have a reasonable opportunity to state their case.

A tribunal might support such claims from employees because a standard process has not been followed. For this reason, it is very important for HR departments to lay down detailed procedures to ensure that such claims are not successful.

Of course, the fact that the statutory procedures have been followed does not automatically mean that a tribunal will consider a dismissal to be fair. Most of the reasons for which an employer might reasonably consider dismissing an employee – inability to do the job, misconduct, persistent absenteeism and so on – are, in principle, acceptable but the employer has to show that appropriate training was offered, warnings given and so on.

9.8.2 Redundancy

Essentially, dismissal because of redundancy (**retrenchment** in the USA) occurs when employees are dismissed because the employer no longer needs people to do their jobs. In these circumstances, most employees will be entitled to compensation based on their age, salary and years of service. The law lays down a minimum level of compensation that must be paid. In practice, some employers pay more than this.

If an employer is intending to make any employees redundant, the employees are entitled to consultation in most cases. The consultation should explain why a person is being made redundant and whether there are any alternatives, such as taking a different role in the organisation. There may also be discussion of reducing staff by not replacing those who are retiring or running a voluntary redundancy scheme.

If there are up to 19 employees being made redundant, there are no rules on how the consultation needs to take place. If the employer is intending to make 20 or more employees redundant over a period of 90 days or less, the consultation must follow the collective redundancy rules.[2] Under the collective rules, the employer must consult with a trade union representative (if there is a union) or with a representative of the employees.

In most cases of redundancy, the employer will be seeking to reduce the number of workers in a particular job category rather than dismiss all such workers. The question of how to select the employees to be made redundant therefore arises. It is common practice to use the **last in, first out principle** – that is, the most recently recruited employees are the first to be made redundant. While there are many reasons for feeling that this is not a desirable policy, it is acceptable to the trade unions and to the courts. If the last in, first out principle is used, it is necessary to consider any possible discrimination, such as disproportionately affecting young people in the organisation.

Dismissal for redundancy can easily become unfair dismissal if individuals are selected for redundancy in some other way. There is a long list of criteria that are not acceptable reasons for selecting who is made redundant, ranging from participation in trade union activities to sex, racial or ethnic origin, sexual orientation, religion and so on.

9.8.3 Constructive dismissal

It sometimes happens that an employer behaves towards an employee in such a way that the employee feels that they have no option but to resign. If the employer's behaviour amounts to a substantial breach of the contract of employment, the law may regard the employer's behaviour as tantamount to dismissal. This situation is known as constructive dismissal and can be the subject of unfair dismissal proceedings, although the fact that it is constructive dismissal does not automatically make it unfair dismissal.

---

2 'Redundancy: Your Rights' (n.d.), Gov.uk, https://www.gov.uk/redundancy-your-rights/consultation.

The following are a few examples of circumstances that might lead to employees resigning in circumstances that would probably amount to constructive dismissal:

- The employer moves an employee's place of work to somewhere 400 km away, at short notice and without consultation.
- The employer requires someone who was employed as an accountant to spend their time acting as a receptionist.
- A senior manager repeatedly countermands instructions issued by a more junior manager.

The regulations regarding dismissal procedures also lay down statutory grievance procedures to be used if an employee has a grievance against their employer. Employees are required to make use of these procedures before they can claim constructive dismissal.

9.8.4 Takeovers and outsourcing

It frequently happens in modern commerce and industry that one company takes over another; this is particularly common in the IT industry. It also happens when an organisation outsources its IT activities (or any other activities). In these circumstances, staff involved are usually transferred to the new employer. This could mean a major change in their employment conditions. In particular, if IT activities are being outsourced from a government department to a private company, there are likely to be major changes affecting security of employment and pension rights.

There are specific regulations in the UK and in the countries of the European Union (EU) governing what happens to employees when an undertaking or part of an undertaking is transferred from one employer to another. These are known as the Transfer of Undertakings (Protection of Employment) (TUPE) regulations. The original TUPE regulations dated back to 1981 but they were replaced by a new set of regulations in 2006, reflecting a change to the underlying EU directive. Following the UK's exit from the EU, the legislation continues to apply as a result of the European Union (Withdrawal) Act 2018.

The purpose of the regulations is to maintain the employees' conditions of employment in these circumstances. If Employer A has taken over Employer B, then all the employees of Employer B will transfer to Employer A on the same terms as their original contracts. It is as if Employer A was the original employer. Also, there is continuity of employment to prevent issues regarding laws that require certain lengths of employment, such as unfair dismissal. There are some exceptions, such as pension rights, but the overall aim is to protect the employees who are moving to the new organisation.

The employees who are being transferred to the new employer cannot be made redundant because of the transfer. There may be legitimate business reasons why, after the transfer, redundancy is considered, such as needing to close a factory or office that is not generating sufficient income. However, the new employer must follow the requirements for any redundancy process.

9.8.5 Public interest disclosures

Until comparatively recently, an employer could dismiss an employee for revealing publicly that, for example, the employer was consistently and wilfully breaking the law. There were several well-known cases in which senior employees revealed that their employers were breaking the law in areas such as price fixing or the disposal of toxic wastes. The employees (so-called **whistleblowers**) were dismissed and, furthermore, because of the high profiles of the cases, they found it impossible to get other jobs in their industry.

The Public Interest Disclosure Act 1998 is intended to protect employees who raise concerns about criminal behaviour, certain types of civil offence, miscarriages of justice, activities that endanger health and safety or the environment, and attempts to cover up such malpractice. Since it is closely tied to the law relating to confidential information, we shall postpone a fuller discussion to Chapter 11.

9.8.6 Wrongful dismissal

For the sake of completeness, we should mention wrongful dismissal. This is significantly different from unfair dismissal. An action for wrongful dismissal is an action for damages brought by an employee against an employer for breach of the contract of employment. An example would be where a notice period is specified in an employee's contract but the employer does not allow the notice period to be taken.

It is an action under the common law and for this reason is not subject to the maximums laid down by the statutes for unfair dismissal. It is typically brought by very senior or highly paid employees who can make a reasonable case for very substantial compensation resulting from their employer's breaking of the contract. For example, some employees may have notice periods to terminate their contracts of one year or even two years. If the employer gives a shorter notice period than is in the contract, the employee may be able to make a compensation claim.

9.9 CONTRACTS OF EMPLOYMENT

Under UK law, every employee has a contract of employment, whether or not it is written down. What this means is that the agreement between an employee and their employer can be enforced in a court of law. The law requires that, if the contract is not written down, the employer must provide the employee with a statement in writing of the major conditions of the employment, including grievance procedures. The written statement consists of two parts. There is the main document, which is known as the **principal statement**. There is also a wider **written statement**. The rules are very detailed as to what information must be given to the employee, and any employer taking on an employee needs to consider them carefully.

A good contract of employment should be written in terms that are easily understood and should avoid legal jargon. Prospective employees should not need to consult a lawyer in order to understand it. They should, however, read it carefully before signing it.

It is an important function of HR staff to ensure that contracts of employment are issued to all employees and that signed copies are retained.

An example of a contract of employment, with some explanatory comments, is included in the Appendix.

9.10 WORKFORCE PLANNING

If the HR department is to ensure that the organisation always has available the staff it needs, it must be able to forecast those needs some time ahead. This is extremely difficult, particularly in software companies. As we move through the spectrum of organisations, from software houses through banking, manufacturing and retailing to policing, health care and the operation of lighthouses, the uncertainty, although always present, is reduced and it becomes possible to predict staff needs much more precisely. For example, for software houses the staff needs will vary according to the types and number of projects at any one time. For the operation of lighthouses, a predictable number of staff are needed to operate each lighthouse at any one time.

In a software company, there are three inputs to the HR planning process:

- **HR plans from existing projects:** These show how many staff of each grade and with which specialised skills will be required in each of the following months.
- **Sales forecasts:** These are subject both to the whims of potential clients and the judgement, good or otherwise, of the sales staff. Sales staff are asked to identify all active sales situations – that is, situations in which they are talking to potential clients about their actual needs, not just trying to establish the company's credentials. They then estimate the staff needs for doing this work, in terms of numbers of staff in the various grades and any special skills required, and assign a probability to winning a contract to carry out the work. The probabilities are carefully defined in something like the manner shown in Table 9.2.

Table 9.2 Example of probabilities assigned to sales forecasts

0.9	Negotiations concluded successfully but no signed contract yet received.
0.7	The company has been offered the business, subject to negotiation on price, contractual conditions, etc.
0.5	The company has submitted a proposal for the business and has been shortlisted, or is in competition with no more than two other companies.
0.3	The company has been asked to submit a formal proposal.
0.1	The client has an identified requirement that is expected to be met by commissioning a software house.

- **Forecasts of the likely staff losses in the coming months:** In the software business, this depends very much on the buoyancy of the market for software developers. This, in turn, seems to depend on the economic cycle, which, as in other capital goods industries, is sensitive to growth rates rather than to the overall production of the economy. However, it is also very strongly affected by events such as decimalisation in 1972 and the problems associated with the year 2000 (the Y2K problem), the UK's exit from the EU (when some EU workers including IT staff left the UK) and the Covid-19 pandemic (which led to changes in areas such as home working and demand for IT). If such events can be predicted in advance, they can generate an enormous demand for staff in the year or two leading up to them. They are followed by an equally large fall, leading to much temporary unemployment, particularly among contractors.

From these inputs, a company can try to predict how many staff will be required each month, with their grades, qualifications and experience, and how many will be available. It can then proceed to produce a plan for recruiting staff if necessary.

In practice, HR prediction in project-based companies never works very well and there are good statistical reasons why it never will. If we are summing 1,000 weighted predictions, the uncertainty in the sum will be quite small, even though the uncertainty in each prediction may be quite large; this follows from what is called the Law of Large Numbers. But, if we are summing only 20 predictions, the uncertainty will still be very large. This suggests that workforce planning should be easier in larger companies and to some extent this is so. However, few project-based companies, even large ones, ever have as many as 100 live sales situations relating to the same pool of staff at any one time. Furthermore, most such companies depend for their success on specialised skills; this means that you cannot treat every employee in a given grade as the same – the fact that you have a grade 5 expert on communications available does not help the project that needs a grade 5 expert on data modelling. And you cannot turn one into the other by sending them on a two-week training course. As a result of all these difficulties, most project-based organisations find themselves see-sawing between being desperate to get new staff for the projects they have won and being desperate to get new projects for the staff they have got.

FURTHER READING

The advisory handbook of the Advisory, Conciliation and Arbitration Service (ACAS), *Discipline and Grievances at Work: The Acas Guide*, and its web pages on redundancy, contracts and agency workers are good sources of information about some of the material covered in this chapter. This information can all be found on the ACAS website:
https://www.acas.org.uk

The UK government publishes information about business transfers, takeovers and TUPE:
https://www.gov.uk/transfers-takeovers

Information about the Education and Skills Funding Agency, including details about apprenticeships, can be found at:
https://www.gov.uk/government/organisations/education-and-skills-funding-agency

The Chartered Institute of Personnel and Development covers employment law matters for HR management:
    https://www.cipd.co.uk

The HMRC Check Employment Status for Tax tool is found at:
    https://www.gov.uk/guidance/check-employment-status-for-tax

10 EQUALITY, DIVERSITY AND INCLUSION

After studying this chapter, you should:

- *understand in general terms what anti-discrimination laws are trying to do and why employers need codes of practice to follow;*
- *know how legislation affects the design of information systems;*
- *understand the role that diversity and inclusion have in organisations.*

10.1 INTRODUCTION

Equality, diversity and inclusion are about creating a more equal society that represents the diversity found in the citizens of a country, and about including and welcoming a variety of views and experience. Together, they address issues relating to discrimination, bullying and harassment. Some of this is underpinned by legislation and some of it is good practice.

Most of this chapter will look at the issue of anti-discrimination legislation, which is about equality in society. It will highlight relevant areas of the legislation and the impact that they may have when designing information systems. In the UK, the legislation applies to all organisations but includes additional requirements for public sector organisations.

While the legislation provides the legal framework for equality, other activities are needed to support the underlying social change. Efforts to encourage diversity are one aspect of this; they seek to involve a wider range of people who represent views and experiences across society. Such efforts are also about normalising diversity in the organisation, not just through recruitment but in the messages that the organisation communicates through its activities. Inclusion is the other essential aspect, which is about people feeling valued and that their views will be listened to and respected. This chapter explores these issues and considers some example changes to working practices.

The anti-discrimination legislation and the practices of diversity and inclusion work together. They support better working environments and promote opportunities for those who may otherwise be disadvantaged. They can also help to build teams that have a wider set of skills and experiences. In the IT setting, this can lead to more effective teams that can better support their users.

10.2 THE DEVELOPMENT OF ANTI-DISCRIMINATION LEGISLATION

Three hundred years ago, the laws of England contained many specific statutes embodying discrimination on the grounds of sex, religion and wealth. To vote, you had to be male and own property. To be admitted to either of the two universities, you had to be male and a member of the Church of England. If you were a woman, when you married all your personal property became the property of your husband.

From 1700 to the 1950s, all these explicit examples of discrimination enshrined in the law were slowly but surely abolished. With a very few exceptions, men and women, whatever their religion and however rich or poor they might be, were treated by the law in the same way. This did not, however, eliminate discrimination. There were, for example, golf clubs that would not admit Jews, medical schools that were very reluctant to admit female students, and professions that it was difficult for anyone not from a wealthy background to enter.

Since the 1960s there has been a plethora of legislation outlawing discrimination and a number of bodies have been established to help enforce the law. The Equality and Human Rights Commission (EHRC) came into being in 2007 to promote and enforce equality and non-discrimination laws in England, Scotland and Wales, replacing several existing bodies. There is a separate body for Northern Ireland. The Equality Act 2010 brought all the existing legislation together in a single Act of Parliament.

It is, however, one thing to make a law giving women the vote, but quite another to legislate effectively to ensure they are treated on an equal footing with men in all matters concerned with employment. Equally, it is one thing to make racial discrimination unlawful but quite another to eliminate racial prejudice. Even if effective legislation can be framed – itself a difficult task – legislation, of itself, is not enough; time is required to bring about the changes of attitude that are necessary if discrimination is to be eliminated.

Information systems professionals need to have an appreciation of anti-discrimination legislation for two reasons. First, as professionals, they will inevitably find themselves in managerial and supervisory positions and the law requires people in such positions to prevent the people they supervise from behaving in a discriminatory manner and to avoid such behaviour themselves. Second, the obligation to avoid certain sorts of discrimination should influence the way in which information systems are designed and constructed. For example, technology exists to simplify the process of making information systems more accessible, which could reduce the possibility of discrimination on the grounds of disability.

While the Equality Act has done a great deal to bring about consistency in the way that the law deals with discrimination, it is a long, complicated and far-reaching piece of legislation. What is presented here is a very limited and simplified picture of the law as it is likely to impinge on the information systems professional.

10.3 WHAT IS DISCRIMINATION?

Discrimination means treating one person or one group of people less favourably than another on the grounds of personal characteristics. The Equality Act 2010 prohibits discrimination on any of the following grounds, known as **protected characteristics**:

- age;
- disability;
- gender reassignment;
- marriage and civil partnership;
- pregnancy and maternity;
- race, colour, ethnic origin or nationality;
- religion or belief;
- sex;
- sexual orientation.

Similar legislation applies across the European Union, in the USA and in many other countries.

Much of the law and much of the debate on discrimination issues relates to employment and related matters. However, the legislation relates to discrimination in other contexts as well – education, the provision of goods and services, letting of premises and so on.

The language used in the Equality Act 2010

There are some ways that the language in the Equality Act 2010 seems out of step with language in use today. For example, the Act uses the term 'transexual', whereas today we typically use other terms including 'transgender', 'trans male', 'trans female' and 'trans'.

The term 'gender reassignment' could suggest that the Act is about protecting people who undergo a medical process to transition from the gender they are assigned at birth to the gender as which they identify. Gender reassignment may involve a medical process, but there is no requirement for that. Instead, the process where a person transitions from the gender they are assigned at birth to the gender as which they identify could include having gone through a process, intending to go through a process, being part-way through a process or having stopped a process. The Act offers protection for each of these situations.

Non-binary and gender-fluid identity are not specifically mentioned in the Act. In 2020, an employment tribunal recognised that non-binary and gender-fluid identity are covered by the Act, following a case brought by Ms Taylor against Jaguar Land Rover in the UK. The case addressed harassment and discrimination experienced by Ms Taylor after coming out as 'gender fluid or non-binary'. The tribunal found in Ms Taylor's favour and Jaguar Land Rover has since improved its equality, diversity and inclusion policies and training.[1] While this decision does not set a legal precedent, it does indicate the way that the 2010 legislation's wording is interpreted in today's context.

The term 'intersex' is not explicitly protected by the Act. However, the Act does protect people on the basis of their sex or their perceived sex. Therefore, there will be situations where intersex individuals are covered by the Act.

10.3.1 Direct and indirect discrimination

Discrimination can be direct or indirect. **Direct discrimination** occurs when one person is treated less favourably than another specifically because of one of the protected characteristics, such as their sex or race. Here are some examples that, on the face of it, would constitute direct discrimination:

- A woman does exactly the same job as a man but is paid less than he is.

- A doctor refuses to treat a Chinese patient on the grounds that he has no room for any more patients but then accepts an English patient.

- A company advertises for a secretary and automatically rejects all the male applicants.

- A landlord seeking to let a flat tells a same-sex couple that the flat is already let but next day lets it to an individual person.

- A company advertises for 'a mature woman to act as the chief executive's personal assistant' or 'a strong young man to work as a trainee zoo-keeper'.

Employment tribunals have increasingly taken the view that harassment and victimisation constitute direct discrimination, and this was formalised under the Equality Act. The Act defines harassment is occurring when a person 'engages in unwanted conduct related to a relevant protected characteristic' and this conduct 'has the purpose or effect of violating [another person's] dignity, or creating an intimidating, hostile, degrading, humiliating or offensive environment [for another person]'. Victimisation means treating a person badly because that person has brought proceedings under the Act, alleged that someone has contravened the Act, or given information or evidence in connection with proceedings under the Act.

Indirect discrimination occurs when general conditions are imposed that have a disproportionate effect on one group.

Here are a few examples that might constitute indirect discrimination:

---

1   'Jaguar Land Rover Ltd Signs a Legal Agreement with EHRC' (2021), Equality and Human Rights Commission, https://www.equalityhumanrights.com/en/our-work/news/jaguar-land-rover-ltd-signs-legal-agreement-ehrc.

- A job is advertised with the requirement that applicants must be at least 180 cm tall. In the UK there are many men over 180 cm tall but very few women. The result is that few women can apply for the job.

- When allocating public housing, a local authority has a policy of giving priority to the children of existing tenants.

- An employer insists that all employees work on Saturdays. This might be held to be indirect discrimination against those who practise Judaism, since Saturday is the Jewish Sabbath.

The Equality Act permits discrimination in cases where it is 'a proportionate means of achieving a legitimate aim'. Where they are associated with employment, direct and indirect discrimination can also be justified if the employer demonstrates that there is an occupational requirement for the potentially discriminatory condition. For example, if a job is advertised for a personal care assistant for a disabled woman, it might be possible to set an occupational requirement that states that the post is only open to women applicants. Use of an occupational requirement needs to be carefully considered and justified. It would be for an employment tribunal to determine whether such a requirement were acceptable.

10.4 DISCRIMINATION ON THE GROUNDS OF SEX

The position of women workers in the 1960s was very different to today. Where formal salary scales were in operation, there would either be separate, lower scales for women or there would be additional allowances for men, especially for married men. A female employee who got married might lose her job or might be transferred to the 'temporary' staff, making her ineligible for bonuses or additional holiday entitlement for long service. Women who had babies were not normally expected to return to work and had no legal right to do so. Outside a few professions, such as nursing and teaching, promotion prospects for women were very poor and there were few women in senior positions. Indeed, it was very difficult for women to gain entry to academic and professional courses in fields such as medicine or the law, which would have qualified them for senior positions.

Discrimination also existed outside the field of employment. Some hotels would refuse to let rooms to unaccompanied women. Building societies applied much stricter criteria when considering whether to offer a mortgage to a single women than to a single man.

10.4.1 Employment

The most important features of the current legislation can be summarised as follows:

- It is unlawful for an employer to discriminate against a person on the grounds of their sex or marital status in terms of the arrangements made for recruitment and selection and the terms on which employment is offered (not just pay but also holiday entitlement, sick pay, notice period, etc.). The Act specifically makes unlawful advertisements that explicitly or implicitly suggest that only persons of one sex will be considered. The Act's principal of equal pay for equal work applies not just to men and women doing the same jobs but also to men and women doing jobs 'of equal value' – that is, where the work is not equivalent but there are equal demands in the work regarding 'effort, skill and decision making'.

- It is unlawful for an employer to discriminate against an employee on the grounds of their sex or marital status regarding opportunities for promotion, transfer, training or any other benefits.

- It is unlawful for an employer to discriminate against an employee on the grounds of their sex or marital status regarding dismissal or redundancy.

- It is unlawful for an employer to victimise an employee for bringing a complaint of sex discrimination or for giving evidence in support of another employee's complaint.

- It is unlawful for any of the following to discriminate against a person on the grounds of sex or marital status: a trade union, a professional body, a registration authority (e.g. the Architects Registration Board; see Section 2.9), an employment agency or a provider of vocational training.

Contract workers are covered by the legislation.

There are a few exceptions to these provisions. The most important is where there is an occupational requirement for a person of a specific sex, as for example in the case of recruiting actors to play roles of a specific sex. There is also a provision that specifically allows political parties to use procedures for selecting candidates for Parliament that ensure that women will be selected.

10.4.2 Education

It is unlawful for a provider of education (public or private; school, college or university) to discriminate against a person on the basis of their sex. This applies when they are offering admission to the establishment or to specific courses, and when they are providing access to the other benefits and facilities the establishment offers.

One example exception to this is that allowance is made for single-sex educational establishments.

10.4.3 Provision of goods and services

It is unlawful to discriminate on the grounds of sex:

- in the provision of goods, facilities or services – this covers accommodation in a hotel, facilities for entertainment and refreshment, banking and insurance services, and so on;

- in selling or letting property.

The main exception to these provisions is for charities that have been founded with the purpose of helping a specific group of people who are all of the same sex – for example, single mothers.

Two consequences of this part of the legislation are that it is unlawful to do the following:

- offer car insurance to women at a lower price than to men despite the fact that women are statistically less likely to be involved in car accidents;
- offer better pensions to men of a given age than to women of the same age despite the fact that men are statistically likely to die sooner.

10.4.4 Remedies

A person who believes that they have been discriminated against in their employment because of their sex – whether by being refused a job, refused a promotion, paid less, not given training opportunities or anything else – can take the matter to an employment tribunal. If the tribunal finds in favour of the complainant (the employee), it can award damages and make recommendations to the respondent (the employer). If the respondent fails to act on the recommendations, the amount of the damages may be increased.

An individual who feels that they have been the victim of sexual discrimination in the other areas covered by the legislation – education or the provision of goods and services – can take action in the civil courts for damages.

The EHRC provides advice and assistance to complainants who feel that they have been subjected to discrimination on the grounds of their sex, whether in their employment or elsewhere. Anyone considering a formal complaint of sex discrimination is well advised to start by consulting the EHRC.

10.5 DISCRIMINATION ON RACIAL GROUNDS

The first race relations legislation in the UK was the Race Relations Act 1965, which made it unlawful to discriminate on the grounds of race or colour by banning people from using public services or entering places such as bars, cinemas or theatres. It also created a new criminal offence of incitement to racial hatred by inflammatory publications or speeches. In 1968, a further Race Relations Act was passed making it unlawful to refuse housing, employment or public services to people because of their ethnic background. Further changes were made to the Race Relations Act in 1976 and 2000. Later, the Race Relations Act and other anti-discrimination legislation were repealed and replaced with the Equality Act 2010.

The specific provisions of the law relating to discrimination on racial grounds are now very similar to those already described relating to discrimination on the grounds of sex. The EHRC has the same responsibilities for providing advice and assistance to complainants.

The implementation of racial discrimination legislation can be more nuanced than that of discrimination relating to some other protected characteristics, such as marital status. The Equality Act does not define the terms 'race', 'colour', 'ethnic origin' or 'nationality'.

Are the English, the Irish, the Scots and the Welsh to be regarded as different racial groups? Is a person whose parents were Afro-Caribbean but who was born and brought up in Cardiff to be regarded as belonging to the Welsh, British or Afro-Caribbean racial groups, or perhaps to all three? Does the requirement that candidates for a job speak a specific language (e.g. Urdu or Welsh) constitute indirect discrimination? These considerations go far beyond what it is relevant to consider here but they illustrate the complexity of legislation in this area.

10.6 DISCRIMINATION ON THE GROUNDS OF DISABILITY

From the 1970s onwards, the UK government had been encouraging the recruitment of disabled employees into the civil service. It had also encouraged employers to take on disabled workers by withholding government contracts from companies that could not demonstrate a commitment to offering opportunities to disabled people. It was not, however, until 1995 that the anti-discrimination legislation was extended to cover discrimination on the grounds of disability, in the Disability Discrimination Act. This was followed in 2001 by the Special Educational Needs and Disability Act, which extended the provisions of the earlier Act to cover education. The provisions of these Acts are now included in the Equality Act 2010 and the EHRC is responsible for advising and assisting complainants.

The Equality Act makes it unlawful to treat a disabled employee or applicant less favourably because of their disability without justification. The justification must be serious and substantial. Therefore, it would be justified to reject a blind applicant for a job as a bus driver or a paraplegic for a job as a lifeguard, and it might be justified to reject a dyslexic applicant for a job as a copy-editor. However, the Act requires the employer to make reasonable adjustments to meet the needs of disabled applicants or employees. This might include adapting a bus so that a disabled applicant could drive it safely, providing a workstation with special hardware and software to make it suitable for use by a partially sighted employee, or supplying aids to allow a dyslexic applicant to work well as a copy-editor.

The Act also makes it unlawful for businesses and organisations providing goods and services to treat disabled people less favourably than other people for a reason related to their disability. Service providers are required to make reasonable changes to make it possible for disabled people to use their services. This has an impact on information systems, which are discussed in Section 10.10.

10.7 DISCRIMINATION ON THE GROUNDS OF AGE

The Equality Act 2010 makes it unlawful to discriminate on the grounds of age. In the field of employment this has meant the end of compulsory retirement ages. It also means that it is probably unlawful for employers to specifically seek to recruit new graduates. (This would be indirect age discrimination because a much smaller proportion of over-50s fall into the category of 'new graduates' than of under-25s.)

The test that discrimination can be justified if it represents 'a proportionate means of achieving a legitimate aim' means, however, that examples such as the following might well be considered lawful:

- special treatment of different age groups to protect them (but note that the age discrimination provisions of the Act do not, in any case, apply to persons under the age of 18);

- different premiums for life insurance policies depending on the age of the person at the time the policy is taken out, and different pension rates depending on the age of retirement (but these must not amount to sex discrimination);

- fixing a maximum age for recruitment based on the need for a reasonable period of employment after training and before retirement;

- fixing a minimum age, a minimum amount of professional experience or a minimum number of years with a company before a person will be regarded as eligible for a given post or eligible for certain employment benefits (e.g. additional annual leave).

The IT industry has traditionally been a youthful one and many companies have discriminated against older job applicants, albeit unconsciously or unintentionally. As the industry itself has grown older, the average age of its employees has been increasing, so this phenomenon has become less marked. Legislation against age discrimination will probably have little direct effect on the industry beyond accelerating this tendency.

10.8 PUBLIC SECTOR EQUALITY DUTY

The Equality Act 2010 includes the **Public Sector Equality Duty**, which places specific requirements on public sector organisations. In addition to adhering to the requirements to promote equality and act against discrimination, public sector organisations must consider the needs of all individuals. This applies to opportunities within the organisation as well as to people who use services that the organisation provides and the policies it defines.

There are three aims for the duty:

- eliminate unlawful discrimination;
- advance equality of opportunity;
- foster good relations.

The first aim is the same for all organisations. The second and third aims are specific to the duty. The Act states that they are about opportunity and relations between 'people who share a protected characteristic and those who do not share it'. Public sector organisations are expected to proactively consider these aims in all parts of their work. This includes working with employees and with the people they serve (e.g. residents accessing a local council's services). It also includes the services that public sector organisations procure from others; as such, public sector organisations have the potential to change the culture in other organisations to fit with the duty.

This duty affects all parts of an organisation, including its IT services. It can affect systems to improve support for accessibility, but it can have wider impacts too. For example, it could include updating IT systems to reflect the use of inclusive personal pronouns (she, he, they, ze).

10.9 POSITIVE ACTION

The Equality Act 2010 includes provision for positive action, which is about taking measures to improve equality in the workplace. This can apply when an organisation 'reasonably thinks' that people who share a protected characteristic:

- 'suffer a disadvantage connected to the characteristic';
- 'have needs that are different from the needs of persons who do not share [the characteristic]';
- have 'disproportionately low' participation in an activity compared with people who do not share the characteristic.

An example is where groups of people with a protected characteristic are under-represented in the management roles in an organisation. An organisation could consider why there is a discrepancy and take positive action to have better representation. One way of doing this could be to adjust job adverts to remove requirements for set hours of work or requirements for travel, which could encourage more applications. Another could be to establish mentoring schemes that target under-represented groups and help them to develop skills needed for more senior roles.

The test of 'reasonably think' is not defined in the Act. There should be some form of evidence to support the actions, but this does not need to be a detailed statistical report. The EHRC provides discussion of this topic in its *Employment Statutory Code of Practice* (see the Further Reading section). For example, a company might observe possible disadvantages, different needs or low participation in an area. To understand these issues, the company could compare what it has observed to what is observed in companies in the same industry or the general population, or it could discuss the issues with trade unions. The company could then identify potential positive actions that could improve the issues it observed. Providing that the actions were supported by the company's research into the issues, the actions might be deemed 'reasonable' in law.

Positive action is voluntary, but it can help organisations to make improvements to equality in the workplace. It can be useful for public sector organisations as they work to comply with the Public Sector Equality Duty.

10.10 INFORMATION SYSTEMS

The requirement to make reasonable adjustments could certainly include adapting information systems so that they can be used by a blind or partially sighted employee, provided this can be done at reasonable cost. And the requirement for service providers to make reasonable adjustments certainly requires that reasonable adjustments should be made to the way that services are provided via the web.

The legislation has a direct effect on information systems professionals in a way that other anti-discrimination legislation does not: it directly influences – or should influence – the way in which information systems are designed. In practice, for the ordinary information systems developer (as opposed to specialists working in areas such as text-to-speech conversion), this translates into the need to make systems usable by the blind, those whose vision is impaired, those whose hearing is impaired, those with conditions that affect their manual dexterity (and so are unable to use a mouse, for example) and those with dyslexia. This need is most apparent, and most likely to be enforceable, when the system includes publicly accessible web pages.

Methods of improving accessibility

A few of the ways accessibility can be improved include:

- Do not rely on subtle colour contrasts, such as yellow text on a green background.

- Provide textual alternatives for non-text content such as diagrams, pictures, audio and videos.

- Make all functions available from the keyboard – some users may have difficulty using a mouse.

- Do not impose time constraints on users, some of whom may read slowly.

- Ensure that the page can be read satisfactorily by a screen reader (i.e. software that converts text on the screen to speech output).

- If animation is used, provide the ability to reduce the intensity (such as slowing an animation so that it is less distracting) or the ability to turn off an animation.

- Provide ways to change the font.

- Make it easy to avoid or correct mistakes – for example, by providing undo and redo functionality when deleting an email.

Within a few years of the start of the World Wide Web, it was recognised that guidance was needed to improve the accessibility of the web for disabled users. Since 1997 the World Wide Web Consortium (W3C) has published guidelines as part of its Web Accessibility Initiative. Perhaps the best known are the Web Content Accessibility Guidelines (WCAG), which are currently at version 2.1 (see the Further Reading section).

The W3C's guidelines specify three levels of compliance:

- Level A is the lowest level of conformance. If a web page does not satisfy the success criteria at this level, one or more groups of disabled people will be unable to access the page.

- Level AA is the next level. If a web page does not satisfy the success criteria at level AA, some groups of disabled people will have difficulty accessing the page.

- Level AAA is the final level. Satisfying the success criteria at level AAA will provide the widest support for people with accessibility needs wishing to access the web page.

Several pieces of software are available to test whether a web page complies with W3C's guidelines.

There have been various studies of access and inclusion relating to websites. *The Web: Access and Inclusion for Disabled People*, from 2004, was conducted by the Disability Rights Commission (a predecessor of the EHRC). It considered a survey of 1,000 home pages. There is also an annual survey conducted by WebAIM, part of Utah State University, that samples 1 million pages each year. These show that many sites have accessibility errors, although the WebAIM Million study shows recent improvements (see the Further Reading section for details).

Common accessibility issues include:

- Page layouts are unclear and confusing.
- Navigation mechanisms are confusing and disorienting.
- There is poor contrast between the text and the background, and colours are used inappropriately.
- Graphics and text are too small.
- Links and images are poorly labelled.

It is striking that the first four of these, and possibly the fifth, are sources of difficulty for all web users. Eliminating these faults would not only improve the accessibility of the web for disabled users but also enhance its usability for everyone.

W3C also produces accessibility guidelines for authoring tools. They are intended to ensure that the authoring tools 'make the authoring tools themselves accessible, so that disabled people can create web content' and 'help authors create more accessible web content'.[2] Authoring tools are an important part of creating and editing content on the web. Making the tools accessible for users and able to produce accessible content is an important part of the Web Accessibility Initiative. IT professionals should consider this when selecting tools or creating new tools.

Quite apart from the ethical and commercial reasons for making web pages accessible to the disabled, there are legal requirements. In 2012 the Royal National Institute of Blind People served legal proceedings against the low-cost airline bmibaby (now defunct) over its failure to ensure web access for blind and partially sighted customers. More recently, there have been similar cases in the USA against companies including Netflix, a range of fashion companies and Domino's Pizza. The requirement laid down in the Equality Act is to make reasonable adjustments to allow access by disabled people. In practice, this probably means that a small company can claim that it does not have the

---

2   'Authoring Tool Accessibility Guidelines (ATAG) Overview' (2020), W3C, https://www.w3.org/WAI/standards-guidelines/atag.

necessary resources to make significant adjustments, but no such defence is available to larger organisations.

Accessibility is not just limited to web pages and web applications. Applications for phones, tablets, laptops and desktops are all capable of using accessibility functionality that is built into the operating systems. For example, iOS and Android developers have access to techniques to improve the accessibility of their applications. Some of these are easily enabled and others take more time for developers to learn and apply. Also, office tools such as word processors and presentation tools now have improved support for highlighting and fixing accessibility issues. As with web pages, making the changes can enhance usability for all users and reduce the likelihood of discriminating against some users.

There is a related issue of access to IT for people who are digitally disadvantaged. For example:

- There are people who have very limited or no experience of using computers or smartphones. Using technology is new and potentially difficult for them.
- There are other people who use computers in public libraries to access websites, including government information websites. They may not have a phone that can be used for two-factor authentication and so may be unable to access some of these websites.

The Equality Act and the accessibility guidelines do not specifically mention such groups of people. As discussed earlier, improving accessibility can help all users of a system. Doing so won't address all of the issues, but it is a positive step. Another action that could help when building IT systems is to have a wider set of experiences on the development team. This can help the team to use those experiences to understand and anticipate the needs of users, leading to better IT systems. The issue of building teams with wider sets of skills and experiences is discussed in Section 10.12.

10.11 AVOIDING DISCRIMINATION

It is not enough for an employer to support anti-discrimination legislation and resolve to comply with it. In an organisation of any size, it is necessary to ensure that all members of the organisation share the employer's resolve. And, even if this is achieved, the organisation may have to deal with such problems as unlawful harassment from customers or unjustified accusations of discrimination. However, effective compliance with the legislation should provide a company with the ability to rebut such harassment and accusations.

Effective compliance with anti-discrimination legislation in the workplace requires three things:

- a suitable written policy that is well publicised and freely and easily available;
- a training programme for new and existing staff to ensure that they are all aware of the policy and its importance;
- effective procedures for implementing the policy.

It is a sad fact that an employer's ability to rebut an accusation of unlawful discrimination may depend as much on the ability to demonstrate that proper procedures have been followed as on whether any discrimination took place.

10.12 DIVERSITY AND INCLUSION

The Equality Act is an important part of tackling discrimination and it has legal consequences if companies fail to take action. In addition to the legislation, the issues of diversity and inclusion are important in making society more equal. Diversity and inclusion have advantages for organisations as well as society. For a technology company, diversity can lead to recruiting a diverse team that has a wider set of skills and experiences that help to build better products for its users. In addition, inclusion can help the company to retain the team members because they recognise that their contributions are valued.

Diversity is about involving a wider range of people in the workforce. This encompasses differences in any of the protected characteristics of the Act and could include other differences, such as in the area of neurodiversity. As well as making available additional skills in the organisation, diversity enables organisations to take account of a wider range of views and experiences, thus enabling a better representation of society.

Diversity is an important step, but it is also necessary to ensure that people are included in the decision-making and other activities of the organisation. Inclusion is about providing a culture where different views are encouraged. It allows people to make suggestions and look at problems with a fresh view, helping to improve what the organisation does.

When an organisation supports diversity and inclusion, there is the real potential to improve equality in the company and in the services and products it provides. In a technology company, a more diverse team can have a breadth of skills and experiences that help the design and development of technology applications. If these people are included in the team's activities and listened to, and if their contributions are valued, there is the potential to produce applications and solutions that support all members of the user community. Unfortunately, improving diversity in a team without also improving inclusion (across all team members) is likely to lead to employees leaving because they don't feel valued.

Increasingly, organisations are adopting policies that promote diversity and inclusion. These policies are a public statement of their commitment to those principles. They are also a way to begin to change the culture within an organisation so that diversity and inclusion become standard activities that all employees can participate in. The policies need to be supported by training for staff so that they understand the motivations and how these efforts will work in the organisation.

Example changes for organisations might include:

- Reviewing job adverts so that they don't include requirements that may discourage some staff from applying. For example, this might include reviewing whether any length of experience is necessary for a role; women who took a career break to have children may have the relevant skills, but they may not be able to demonstrate that they have the length of experience.

- Encouraging applications to speak at a conference and emphasising that applications are particularly welcome from groups that are normally under-represented. If there are panel discussions at the conference, then steps should be taken to have a diverse panel.

- Introducing inclusivity policies for conferences which emphasise that everyone should be able to feel welcome, included and safe at the conference. Such a policy sets expectations and provides a mechanism to ask people to leave if they behave inappropriately to others at the conference.

- Introducing unconscious bias training in the organisation. This is about raising awareness of ways in which we act and the possibility of bias towards others. Such bias is often manifested in the form of decisions that are taken quickly due to things like stereotypes or possibly due to influence by the views of others. For example, when reviewing job applications and producing a shortlist for interview, we may dismiss an application from an older person because we think that they won't be as prepared as younger applicants to work long hours. These quick decisions may cause us to discriminate as well as miss out on opportunities and skills that would enhance the organisation.

- Improving the range of pictures used in documents and publicity material. This helps to provide a more diverse set of images that more people can relate to. For example, publicity materials for education courses could include pictures with a diverse range of students. This can help potential students to identify themselves with the publicity and see that they could be part of the courses and learning community.

- Promoting guidelines about the use of personal pronouns, including examples so that it is understood how to use them.

- Supporting flexible working, such as job sharing, flexible hours and remote working. This can help to provide ways of working that are more inclusive of those who want flexibility for commitments such as family or caring, or for people who just want to balance work with other activities.

BCS has adopted a policy of making diversity and inclusion its standard way of functioning. It has a particular focus on the impact of diversity and inclusion in the IT industry. Over six years, BCS has been tracking the representation of different groups in the IT labour market. The reports on this topic published in 2021 covered age, disability, women in IT and ethnicity. The reports show that in each area, there is under-representation (of older people, disabled people, women and people from ethnic minority backgrounds) in the IT sector. Over time, these reports will help the industry to track changes and will inform policies to reduce under-representation.

In 2021 BCS published the book *Women in Tech: A Practical Guide to Increasing Gender Diversity and Inclusion*, which provides a detailed look at issues relating to equality, diversity and inclusion. The book looks at women in computing education, encouraging recruitment and retention, career advancement of women in IT and unconscious bias. It notes the importance of the Equality Act and its role in setting out the legal requirements around equality, but it also notes that there have been slow rates of change. It explores ways that change could be accelerated, and it is recommended for those in the IT industry who wish to further understand these issues.

In considering the business case for diversity and inclusion, *Women in Tech* notes that as well as the moral reasons for improving equality, diversity and inclusion, and the legal requirements of the Act, there are reports that show that it is good for business. Such reports show that companies with more diverse gender representation in management teams have improved financial results. Reasons for these business benefits can include better decision making, incorporating a wider set of views, and employees who feel empowered to suggest change.

Training and discussion are essential in bringing about changes in equality, diversity and inclusion. Senior management and the HR department can set the company's aims and define ways to regularly promote these aims throughout the workforce. And as organisations adopt and promote policies, there is the potential to influence other organisations, such as suppliers and customers, to do the same.

FURTHER READING

The Equality Act 2010 can be accessed at:
> https://www.legislation.gov.uk/ukpga/2010/15

The EHRC's website contains much information and guidance about the Equality Act. In particular, it contains the *Employment Statutory Code of Practice*, which covers the Equality Act 2010 as it applies to employment:
> https://www.equalityhumanrights.com

ACAS (the Advisory, Conciliation and Advisory Service) also provides much helpful advice relating to equality issues at work:
> https://www.acas.org.uk

The details of BCS's book on women in computing are as follows:
> Arnold, G. (ed.) (2021) *Women in Tech: A Practical Guide to Increasing Gender Diversity and Inclusion*. BCS, Swindon.

The 'Diversity and Inclusion' section of the BCS website includes reports about diversity:
> https://www.bcs.org/policy-and-influence/diversity-and-inclusion

The UK government has published a guide to the use of the WCAG:
> 'Understanding WCAG 2.1' (n.d.), Gov.uk. https://www.gov.uk/service-manual/helping-people-to-use-your-service/understanding-wcag.

The Disability Rights Commission's study on access can be found here:
> Disability Rights Commission (2004) *The Web: Access and Inclusion for Disabled People*. The Stationery Office, London.

The latest WebAIM Million report is available here:
> https://webaim.org

11 INTELLECTUAL PROPERTY RIGHTS

After studying this chapter, you should:

- *be familiar with the different types of intellectual property that are relevant to IT and understand their applicability;*
- *understand the rights attached to the different kinds of intellectual property and the ways in which these rights can be enforced;*
- *be aware of the issues that are at the root of current debates about intellectual property rights.*

11.1 WHAT IS INTELLECTUAL PROPERTY?

If someone steals your bicycle, you no longer have it. If someone takes away a computer belonging to a company, the company no longer has it.

This seems very obvious. In fact, it hides an important and subtle point. If you invent a drug that will cure all known illnesses and leave the formula on your desk, someone can come along, read the formula, remember it, and go away and make a fortune out of manufacturing the drug. But you still have the formula even though the other person now has it as well. This shows that the formula – more generally, any piece of information – is not property in the same way as a bicycle.

The legal definition of theft involves taking away a piece of someone's property with the intention to permanently deprive them of it. As we have just seen, this cannot apply to a piece of information.

Property like bicycles or computers is called **tangible property** – that is, property that can be touched. It is protected by laws relating to theft and damage. Property that is intangible is known as **intellectual property**. It is governed by a different set of laws, concerned with **intellectual property rights** – that is, rights to use, copy or reveal information about intellectual property.

Intellectual property crosses national borders much more readily than tangible property and the international nature of intellectual property rights has long been recognised. The international law relating to trademarks and patents is based on the Paris Convention, which was signed in 1883. The Berne Convention, which lies at the heart of international copyright law, was signed in 1886.

Rapid changes in technology and the commercial developments that follow them present the law with new problems. The law relating to intellectual property rights is evolving very rapidly and most of this evolution is taking place at a global level or at the level of regional groupings of countries, rather than at the level of individual countries. For the UK, European Community law regarding intellectual property rights when the UK was in the European Union (EU) was critically important, and it remains of interest despite Brexit; however, this law is itself much influenced by developments elsewhere, particularly in the USA.

Software can be very valuable, as the balance sheets of companies such as IBM, Microsoft and Oracle show. But software is intangible property. The industry can therefore only protect its assets by using intellectual property rights – hence the importance of the topic for information systems engineers and hence the length of this chapter.

11.2 DIFFERENT TYPES OF INTELLECTUAL PROPERTY RIGHTS

There are several different rights that relate to intellectual property. In this book, we are only concerned with those that are relevant to software and the information systems industry. These rights should be looked on as a package; different rights may be used to protect different aspects of a piece of software:

- **Copyright** is, as the name suggests, concerned with the right to copy something. It may be a written document, a picture or photograph, a piece of music, a recording, or many other things, including a computer program.

- **Patents** are primarily intended to protect inventions by giving inventors a monopoly on exploiting their inventions for a certain period.

- **Confidential information** is information that a person receives in circumstances that make it clear that they must not pass it on. The right of confidentiality is not an intellectual property right under UK law but it is often treated in a similar way.

- **Trademarks** identify the product of a particular manufacturer or supplier.

Any or all of these rights can be used to protect a piece of software. Suppose, for example, that a company has developed an innovative computer game called *Spookcatcher*. The game is marketed in packaging that features the name superimposed on the image of a ghost. It comes with an add-on device that the company has invented called a 'wailer'. This attaches to the computer and emits very convincing ghostly wails at suitable points in the action. The software uses some very clever data structures developed within the company that make it possible to achieve very high performance.

The law of copyright automatically protects the source code and all documentation of the package from copying. The company might be able to patent the wailer, in which case no one else would be able to produce a similar product. The law relating to confidential information could be used to prevent any employee who left to join a competitor from passing on details of the clever data structure. And the name (with the associated logo) could be registered as a trademark to prevent other companies from using it on their products.

In the next four sections we shall discuss each of these rights separately and explain the conditions under which they come into existence and what their effects are. The use of internet domain names can conflict with trademarks and, arguably, domain names are themselves a special type of intellectual property. We therefore discuss trademarks and domain names separately in Sections 11.6 and 11.7 respectively.

11.3 COPYRIGHT

As the name suggests, copyright is associated primarily with the right to copy something. The 'something' is known as the 'work'. The Copyright, Designs and Patents Act 1988 defines the types of work that are protected by copyright law. The types that concern us here are 'original literary, dramatic, musical or artistic' works. The Act states that the term 'literary work' includes a table or compilation, a computer program, preparatory design material for a computer program and certain databases.

Copyright comes into existence when a work is written down or recorded in some other way. It is not necessary to register it in any way.

11.3.1 The rights of the copyright owner

Copyright law gives the owner of the copyright certain exclusive rights. The rights that are relevant to software and, more generally, to written documents, are the following:

- **The right to make copies of the work:** Making a copy of a work includes copying code from a disk into random access memory (RAM) in order to execute the code. It also includes downloading a page from the World Wide Web to view on your computer, whether or not you then store the page on your local disk.

- **The right to issue copies of the work to the public:** This applies whether or not they are charged for.

- **The right to adapt the work:** This includes translating it – whether from English to Chinese or from C to Java (for example).

In other words, no one can do any of these things without the copyright owner's permission. In some cases, the permission may be implied rather than explicit. The act of making a document available on the web implies that people are allowed to view it over the internet, which involves copying it into the memory of their own computer; however, it does not necessarily extend to allowing people to store copies on their local disk or to print it.

In general, these rights last for 70 years after the death of the author (not the owner); there are, however, many exceptions and special cases. This is far longer than is likely to be commercially relevant for software, although there is software still in use that was written well over 30 years ago.

It is very important to realise that copyright law does not give the owner of the copyright any power to prevent someone else using or publishing identical material, provided they did not produce it by copying the copyright work. (This is in marked contrast to patent law.) This means that programmers do not need to worry that they will be breaching copyright if they inadvertently produce code that is identical to that produced by another programmer somewhere else – something that can easily happen.

11.3.2 What you can do to a copyright work

The law specifically permits certain actions in relation to a copyright work. Some of these are of particular relevance to software.

First, it is explicitly stated that in most cases it is not an infringement of copyright to make a back-up of a program that you are authorised to use. However, only one such copy is allowed. If the program is stored in a filing system with a sophisticated back-up system, multiple back-up copies are likely to come into existence.

Second, you may in most cases 'decompile' a program in order to correct errors in it. You may also, again in most cases, decompile a program in order to obtain the information you need to write a program that will 'interoperate' with it, provided this information is not available to you in any other way.

Third, you can sell your right to use a program in much the same way that you can sell a book you own. However, when you do this, you sell all your rights. In particular, you must not retain a copy of the program.

11.3.3 Databases

According to the Copyright and Rights in Databases Regulations 1997, copyright subsists in a database if 'its contents constitute the author's own intellectual creation'. There are many databases that do not satisfy this criterion but that, nonetheless, require a lot of effort and a lot of money to prepare. Examples might include databases of hotels, of pop songs or of geographical data. In order to encourage the production of such modest but useful databases, the 1997 regulations created a special intellectual property right called the **database right**. The database right subsists in a database 'if there has been substantial investment in obtaining, verifying or presenting the contents of the database'. It lasts for 15 years and prevents anyone from extracting or reusing all, or a substantial part of, the database without the owner's permission. Fifteen years is much less than the protection given by copyright but is, in practice, likely to be longer than the commercially valuable life of a database, unless it is updated. If it is updated, however, a new 15-year period will start. Many databases have both copyright and database right protection at the same time. A database must have an element of intellectual creativity in order to have copyright protection in addition to database right protection.

11.3.4 Ownership and licensing

As a general rule, the copyright in a work belongs initially to its author. If the work is jointly written by several authors, they jointly own the copyright. There is one important exception to this. If the author is an employee and wrote the work as part of their job, then the copyright belongs to the employer, unless there is an explicit, written agreement to the contrary. Note that the copyright nevertheless extends to 70 years after the author (or the last of the joint authors) dies, even though it is very improbable that it will be possible to trace their names. It is one reason companies are advised to keep notes for long periods on who wrote a copyright work.

The employer owns the copyright only if the author is legally an employee. If the author is an independent contractor, they will own the copyright unless there is an agreement to the contrary. For this reason, if a company commissions an independent contractor (freelance programmer) to write software, it is important to have a formal agreement regarding ownership of the copyright in the resulting software.

These issues are dealt with in more detail in Section 12.4.3.

11.3.5 Copyright infringement

Anyone who, without permission, does one of the things that are the exclusive right of the copyright owner is said to infringe the copyright. There are two sorts of infringement. **Primary infringement** takes place whenever any of the exclusive rights of the copyright owner are breached. It is a matter for the civil courts and the usual remedies are available: a claim for damages or an injunction to refrain from the infringement are the most likely. **Secondary infringement** occurs when primary infringement occurs in a business or commercial context. In the case of software, this could involve trading in pirated software or it could involve using pirated software within a business. This is a much more serious matter and may result in criminal proceedings leading to a substantial fine or imprisonment and the confiscation of the copying equipment, as well as civil damages.

Software and other material distributed in digital form is now often protected against copying by some sort of technical device. Inevitably, information about how to circumvent this protection has appeared on the internet and ready-made devices to do it are available from certain sources. The Copyright, Designs and Patents Act provides that anyone who publishes such information or makes, imports or sells such devices will be treated in the same way as if they were infringing the copyright in a protected work.

There are some cases in which it may be difficult to demonstrate that copying has taken place. Books of mathematical tables fall into this category, because the numbers in them have an objective existence – the square root of 2 correct to four decimal places is 1.4142, regardless of who calculated it. In order to protect their copyright, the compilers of mathematical tables commonly insert a few small, random errors (one unit in the last decimal place) in their tables. Anyone who copies the tables rather than recalculating them will reproduce the errors and this can be adduced as evidence to show that copying has taken place. A similar technique could be used to help demonstrate that copying of source code had taken place. In this case, the writer could insert the occasional statement that had no functional effect. If the code were copied, the presence of such statements would be convincing evidence of the fact.

Copyright infringement is one of the commonest reasons for litigation in the IT industry. What follows is a description of one such case. The action, which was heard in the High Court of Justice in 1999, concerned a system for inter-dealer bond broking, a somewhat esoteric financial activity in which both Cantor Fitzgerald (CF) and Tradition (UK) were involved.

The managing director of CF, Michael Howard, was dismissed and obtained employment with Tradition, taking with him Christopher Harland, a senior member of the team who had worked on CF's system, as well as two very capable junior members of staff. It took them less than three months to develop a system for Tradition that was a significant improvement on the CF system but had many features in common with it. The claimants alleged that this must have been a copy of their system. They therefore brought an action for copyright infringement (and breach of confidence; see Section 11.5) against Tradition itself and against Howard and Harland.

There were many complicating factors in this action and a great deal of effort was needed to establish the facts of the case. In essence, however, it appeared that:

- When the staff left CF, they took a copy of the source code of the system with them.
- After he had left CF, Harland logged into CF's system and took a copy of a substantial data file.
- Howard and Harland initially expected to implement a system for Tradition that would have been very largely a copy of CF's system and intended to conceal this copying.
- The system eventually implemented was very different from CF's system in internal structure and substantially better but contained a comparatively small amount (no more than 4%) of code copied from the CF system.
- The programmers used the copy of the CF system that they had taken both for reference and for testing.

The judge ruled that Howard, Harland and the programmers (who were not sued individually) had infringed copyright and that Tradition, as their employer, was also liable. The extent of the liability was, however, very much limited by the fact that only a small proportion of the system had been copied. Many of the claims made by CF were unjustified.

When CF started the action against Tradition, Howard denied that there had been any copying. This led Tradition to spend a great deal of money on a line of defence that ultimately had to be abandoned. The judge ruled also that, by not telling Tradition about the copying while the system was being developed, Howard had failed in his duty to his employer. For these reasons, therefore, Howard was obliged to indemnify Tradition against its costs and damages.

The circumstances of this case are not unusual and it serves to demonstrate how easily behaviour that may seem only marginally dishonest can result in expensive litigation.[1]

11.3.6 Where does copyright law come from?

The primary source of law relating to copyright in the UK is the Copyright, Designs and Patents Act 1988; important amendments to the Act were made by the Copyright

---

1   For further details of this case, see 'Infringement of Copyright in Software' (2000), Humphreys & Co, https://www.humphreys.co.uk/articles/infringement-of-copyright-in-software.

(Computer Programs) Regulations 1992, the Copyright and Rights in Databases Regulations 1997, and the Copyright and Related Rights Regulations 2003. Many of these amendments were made in order to comply with EU legislation and the description of copyright given here is broadly valid throughout the EU. Following Brexit, the UK is free to modify its laws relating to copyright but, up to the time of writing (2022), it has not chosen to do so, although it has chosen not to implement the latest EU copyright directive (2019/790) so far.

A large number of countries (179) are signatories to the Berne Convention, last revised in 1979. Countries that sign the Berne Convention agree to establish national laws protecting copyright along the lines described above. In practice, details such as the length of time for which protection is provided may vary, as may the enthusiasm with which countries pursue cases of copyright infringement.

11.4 PATENTS

11.4.1 What is a patent?

A patent is a temporary right, granted by the government, enabling inventors to prevent other people from exploiting their invention without their permission. Unlike copyright, it does not come into existence automatically; the inventor must apply for the patent to be granted. However, the protection it gives is much stronger than copyright, because the grant of a patent allows the person who owns it (the **patentee**) to prevent anyone else from exploiting the invention, even if they have discovered it for themselves either before or after the grant of the patent.

Patents were originally intended to encourage new inventions, and in particular to encourage the disclosure of those new inventions. Inventors are often hesitant to reveal the details of their invention, for fear that someone else might copy it. A government-granted temporary monopoly on the commercial use of their invention provides a remedy against this fear, and so acts as an incentive to disclose the details of the invention. After the monopoly period expires, everyone else is free to exploit the invention. And, because of the disclosure made by the inventor, it is very easy to do so.

The temporary monopoly also gives inventors a chance to recoup the investments they make during the development of their invention. They can, for instance, use the patent to monopolise the market, excluding possible competitors by enforcing the patent. They might then set a high price and make a nice profit. They could also request money from others in return for a licence to exploit the invention. The licensing fee then provides extra income. Licensing a patent can be a very lucrative business.

11.4.2 What can be patented?

In Europe, the law relating to patents is based on the European Patent Convention. This was signed in 1973 by 27 European countries and came into force in 1978. The UK's obligations under the convention were implemented in the Patents Act 1977, although there have been some subsequent modifications. The 1977 Act states that an invention can only be patented if it:

- is new; *and*
- involves an **inventive step** (described below); *and*
- is capable of industrial application; *and*
- is not in an area specifically excluded.

Similar criteria apply in all the countries that are signatories to the convention.

The requirement that the invention must be new means that it must not have been disclosed or used publicly before the date on which the patent application was made. This applies as much to publication or use by the inventor as by anyone else. Thus, if Alexander Graham Bell had demonstrated the telephone or written an article about it before he applied for his patent, the patent would not have been granted.

When a patent application is filed in the UK, officials at the Intellectual Property Office (UKIPO; also known as the Patent Office) will search existing patents as well as the literature in the area to see whether the invention has been described before. The searches will not be limited to the literature published in the country where the application is made and they may go back many years. Provided it is publicly available (even if very difficult to access), any publication describing the invention, no matter how obscure the source, will lead to the rejection of the application.

The requirement for an inventive step essentially means that the invention should not be obvious. In other words, it must not be something that anyone reasonably competent in the field would have produced if faced with the same requirements. Thus, leaving aside any other considerations, a program to print invoices for a company is unlikely to satisfy the requirement for an inventive step, even if no one has ever written precisely the same program before, because any competent programmer would have written very much the same program.

The requirement for the invention to be capable of industrial application is simply a requirement that the invention must have a practical application (sometimes referred to as a **technical effect**).

Following the European Patent Convention, the Patents Act 1977 excludes the following:

- **Scientific theories:** The theory of gravity cannot be patented, although a machine that uses it in a novel way could be.
- **Mathematical methods:** This means, for example, that the methods used for carrying out floating-point arithmetic cannot be patented. A machine that uses the idea can, however, be patented.
- **A literary, dramatic, musical or artistic work or any other aesthetic creation:** As we have already seen, these are protected by copyright.
- **The presentation of information:** Again, this is covered by the law of copyright.
- **A scheme, rule or method** for performing a mental act, playing a game or doing business, or a program for a computer.

The last of these exclusions is the one that will be by far the most important to the readers of this book and we shall discuss it at length in Section 11.4.5.

11.4.3 Obtaining a patent

Unlike copyright – which comes into existence automatically when the protected work is recorded, whether in writing or otherwise – a patent must be explicitly applied for. Applying for a patent can be an expensive and time-consuming business.

Patents are granted by national patent offices. Inventors who want protection in several different countries must, in principle, apply separately to the patent offices of each country. In practice, there are schemes run by the European Patent Office (EPO) and the World Intellectual Property Organization (WIPO) – an international organisation with 177 states as members – that provide some assistance by simplifying the process of applying for patents in several countries simultaneously and by reducing its cost. The EPO is not an EU body but a European one and so is unaffected by Brexit. A **European patent** is simply a bundle of national patents, often including a UK one.

The requirement that an invention must be new if a patent is to be granted means that the date at which the patent application is first filed is critical, because it is at this date that the invention must be new. If someone else filed a similar application the day before, then that one will have priority. An initial application to one national patent office is enough to establish priority, provided it is followed within 12 months by the submission of a full patent specification to the national patent offices of all the countries in which a patent is sought, possibly through the EPO or the WIPO.

The full patent specification needs to be prepared by a specialist patent attorney and it can take up to four years for the process of obtaining patents to be completed.

Because computing is a global industry, any patents relating to computing need to be taken out in enough countries to make sure that the market in which the invention is not protected is too small to attract a competitor.

In 2022, progress was made on a new right known as the **unitary patent**, or single patent for the EU. However, as the UK has left the EU, this single EU-wide patent will not be available in the UK.

11.4.4 Enforcing a patent

The grant of a patent is not a guarantee that it can be effectively enforced. If you own a patent and you find that someone is infringing it, you may have to go to the courts to enforce your rights. In the court hearing, the offender can challenge your patent on the grounds that it does not satisfy the four criteria listed at the start of Section 11.4.2. The commonest challenge is on the grounds of **prior art** – that is, that the invention is not new. Publication anywhere of the invention – even by display of a prototype at a trade fair or discussion of the invention at a university conference, or even disclosure to a very few people with no non-disclosure agreement in place – means the patent then is subject to challenge if that publication occurs before the application is submitted. The other likely challenge is that it does not involve an inventive step – in other words, that anyone of reasonable competence in the field could have produced the invention simply by following established practice.

The problem is that enforcing a patent that you own or challenging a patent held by someone else is a time-consuming and expensive process. This means that if an individual or a small company owns a patent, a large company can challenge that patent or even blatantly infringe it, knowing that the holder of the patent cannot afford to contest the challenge effectively.

11.4.5 Software patents

For many years, the US Patent and Trademark Office refused to grant patents for any invention that involved a computer program. In 1981, however, it was ordered by the US Supreme Court to grant a patent on a method of curing rubber, the novel element of which was a computer program to calculate the optimal way of heating the rubber.

Very roughly, the position in the USA is now that software can be patented if:

- it is part of a product that is itself eligible to be patented;
- it controls a process that has some physical effect (e.g. curing rubber);
- it processes data that arises from the physical world.

As we have seen, the European Patent Convention and the Copyright, Designs and Patents Act 1988 both state unequivocally that a patent cannot be granted for a computer program. Despite these provisions, the EPO has been granting patents for software since 1998, as has the UKIPO. Patent offices in the different European countries have adopted different policies towards the patenting of software, with the result that there is much confusion about what is and is not patentable. The result is that there has been a conflict between the law and practice, a very undesirable situation.

In order to clarify the situation, the European Commission produced a draft directive (COD 2002/0047). When this was submitted to the European Parliament, it was extensively modified. The resulting version has been heavily criticised and no new legislation has emerged. The confusion therefore looks set to continue.

The question of software patents has proved to be extremely controversial. There are very many websites and many organisations dedicated to opposing the idea of software patents. The arguments for and against the patenting of software can be summed up as follows.

On the one hand, it is illogical and unfair that something that would be clearly patentable if implemented completely in hardware should not be patentable if implemented completely in software. Furthermore, patents encourage investment because:

- A patent is a well-defined asset that allows shareholders and, in particular, venture capitalists to be confident that their investment is producing something of value.
- Patents ensure that the benefit of research and development accrues to the people who financed it.

A vast number of patents relating to inventions in software equipment and relating to the technology have been granted where it has been possible to show the patent is not for software 'as such' and there is an invention involved.

On the other hand, the software industry has been immensely productive and successful in many cases without patents. Much of its success is due to the efforts of small companies. Patents are not helpful to small companies as, even if they can afford to file for patents, they cannot afford to defend their patents or defend themselves against invalid claims for patent infringement coming from large companies.

Additionally, many of the patents granted are 'bad' patents because they are not new or because there is no inventive step. A great deal of software was written before software patents were thought possible. This means the records of prior art are very patchy. Although such patents could not be successfully defended in court, the threat of patent litigation, which is always likely to be both expensive and protracted, could restrict the activities of many smaller companies or even force them out of business.

11.5 CONFIDENTIAL INFORMATION

As we have already explained, information cannot be 'stolen'. Nevertheless, it is possible to take action in a civil court to prevent someone from using or revealing information that they have received in confidence. The critical point is that the information must have been given to that person in circumstances that give rise to what is known as an **obligation of confidence**. Rights of confidentiality are not intellectual property rights under UK law but are often treated in a similar way.

It is common for an obligation of confidence to come into existence as a result of a specific clause in a contract. Contracts for consultancy services or the provision of bespoke software will invariably include specific clauses binding each party to keep confidential any information it obtains about the operations or products of the other. Non-disclosure agreements are agreements that are specifically intended to set up obligations of confidence. It is common, for example, when two companies are discussing a possible collaboration, for each side to sign such a non-disclosure agreement to protect the information that they exchange.

Where there is no specific contractual term that creates an obligation of confidence, such an obligation may still exist under equity, that part of the law that reflects general notions of fair dealing. Under equity, an obligation of confidence exists whenever a reasonable person, placed in the position of the recipient of the information, would reasonably understand that the information was being given to them in confidence.

One important aspect of confidential information relates to ideas that are likely to be the subject of a patent application. Because the application may be rejected if it can be shown that the ideas had already been made public, it is important that the inventor only discusses them in conditions where an obligation of confidence exists, whether this is through the signing of a non-disclosure agreement or otherwise.

Another important example of confidential information is information about current sales prospects. Many software companies will be engaged in sales negotiations with a range of prospective customers and a knowledge of the content of these negotiations could certainly enable a competitor to gain a considerable advantage. If a member of the sales staff of Company X gave notice of their intention to leave and join a competitor, Company Y, it would be unwise to rely purely on the obligation of confidence, however clearly this was spelled out in the contract of employment. The problem is that it might be very difficult to prove that the salesperson had revealed crucial information that subsequently enabled Company Y to win a contract that Company X was expecting to win. For this reason, it is common for sales staff, and other staff who are likely to have sensitive knowledge about sales negotiations, to be employed on contracts that specify comparatively long periods of notice – typically three or six months. When such employees give notice, they are immediately removed from sensitive work and assigned to such important and worthy tasks as reorganising the company's technical library.

Confidential information is not at all the same thing as professional skill and expertise. If, as part of your employment, you learn to program in Perl or to design using Unified Modelling Language, you take these skills with you and are entitled to use them in your new employment.

An obligation of confidentiality is not absolute. A court may rule that it is in the public interest that certain confidential information is disclosed. While this rules out an action for breach of confidence, it does not prevent an employee who discloses such information from being dismissed. Over the years, there have been a number of well-publicised instances in which employees have disclosed confidential information about malpractice on the part of their employer; they have done this because they felt strongly that the malpractice – be it illegal price fixing or serious environmental damage – should be stopped. For a long time, there was nothing to protect such employees, who are often known as **whistleblowers**, from being fired by their employers, often in such circumstances that it was difficult or impossible for them to get another job. There are, however, many more instances in which employees have been victimised for drawing their employer's attention to matters that the employer would rather not be told about. The authors know of one instance in which an employee was effectively dismissed for drawing his employer's attention to systematic fraud going on in the organisation.

In 1998, the UK Parliament passed the Public Interest Disclosure Act, which provides some protection for employees in these circumstances. First, the Act defines what sort of disclosure of information is covered. A **qualifying disclosure** – that is, a disclosure to which the Act applies – means any disclosure of information that the person making the disclosure reasonably believes shows that one or more of the following has occurred or is about to occur:

- a criminal offence;
- failure to comply with a legal obligation;
- a miscarriage of justice;
- danger to health and safety;
- environmental damage;
- information showing that any of these has been concealed.

A worker making a qualifying disclosure will only be protected against victimisation if the disclosure is made in the right circumstances. In this case, the disclosure is known as a **protected disclosure**. The rules defining the circumstances in which a disclosure becomes protected are complicated but they encourage the worker first of all to raise the matter internally – many employers have produced codes of practice on public interest disclosure, which specify who the worker should make the disclosure to and the procedures for handling it. In more serious cases, or if the internal route has proved ineffective, it may be appropriate to disclose the information to a professional body or to a public official. Only in the most serious of cases will disclosure to the media be protected.

The 1998 Act has had only a limited effect and a private members' bill, the Public Interest Disclosure (Protection) Bill, was introduced in Parliament in 2019. This would have had the effect of substantially extending the protection offered by the 1998 Act but it failed to pass through Parliament.

The UK did bring the EU directive on trade secrets into force through the Trade Secrets (Enforcement, etc.) Regulations 2018 before Brexit. In a few, but not most, areas, these regulations add to the existing common law of confidentiality. These regulations emphasise the need to take reasonable steps to keep information secret for it to be classed as a **trade secret**.

11.6 TRADEMARKS AND PASSING OFF

The law regarding trademarks in the UK is based on the Trade Marks Act 1994, which consolidated and updated existing legislation. The Act defines a trademark as:

> Any sign capable of being represented graphically which is capable of distinguishing goods or services of one undertaking from those of other undertakings. A trade mark may, in particular, consist of words (including personal names), designs, letters, numerals or the shape of goods or their packaging.

Some of the best-known examples of trademarks include the name Coca Cola, the characteristic shape of the Coca Cola bottle and the large M that serves to advertise McDonald's fast food outlets. Microsoft is a trademark, as are the names of many Microsoft products, such as Outlook.

Provision is made for registering trademarks and most trademarks are now registered. In the UK this is done through the UKIPO. It maintains a database of registered trademarks and their owners that can be searched over the internet. Trademarks are associated with particular classes of products so that it is quite possible for the same trademark to belong to several different owners because each has registered it for a different class of product. There are comprehensive rules limiting what can be registered as a trademark. In particular, trade marks including place names or the names of people are subject to stringent conditions.

The 1994 Act makes it an offence to:

- apply an unauthorised registered trademark (i.e. a registered trademark that you do not own or do not have the owner's permission to use) to goods;

- sell or offer for sale (or hire) goods or packaging that bear an unauthorised trademark;

- import or export goods that bear an unauthorised trademark;

- have, in the course of business, goods for sale or hire goods (or packaging) that bear an unauthorised trademark.

In most circumstances, the offence will be criminal and punishable by a fine or up to two years' imprisonment. However, trademark owners can also bring civil proceedings to claim for the financial damage they may have suffered. The 1994 Act and subsequent detailed regulations referred to EU Council regulations. Following Brexit, new legislation was introduced to make essentially the same provisions but without reference to EU law. Those in the EU are able, if they choose, to register an EU-wide trademark – a European Trade Mark. However, this option is not available in the UK so a UK registration is needed separately there.

Under the General Agreement on Tariffs and Trade (GATT), to which most countries are signatories, countries that do not have suitable laws to protect trademarks (or intellectual property rights more generally) or where such laws are not effectively enforced will face trade sanctions. It was hoped that this would stamp out the flagrant piracy of trademarks but it has only had a limited effect.

Even where a trademark is not registered, action can be taken in the civil courts against products that imitate the appearance or 'get-up' of an existing product. This is known as the **tort of passing off**. It is, however, usually better to register the trademark than to rely on protection under civil law, because the legal action involved in defending it will be much more straightforward.

Trademarks are an effective way of protecting retail packaged software from piracy. Given that pirated software can be distributed over the internet with no physical packaging, it is desirable to display the trademark prominently when the software is loaded, as well as displaying it on the packaging.

11.7 DOMAIN NAMES

Internet domain names are ultimately managed by the Internet Corporation for Assigned Names and Numbers (ICANN). ICANN is an internationally organised, non-profit-making corporation. Its main responsibility is ensuring the **universal resolvability** of internet addresses – that is, ensuring that the same domain name will always lead to the same internet location wherever it is used from and whatever the circumstances. In practice, ICANN delegates the responsibility for assigning individual domain names to other bodies, subject to strict rules.

Domain names were originally meant to be used just as a means of simplifying the process of connecting one computer to another over the internet. However, because they are easy to remember, they have come to be used as a way of identifying businesses. Indeed, they are frequently used in advertising. Conversely, it is not surprising that companies should want to use their trademarks or their company names as their internet domain names.

The potential for conflict between trademarks and domain names is inherent in the two systems. Trademarks are registered with public authorities on a national or regional basis. The owner of the trademark acquires rights over the use of the trademark in a specific country or region. Identical trademarks may be owned by different persons in respect of different categories of product. Domain names are usually allocated by a non-governmental organisation and are globally unique; they are normally allocated on a first-come, first-served basis. This means that if different companies own identical trademarks for different categories of product or for different geographical areas, only one of them can have the trademark as a domain name, and that will be the first to apply.

The inconsistencies between the two systems of registration have made it possible for people to register, as their own domain names, trademarks belonging to other companies. This is sometimes known as **cyber-squatting**. Cyber-squatters then offer to sell these domain names to the owner of the trademark at an inflated price. It is usually cheaper and quicker for the trademark owner to pay up than to pursue legal remedies, even when these are available.

In 1999 the WIPO published a report entitled *The Management of Internet Names and Addresses: Intellectual Property Issues*. The report recommended that ICANN adopt a policy called the Uniform Domain-Name Dispute-Resolution Policy (UDRP), which includes specific provisions against cyber-squatting. This policy has proved reasonably effective. In the 20 years from 2000 to 2019 inclusive, over 50,000 complaints were dealt with by the WIPO Arbitration and Mediation Center. Users often find the system much easier to use than suing for breach of trademark as the UDRP procedure is entirely online with no need to attend court.

In 2001, WIPO published a second report, *The Recognition of Rights and the Use of Names in the Internet Domain System*. This addresses conflicts between domain names and identifiers other than trademarks. Examples of such conflicts are the use of personal names in domain names and the use of the names of particular peoples or geographical areas by organisations that have no connection with them. These conflicts are more difficult to deal with than conflicts between trademarks and domain names because the international framework that underlies trademarks is missing in these other cases.

FURTHER READING

The material in this chapter is covered in more detail in:
Holt, J. and Newton, J. (2020) *A Practical Guide to IT Law*. BCS, London.

Software patents and the patenting of business methods are highly controversial topics that generate a great deal of material on the web and elsewhere. In particular, much space was devoted to trying to prevent the EU from following in the steps of the USA and allowing a wide range of software and business methods to be patented. An excellent summary of the position on software patents in the USA can be found at:
'Software Patent' (n.d.) Bitlaw. https://www.bitlaw.com/software-patent/index.html.

The website of the WIPO can be found at:
https://www.wipo.int/portal/en/index.html

In 2015, the UK Department for Business, Energy and Industrial Strategy produced a document on whistleblowing:

> Department for Business, Energy and Industrial Strategy (2015) *Whistleblowing: Guidance and Code of Practice for Employers*. https://www.gov.uk/government/publications/whistleblowing-guidance-and-code-of-practice-for-employers.

The WIPO's reports on domain names are available at:

> World Intellectual Property Organization (1999) *The Management of Internet Names and Addresses: Intellectual Property Issues*. https://www.wipo.int/export/sites/www/amc/en/docs/report-final1.pdf.
>
> World Intellectual Property Organization (2001) *The Recognition of Rights and the Use of Names in the Internet Domain System*. https://www.wipo.int/export/sites/www/amc/en/docs/report-final2.pdf.

12 CONTRACTS AND LICENCES

After studying this chapter, you should:

- *understand what a contract is and how it comes into existence;*
- *be aware of the different types of contract appropriate to different situations in IT;*
- *understand the main issues that need to be addressed in the different types of IT contract;*
- *be aware of contractual issues regarding liability for defective software.*

12.1 WHAT IS A CONTRACT?

A contract is simply an agreement between two or more persons (the **parties** to the contract) that can be enforced in a court of law. The parties involved may be legal persons or natural persons. There is no specific form for a contract; in particular, in England, Wales and Northern Ireland, a contract need not be written down, although it usually is. What is essential is:

- all the parties must intend to make a contract, and there must be an offer and an acceptance of the offer;
- all the parties must be competent to make a contract – that is, they must be old enough and of sufficiently sound mind to understand what they are doing;
- there must be a **consideration** – that is, each party must be receiving something and providing something; *and*
- there must be the intention to create a legal relationship.

Contract law is largely based on common law. It has a long history and is immensely complicated. Contract law in Scotland is significantly different from that in the rest of the UK.

The existing contract law showed itself perfectly adequate to handle contracts for the supply of computers, software and associated services. However, the coming of the internet and e-commerce has created a need for new provisions to deal with such matters as electronic signatures and which country's laws should govern transactions made over the internet when the parties to the transaction are in different countries.

In this chapter we shall not be much concerned with the law relating to contracts. We shall be much more concerned with what should go into contracts for providing software and services in different circumstances and with issues of liability when software fails.

12.2 LICENCE AGREEMENTS

When customers buy software, they are buying a copy of the software together with the right to use it in certain ways. The agreement that covers such purchases is a type of contract known as a **licence agreement**. There are many different types of restriction that a licence agreement may place on the extent to which a customer can use the software. Here are some examples:

- A licence may allow the **licensees** (i.e. the people to whom the software is licensed) to use one copy of the software on their computer. This is the type of licence commonly granted when software such as a computer game is purchased from a retail outlet.

- A licence may allow licensees to run the software on a server on their local-area network and allow it to be used by any number of users simultaneously, up to some agreed maximum number. This type of licence is used, for example, for large multi-user database management systems and for applications such as accounting packages intended for the corporate market.

- A licence may allow licensees to run as many copies of the software as they wish on computers at specified premises. This is often known as a **site licence**.

There are several things that a software vendor may be concerned about when providing a customer with a licence to use one of its products:

- making sure that it is not giving away any of its own rights in the software;

- limiting the extent to which the customer can use the software, so that, if customers want to use it more extensively, they must pay an additional licence fee;

- ensuring a regular income from support activities, possibly an annual maintenance charge, possibly fees for consultancy services;

- ensuring that, as far as is possible, it will not be liable for any defects in the software.

It is very common for the owner of the copyright in a piece of software to license other people or organisations to carry out some of the activities that are otherwise the exclusive right of the copyright owner. The copyright remains the property of the owner but the licensees acquire certain rights. There are many different types of licence in use. We have already seen examples of licences for different types of usage but there are other types of licence – for example, the licensee may itself be a marketing company that is granted the right to license other people to use the software. Companies that produce software packages frequently do not have the expertise to market the software outside their own countries and they therefore license agents to sell it for them in other countries. Computer games are usually produced by fairly small companies that have no capacity to market their games. Instead, they license large international companies to market them.

Licences themselves may be granted **in perpetuity** (i.e. for ever) or for some **fixed period**. Licences for retail software are usually granted in perpetuity. Licences for corporate software, however, are typically granted on an annual basis; the initial fee may be larger than the fee for the annual renewal. Marketing licences are normally granted for a fixed period.

The owner of the copyright can transfer ownership to someone else. This is known as **assignment of the copyright** and must be done in writing. In this case, the new owner of the copyright has all the rights that the previous owner had.

12.3 OUTSOURCING

Outsourcing, sometimes known as facilities management, is the commercial arrangement under which a company or organisation (the customer) hands over the planning, management and operation of certain functions to another organisation (the supplier). This definition covers many common situations – most of us, for example, choose to give the responsibility for supplying our home with electricity to a company that specialises in this, rather than buying our own generator and doing it ourselves; in other words, we outsource the supply of electricity.

The past 40 years have seen a rapid increase in outsourcing in the UK. This was led by the civil service. Civil service salaries were low in comparison with salaries in the IT industry so the civil service had great difficulty in retaining competent IT staff. This difficulty was reflected in the poor quality of government information systems. Outsourcing IT provision to specialist companies provided a means of overcoming this problem while, at the same time, allowing the government to reduce the number of civil servants, a political objective to which it was committed.

The logic behind outsourcing is that a company that specialises in a particular area, be it IT or office cleaning, is likely to be able to make a better job of running services than an organisation whose main area of expertise is elsewhere. Forty years ago, companies would employ their own staff to develop software, run the staff canteen, clean the offices, carry out market research and so on. Nowadays, they are likely to outsource all these operations to specialist companies so that they can concentrate on their **core business** – that is, the business that is the main source of their revenue. Changes in the tax system from April 2021 have made it somewhat less attractive for IT professionals to set up their own companies (see Section 9.6). This has led to a small decline in outsourcing but it nevertheless continues to be practised widely.

IT outsourcing contracts are inherently complex and depend very much on individual circumstances. It is not appropriate to go into detail here about such contracts but the following is a list of just some of the points that need to be addressed:

- how performance is to be monitored and managed;
- what happens if performance is unsatisfactory;
- which assets are being transferred;
- staff transfers;

- audit rights;
- contingency planning and disaster recovery;
- intellectual property rights in software developed during the contract;
- duration of the agreement and termination provisions.

The first two items above are key elements in IT outsourcing and are often treated as a separate annex to an agreement known as a **service level annex**. The term **service level agreement** is often used but is misleading, since the annex is not a stand-alone agreement or contract.

12.4 FIXED PRICE CONTRACTS FOR BESPOKE SYSTEMS

The first type of contract we shall consider is the type that is used when an organisation is buying a system configured specifically to meet its needs. Such systems are known as **bespoke** or **tailor-made** systems. A bespoke system may consist of a single PC equipped with a word processor, a spreadsheet and a set of macros adapted to the customer's needs or it may consist of several thousand PCs spread across 50 offices in different parts of the world, connected by a wide-area network, with large database servers and a million lines of specially written software.

Typically, the contract for the supply of a bespoke system consists of three parts:

- A short **agreement**, which is signed by the parties to the contract. This states who the parties are and, very importantly, says that anything that may have been said or written before does not form part of the contract. The short agreement will usually reference:
  - the **standard terms and conditions**, which are normally those under which the supplier does business; *and*
  - a set of **schedules** or **annexes**, which specify the particular requirements of this contract, including what is to be supplied, when it is to be supplied, what payments are to be made and when, and so on.

This structure applies to fairly large contracts. Many small-scale development projects are carried out perfectly satisfactorily using much simpler contracts, often no more than an exchange of letters.

We shall look at the standard terms and conditions for the provision of large bespoke systems for a fixed price in some detail, not because such contracts occur very frequently but because they illustrate many of the issues that can arise in IT contracts.

12.4.1 What is to be produced

It is clearly necessary that the contract states what is to be produced. There are usually two levels of reference here: the standard terms and conditions refer to an annex and the annex then refers to a separate document that constitutes the requirements specification. It is important that the reference to the requirements specification identifies that document uniquely; normally this will mean quoting a date and issue number.

Information systems engineers will be familiar with the problems of producing requirements specifications. A specification sets out the detailed requirements of the client. Ideally, the specification should be complete, consistent and accurate and set out all that the client wants to be done in the performance of the contract. Unfortunately, we know that it is very difficult to achieve this ideal standard and, even if we succeed, the requirements of the client may evolve as the contract proceeds, and sometimes the changes may be substantial. How are these changes to be accommodated by a contract that, in a sense, freezes the requirements of the parties to those at one particular time by incorporating the original specification into the contract? The answer is that the contract should provide a procedure for making variations to the specification or job description, then follow this through by providing a method of calculating payment for work done to facilitate the changes, and also perhaps provide for a variation of the level of anticipated performance, and maybe also vary the method of acceptance testing. In other words, the contract should anticipate events and provide an agreed formula for modification.

12.4.2 What is to be delivered

Producing software for a client is not, usually, a matter of simply handing over the text of a program that does what is required. It is important, therefore, that the contract states (usually in an annex) what precisely is to be provided. The following is a non-exhaustive list of possibilities:

- source code;
- command files for building the executable code from the source and for installing it;
- documentation of the design and of the code;
- reference manuals, training manuals and operations manuals;
- software tools to help maintain the code;
- user training;
- training for the client's maintenance staff;
- test data and test results.

12.4.3 Ownership of rights

When an organisation commissions bespoke software from another company, it is important that both sides think carefully about the licensing and ownership of the copyright and other intellectual property rights in the software produced. Ownership in physical items such as books, documents or discs will usually pass from the software house to the client, but the intellectual property rights present more problems. As we described in Chapter 11, software is potentially protectable by a number of intellectual property rights, such as copyright, design rights and trademarks, and rights of confidentiality may also apply to it. There was a time when the customer would expect to take ownership of the copyright in all the software supplied. This is no longer realistic.

Parts of the software supplied are likely to be proprietary products that the supplier has developed to enable it to construct such systems quickly and efficiently; they are part of its fixed assets and it would be absurd to transfer ownership of them to a customer. Other parts of the software may be products acquired from other sources (possibly open-source software) and the supplier will not have the right to assign copyright in them. The customer's needs can almost certainly be satisfied by a suitable licence. However, customers must take into account the long-term need for maintenance and ensure that they have the right, for example, to give another contractor access to the source code and documentation for maintenance purposes.

As mentioned in Section 11.3.4, if the contract says nothing about ownership of intellectual property rights in bespoke software, then the default position under the Copyright, Designs and Patents Act 1988 is that the supplier/licensor retains all ownership of these rights and all the customer obtains is a licence to use the software, which the courts have held should be the most limited licence necessary to make the contract effective. It is preferable, however, to set out expressly the detailed terms of the licence or whether ownership of intellectual property rights in bespoke elements of the software will pass to the customer. Sometimes a contract will state that ownership will be transferred only after full payment has been made.

12.4.4 Confidentiality and data protection

It is almost inevitable that, when a major bespoke software system is being developed, the two parties will acquire confidential information about each other. The commissioning client may well have to pass confidential information about its business operations to the software house. On the other side of the coin, the software house may not want the client to divulge to others details of the programme content or other information gleaned about its operations by the client. It is usual in these circumstances for each party to promise to maintain the confidentiality of the other's secrets, and for express terms to that effect to be included in the contract. The law relating to confidential information was discussed in Section 11.5.

In some cases the system being provided will be processing large amounts of personal data. This is typically the case with human resources applications and customer relationship systems. In such cases detailed data protection clauses will be needed. These will usually be placed in a separate annex, as required by the UK General Data Protection Regulation (GDPR) (see Section 13.2.4) and the amended Data Protection Act 2018.

12.4.5 Payment terms

The standard terms and conditions will specify the payment conditions – that is, something along the lines that:

Payment shall become due within thirty days of the date of issue of an invoice. If payment is delayed by more than thirty days from the due date, the Company shall have the right, at its discretion, to terminate the contract, or to apply a surcharge at an interest rate of 2% above the bank base lending rate.

In practice, such clauses are only brought into effect in extreme cases, since using them is likely to destroy the goodwill between supplier and client on which the success of the project depends.

It would be unusual, in a project of any significant length, for all payment to be delayed until the work is complete and accepted. An annex will usually specify a pattern of payments like the following:

- an initial payment of, say, 15% of the contract value becomes due on signature of the contract;
- further stage payments become due at various points during the development, bringing the total up to, say, 65%;
- a further 25% becomes due on acceptance of the software;
- the final 10% becomes due at the end of the warranty period.

Such a pattern has advantages for the supplier in that it reduces the financial risk arising from possible insolvency of the client or from default for other reasons and it reduces possible cash flow difficulties. If the client is not prepared to accept a payment pattern of this type, the supplier is likely to demand a premium to cover the increased risk and the costs of financing the development. In negotiating the payment pattern, the supplier will usually seek to have the stage payments become due on fixed calendar dates while the client will try to have them tied to the achievement of specific project milestones (e.g. approval of the design specification).

12.4.6 Calculating payments for delays and changes

It happens not infrequently that progress on the development of a piece of software is delayed by the failure of the client to meet obligations on time. While the supplier will be expected to use its reasonable endeavours to rearrange activities so as to avoid wasting effort, this is not always possible. The contract should therefore make provision for payments to compensate for the wasted effort – incurred, for example, when the client fails to provide information on a due date or when changes are requested that result in extra work.

The contract must specify the process by which these extra payments are to be calculated. Typically, an annex will include daily charging rates for each grade of staff employed on the contract and the amount of extra effort to be paid for will be agreed at progress meetings.

Delay payments and payments for variations to the original requirements are, perhaps, the commonest cause of contractual disputes, not only in software engineering but also in most other contracting industries – the construction industry is a notorious example. One reason for this is that competitive bidding for fixed price contracts often means that the profit margin on the original contract is very low so that companies seek to make their profit on these additional payments.

12.4.7 Liquidated damages clauses

The previous subsection dealt with compensation for delays caused by the client; delays caused by the supplier are handled differently.

The normal mechanism used is to include a liquidated damages clause which provides that the sum payable to the supplier is reduced by a specified amount for each week that acceptance of the product is delayed, up to a certain maximum. Thus, on a contract of value £1 million, the amount might be specified as £5,000 per week up to a maximum of £100,000.

Following a judgement in the High Court in 2015, so-called **penalty clauses** – that is, clauses that levy an excessive monetary charge against a defaulting party that is unrelated to the actual harm suffered – are unenforceable in UK law and the term should be avoided. The liquidated damages should be a reasonable pre-estimate of the loss likely to be suffered through the delay. The contract should make clear whether the liquidated damages are the sole remedy for the delay or whether they are without prejudice to other rights, the latter meaning that the liquidated damages could be claimed and a claim for breach of contract could be brought.

Delays in delivering working software are notoriously common; it might therefore be expected that contracts for the supply of software would normally include such a liquidated damages clause. Paradoxically, such provision is comparatively rare. There are three reasons for this:

- Suppliers are very reluctant to accept such clauses and anything stronger than the example quoted above is likely to lead to reputable suppliers refusing to bid.
- If the contract is to include such clauses, the bid price is likely to be increased by at least half the maximum value of the liquidated damages amount.
- If the software is seriously late and the liquidated damages sums approach their maximum, there is little incentive for the supplier to complete the work since it will already have received in stage payments as much as it is going to get.

It should be realised that the cost of delays on fixed price contracts is very high, regardless of liquidated damages payments. Every delay eats into the supplier's profit margin. As a result, suppliers are strongly motivated to produce the software on time and delay is usually the result of genuine technical difficulties (or incompetence!) rather than lack of motivation.

12.4.8 Obligations of the client

In almost all cases where work is being carried out for a specific client, the client will have to fulfil certain obligations if the contract is to be completed successfully. The following is a (non-exhaustive) list of possibilities:

- provide documentation on aspects of the client's activities or the environment in which the system will run;
- provide access to appropriate members of staff;

- provide machine facilities for development and testing;
- provide office accommodation and secretarial facilities for the company's staff when they are working on the client's premises;
- provide data communications facilities to the site.

The general terms and conditions will normally state that a list of specific obligations and the dates at which they will be required is given in an annex. It will also state that failure to meet these obligations may render the client liable for delay payments.

12.4.9 Standards and methods of working

The supplier is likely to have company standards, methods of working, quality assurance procedures and so on, and will normally prefer to use these. More sophisticated clients will have their own procedures and may require that these be adhered to. In some cases, the supplier may be required to allow the client to apply quality control procedures to the project. The contract must specify which is to apply.

12.4.10 Progress meetings

Regular progress meetings are essential to the successful completion of a large fixed price contract and it is advisable that standard terms and conditions require them to be held. The minutes of progress meetings, duly approved and signed, should have contractual significance in that they constitute evidence that milestones have been reached (so that stage payments become due) and that delay payments have been agreed.

12.4.11 Project managers

Each party needs to know who, of the other party's staff, has day-to-day responsibility for the work and what the limits of that person's authority are. The standard terms and conditions should therefore require each party to nominate, in writing, a project manager. The project manager must have at least the authority necessary to fulfil the obligations that the contract places on them. It is particularly important that the limits of their financial authority (i.e. the extent to which they can authorise changes to the cost of the contract) are explicitly stated.

12.4.12 Acceptance procedure

Acceptance procedures are a critical part of any fixed price contract as they provide the criteria by which successful completion of the contract is judged. The essence of the acceptance procedure is that the client should provide a fixed set of acceptance tests and expected results and that successful performance of these tests will constitute acceptance of the system. The tests must be provided at or before the start of the acceptance procedure; within reason, there may be as many tests as the client wishes but extra tests cannot be added once the test set has been handed over. The purpose of this restriction is to ensure that the acceptance procedure can be completed in reasonable time.

Other points to be addressed under this heading include who shall be present when the tests are carried out and what happens if the tests are not completed successfully.

12.4.13 Warranty and maintenance

Once the product has been accepted, it is common practice to offer a warranty period of, typically, 90 days. Any errors found in the software and reported within this period will be corrected free of charge. This clause is, of course, subject to negotiation; reducing or eliminating the warranty period will reduce the overall cost of the contract and prolonging the period will increase it.

Once the warranty period is over, the supplier may offer, or the client demand, that maintenance will continue to be available on request. Since such maintenance is likely to involve enhancement of the software rather than simply correction of faults, the resources required are unpredictable – the client almost certainly does not know what enhancements will be required in two years' time. For this reason, a fixed price for the maintenance will not be appropriate. Maintenance will therefore usually be charged on a time and materials basis; the client may be required to commit to taking a fixed number of days of effort each year in order to compensate the supplier for the need to retain knowledge of the system.

12.4.14 Inflation

In lengthy projects or projects where there is a commitment to long-term maintenance, the supplier will wish to ensure protection against the effects of unpredictable inflation. To handle this problem, it is customary to include a clause that allows charges to be increased in accordance with the rise in costs.

The clause should state how often (e.g. once a year, twice a year) charges can be increased and how the effect on the overall price is to be calculated.

12.4.15 Indemnity and liability

It could happen that, as a result of the client's instructions, the supplier is led unwittingly to infringe the intellectual property rights of a third party or that, through carelessness or dishonesty, the supplier provides a system that infringes such rights – perhaps through using proprietary software as a component of the system delivered. For this reason, it is advisable to include a clause under which each party indemnifies the other (i.e. guarantees to cover any costs to which the other party becomes subject) for liability arising from its own faults in this respect. Usually the party indemnifying the other will want full control of any legal claims and actions and a clause in the contract stating that no settlement of any claim against the party being indemnified is made without the consent of the party having to pay (i.e. the one who gave the indemnity).

Most contracts will also limit the liability of the supplier to the price paid for the software/ services or to a fixed amount and, in addition, exclude liability for consequential and similar loss. However, they must not under UK law exclude liability for death and personal injury caused by negligence, nor for fraud, so these categories are usually omitted from the exclusion of liability clause. Nevertheless, liability under intellectual property confidentiality and data protection law losses caused by the other party is usually not so capped nor excluded on either side. As these clauses are surrounded by much law and regulation, it is best to take legal advice before changing them. For example, exclusions that are unreasonable or unfair may be void whereas accepting more liability albeit capped may put the supplier in a better, not a worse, position than an attempt to exclude all liability, which would inevitably be void. This is discussed further in Section 12.7.

12.4.16 Termination of the contract

There are many reasons why it may become necessary to terminate a contract before it has been completed. It is not uncommon, for example, for the client to be taken over by another company that already has a system of the type being developed, or for a change in policy on the part of the client to mean that the system is no longer relevant to its needs. It is essential, therefore, that the contract make provision for terminating the work in an amicable manner. This usually means that the supplier is to be paid for all the work carried out up to the point where the contract is terminated, together with some compensation for the time needed to redeploy staff on other revenue-earning work. The question of ownership of the work so far carried out must also be addressed.

12.4.17 Mediation, arbitration and court action

Litigation (court action) and formal arbitration are always expensive and risky. Contracts often therefore contain a clause saying that, in the event of a dispute that they cannot solve themselves, the parties agree to take the dispute first to mediation through a body such as the Centre for Effective Dispute Resolution. If that fails then the contract will specify whether disputes go to court or to arbitration. Arbitration can be more expensive than going to court because the parties have to pay the arbitrator and hire arbitration rooms, and will usually have to pay solicitors and barristers as for court action. This is to be contrasted with mediation, which can precede court action or formal arbitration, and is much cheaper but may not result in a settlement. Arbitration is confidential and court action is not, and each party needs to weigh up which it prefers. In the case of computer-related contracts, it is usually stated that the arbitrator is to be appointed either by the president of BCS or by the president of the Institution of Engineering and Technology. Both bodies maintain lists of qualified arbitrators who have the necessary technical understanding.

An arbitration clause will usually state that, if arbitration is required, it will take place in accordance with the Arbitration Act 1996. This Act of Parliament lays down a set of rules for arbitration that cover many eventualities, and reference to it avoids the need to spell these out in detail; most of the provisions of the Act are optional, in the sense that they come into effect only if the contract contains no alternative provision. If instead of arbitration the courts will have jurisdiction, then the contract should state which courts are intended – for example, the courts of England and Wales.

12.4.18 Applicable law

Where the supplier and the client have their registered offices in different legal jurisdictions or performance of the contract involves more than one jurisdiction, it is wise to state under which laws the contract is to be interpreted. Even then both parties may later dispute this unless they are in a jurisdiction with rules deciding the matter – for example, where both are in the European Union (EU).

12.5 CONSULTANCY AND CONTRACT HIRE

Contract hire is an arrangement in which the supplier agrees to supply the customer with the services of a certain number of staff at agreed daily or hourly charge rates. The customer takes responsibility for managing the staff concerned. Either party can terminate the arrangement at fairly short notice, typically one week, either in respect of a particular person or as a whole. The supplier's responsibility is limited to providing suitably competent people and replacing them if they become unavailable or are adjudged unsuitable by the client.

The contract for such an arrangement is usually fairly simple. Payment is on the basis of a fixed rate for each person day worked; the rate depends on the experience and qualifications of the staff.

Contract hire agreements are very much simpler than fixed price contracts because the supplier's involvement and responsibility are so much less. Issues such as delay payments, acceptance tests and many others simply do not arise; however, as mentioned in Section 12.4.3, ownership of intellectual property rights generated in the course of the work must be addressed otherwise the customer/buyer will not own such rights.

Contract hire is sometimes referred to disparagingly as 'body shopping'. Closely related are the freelance agreements under which individuals sell their own services, whether as a sole trader, as a partnership or through the individual's own personal service company, to clients on a basis similar to contract hire.

Consultancy is essentially an up-market version of contract hire. Consultants are experts who are called in by an organisation to assess some aspect of its operations or its strategy and to make proposals for improvements. This means that the end product of a consultancy project is usually a report or other document.

Consultancy projects are usually undertaken for a fixed price but the form of contract is very much simpler than the fixed price contracts so far described. There are two reasons for this. First, the sums of money are comparatively small and neither side stands to lose a great deal. Second, while it is possible to demonstrate beyond doubt that a piece of software does not work correctly and thus that the supplier has failed to fulfil the contract, it is not usually possible to demonstrate unequivocally that a report fails to fulfil a contract. The client has to rely on the desire of the supplier to maintain a professional reputation and in practice this usually proves sufficient to ensure that the work is of an acceptable standard.

There are four important aspects of a consultancy contract:

- **Confidentiality:** Consultants are often in a position to learn a lot about the companies for which they carry out assignments and may well be in a position to misuse this information for their own profit.

- **Terms of reference:** It is important that the contract refers explicitly to the terms of reference of the consultancy team and, in practice, these are perhaps the commonest source of disagreements in consultancy projects. As a result of their initial investigations, the consultants may discover that they need to consider matters that were outside their original terms of reference but the client may be unwilling to let this happen, for any one of a number of possible reasons.

- **Liability:** Most consultants will wish to limit their liability for any loss that the customer suffers as a result of following their advice. Customers may not be happy to accept this although they commonly do accept a limit of liability (e.g. to the price paid under the contract) and, in some cases, may insist on verifying that the consultant has adequate professional liability insurance.

- **Control:** This relates to who has control over the final version of the report. It is common practice for the contract to require that a draft version of the final report be presented to the client. The client is given a fixed period to review the report and, possibly, ask for changes. The revised version that is then submitted by the consultant should be the final version.

12.6 TIME AND MATERIALS

A time and materials contract (often referred to as a **cost plus contract**) is somewhere between a contract hire agreement and a fixed price contract. The supplier agrees to undertake the development of the software in much the same way as in a fixed price contract, but payment is made on the basis of the costs incurred, with labour charged in the same way as for contract hire. The supplier is not committed to completing the work for a fixed price, although a maximum payment may be fixed beyond which the project may be reviewed. Many of the complications of fixed price contracts still occur with time and materials contracts – ownership of rights, facilities to be provided by the client, progress monitoring arrangements, for instance – but others, such as delay payments and acceptance testing, do not. This is not to say that no acceptance testing is done, only that it has no contractual significance since nothing contractual depends on its outcome.

It may be wondered why any client should prefer a time and materials contract to a fixed price contract – surely it is better to have a contract that guarantees performance for a fixed price rather than one in which the price is indeterminate and there is no guarantee of completion? In the first place, it often happens that the work to be carried out is not sufficiently well specified for any supplier to be prepared to offer a fixed price; part of the supplier's task will be to discover what is required and to specify it in detail. Second, a supplier always loads a fixed price contract with a contingency allowance, to make provision for the risk that unexpected factors will cause the project to require more resources than originally estimated. If all goes well, the supplier makes an extra profit; this is the reward for risk taken. By accepting a time and materials contract, this risk and the possibility of extra profit (in the form of a lower cost) are effectively transferred to the client, who also avoids the dangers of having to pay excessive sums to have minor changes incorporated into the specification. All this having been said, it remains the case that there has been a strong movement away from time and materials towards fixed price, noticeably in the defence field.

12.7 LIABILITY FOR DEFECTIVE SOFTWARE

Suppliers of software and hardware are very reluctant to give a contractual commitment that it is fit for any purpose whatsoever. Standard terms and conditions will invariably contain a clause that tries to limit the supplier's liability if it turns out that the software or hardware is defective, as briefly mentioned in Section 12.4.15. The law, however, limits how far such clauses can be effective.

Most contracts will limit the extent of any liability either to the purchase price of the product or to some fixed maximum figure. This means that, if the product completely fails to work, the supplier agrees to refund the purchase price or possibly a bit more if some other maximum is specified.

The Unfair Contract Terms Act 1977 restricts the extent to which clauses in standard terms and conditions limiting liability can be effective. In particular, it is not possible to limit the damages payable if a defect in the product causes death or personal injury. This applies as much to software as it does to motor vehicles, say. Thus, if a company supplies software to control a light railway link and a defect in the software leads to an accident in which people are killed or injured, then any clause in the contract for the supply of that software that claims to restrict liability will not be enforceable in respect of the claims for damages for the deaths and injuries.

This restriction is an important one for software companies that produce critical systems (see Section 2.9). However, although this is very relevant when buying, say, a car, it is not very relevant to most individuals or companies when dealing with software, because the software that they use or develop is very unlikely to cause death or personal injury. They are much more likely to be concerned about software that doesn't do what it was claimed to do or that has too many bugs to be usable. However, if the exclusion from the limitation of liability clause for death and personal injury claims is not made in the contract, then the entire clause excluding liability is void and there is no limit on the supplier's liability for any kind of loss. Changes to clauses limiting or excluding liability should therefore be made very carefully indeed, otherwise what may look like a better clause could in law be worse for the buyer or supplier.

At this point we need to distinguish between consumer sales and non-consumer sales. For a sale to be treated as a consumer sale, the buyer must be a private person, the buyer must buy from a seller who is acting in the course of a business, and the goods must be of a type ordinarily supplied for private use or consumption. In a consumer sale, the requirements of the Consumer Rights Act 2015 (which has specific rules relating to digital downloads sold to consumers and now contains the law on exclusion of liability in consumer contracts), the Sale of Goods Act 1979 and the Supply of Goods and Services Act 1982 cannot be excluded. The most important requirement of the Consumer Rights Act and the Sale of Goods Act in the context of software is that goods sold must be as described and fit for the purpose for which such goods are commonly supplied. This means, for example, that if you buy a printer for use with your computer at home, it must be capable of printing reliably and clearly, at a usable speed.

There is, unfortunately, a problem about software. Because software is intangible, it has never been satisfactorily decided whether or not it comes under the definition of 'goods' and hence it is not clear whether the Sale of Goods Act applies to the sale of software. This is why the Consumer Rights Act's provisions about 'digital downloads' was brought in for consumer contracts only. For business-to-business sales of software, it is generally thought the Sale of Goods Act does apply to the sale of retail software or software sold as a package but that it would not apply to bespoke software, which would therefore come under the Supply of Goods and Services Act. This only requires that 'reasonable skill and care' are used. This is a very difficult test to apply and, in practice, would provide little protection.

The Unfair Contract Terms Act again comes to the rescue and for consumer sales so too does the Consumer Rights Act. They allow liability to be limited or excluded only to the extent that it is reasonable to do so.

The view that a court will take depends very much on the circumstances of a particular case but a particularly illuminating example is the 1996 case of *St Albans City and District Council v International Computers Limited.*[1] The facts were that the council had ordered a computer system from ICL to enable it to compute the Community Charge (a system of local taxation that is no longer in use) for the forthcoming year. ICL insisted on using its standard terms and conditions, which stated that its liability 'will not exceed the price or charge payable for the item of Equipment, Program or Service in respect of which liability arises or £100,000 (whichever is the lesser)'. Errors in the software and incorrect advice from ICL's project manager meant that the population of the area was overestimated, so the residents were undercharged and the council lost £1.3 million.

The judge at the initial hearing found that the software was not fit for the purpose for which it had been provided and that ICL's project manager had been negligent. ICL was therefore in breach of contract. The clause limiting liability had to be measured against the requirement of reasonableness. The judge noted that ICL was a substantial organisation with worldwide product liability insurance of £50 million; that all potential suppliers of the system dealt on similar standard terms; that the council was under pressure to install the system before the Community Charge was introduced; and that although the council was a business and not a consumer, it did not usually operate in the same commercial field as a normal business and it would be impractical for it to insure against commercial risks. On balance, the judge found that the clause limiting liability to £100,000 was not reasonable and was therefore ineffective. ICL appealed, but the Court of Appeal confirmed the judgement. However, the value of this case as a precedent will be limited, for each case turns on its facts.

1 *St Albans City and District Council v International Computers Limited* [1996] EWCA Civ 1296, BAILII, http://www.bailii.org/ew/cases/EWCA/Civ/1996/1296.html.

FURTHER READING

The following book from 2020 covers the material in this chapter in more detail, as well as other relevant topics:

Holt, J. and Newton, J. (ed.) (2020) *A Practical Guide to IT Law* (3rd edition). BCS, Swindon.

Although now rather dated, the following book covers IT outsourcing in depth and is written specifically for information systems professionals. It contains one chapter dedicated to contractual matters:

Sparrow, E. (2012) *Successful IT Outsourcing*. Springer, London.

13 DATA PROTECTION, PRIVACY AND FREEDOM OF INFORMATION

After studying this chapter, you should:

- *be able to identify situations in which legislation relating to data protection, privacy and freedom of information is likely to impose obligations on you;*
- *understand, in straightforward cases, what your obligations are, in respect of data protection, privacy and freedom of information;*
- *be able to recognise more complicated situations in which you need to ask for expert advice.*

13.1 INTRODUCTION

On 25 May 2018, the General Data Protection Regulation (GDPR) became law across all member countries of the European Union (EU). From one perspective, the GDPR is an evolution of data protection laws that have been developed in Europe since the 1970s. The GDPR updates these laws to reflect modern concerns about how organisations collect, track and use data about citizens and residents in the EU. From another perspective, the new potential for financial penalties means that senior executives are taking action to improve data protection within their organisations; their aim is to limit the risk of being fined. This is a law made in the EU, but it has implications for companies worldwide that have some role in processing data about EU citizens and residents. Since the UK has left the EU, the former has adopted similar laws, known as the UK GDPR, which are part of the Data Protection Act (DPA) 2018.

A related but more general concern is that of individual privacy. Most people feel that they are entitled to keep personal information, such as their bank balance, their medical history or how they vote in elections, private. This extends to other things that do not obviously fall under the heading of information – personal correspondence, phone calls or photographs taken on private occasions, for example. In UK law, the Human Rights Act 1998 expressly includes a right of privacy from the European Convention on Human Rights. The convention states, in section 8(1), 'Everyone has the right to respect for his private and family life, his home and his correspondence.' Concern over telephone tapping and email monitoring, by employers as much as by the security services, led to the Regulation of Investigatory Powers Act 2000, and later to amendments contained in the Investigatory Powers Act 2016.

Although most people will accept that individuals have a right to privacy, they do not feel that this should extend to governments. Governments are traditionally reluctant to release information to their citizens, even when no question of security arises. There have been many cases where governments have appeared to have kept information secret to avoid acknowledging their responsibilities or compensating individuals for government mistakes or to protect the state. As a result, there has been pressure for more open government and for legislation that will guarantee freedom of information. Australia, Canada, the USA and a few other countries enacted such legislation in the 1970s and 1980s. In the UK it had to wait for the passing of the Freedom of Information Act 2000, although the UK has had for decades a process for release of state papers after the expiry of specific periods. Many countries still have no legislation in this area.

13.2 DATA PROTECTION

Data protection laws have evolved to meet the challenges of their time. In the 1970s, there was growing concern about the way that data about individuals was being used. In particular:

- Large amounts of data about individuals were being collected and stored in computers.

- Some of the data was being used for purposes different from those intended when the data was collected.

- Unauthorised people could gain access to the data.

- The data might be out of date, incomplete or incorrect.

This led to the Council of Europe Convention for the Protection of Individuals with regard to Automatic Processing of Personal Data (Convention 108). The first UK legislation in this area – the DPA 1984 – was designed to implement the provisions of the convention. The Act provided various protections for individuals, but technology moved on and raised new concerns.

By the mid-1990s, more individuals and businesses were starting to regularly use the internet. There were new ways for organisations to gather and process data, with the potential for more sinister uses of this data by some organisations. These concerns led to the European Data Protection Directive in 1995. The UK's implementation of the directive was by the DPA 1998.

By the mid-2010s, internet technology had become ubiquitous, and it connected people in new ways. Individuals started sharing data about themselves on an unprecedented scale through social media. A person's browsing history could be tracked by companies and linked to their activity on social media sites. Linking these items of data together, companies can build profiles about individuals. These profiles can be used to target marketing campaigns to help show relevant adverts to people. There is also the potential to use these profiles to target other messages, such as political messages, to influence people.

As mentioned, in 2016 the EU introduced the GDPR, and in 2018 it became law throughout all EU member states, including the UK. Unlike EU directives (including the

1995 directive), an EU regulation becomes law without any further action by a member state. The GDPR updated the protections for all EU citizens.

In 2021, the UK completed its formal exit from the EU. Although the UK is not covered by the GDPR now that it is outside the EU, the UK made a tailored version of the GDPR as part of the DPA 2018; this tailored version is known as the UK GDPR and it came into force from 1 January 2021. Data protection law in the UK is contained in the DPA 2018 and the UK GDPR. The UK legislation is substantially based on the EU's GDPR, so what is written about UK GDPR in this chapter is similar to or the same as the EU GDPR; the UK and EU legislation may diverge in future. There are also related regulations about spam and electronic marketing, which are discussed in Chapter 14.

This chapter focuses on the UK GDPR. Details about the UK GDPR are found in the DPA 2018 and the UK GDPR legislation, so reference to both is needed in practice. When the EU's legislation is referred to in this chapter, the term 'EU GDPR' is used.

13.2.1 Protected data

The DPA 2018 covers **personal data** about 'identified or identifiable living natural persons'. Examples of data can include, but are not limited to, names, addresses, email addresses, social media accounts, ethnicity, images on CCTV recordings, web browser cookies, computer IP addresses, religious beliefs and political opinions.

Data is a set of facts, and information is the result of processing the data and interpreting it. For example, a set of data could be GPS readings from a person's smart watch. Information could be gained by processing that data, where we learn typical routes a person takes and on which days and times they take those routes. Although data and information are different concepts, the legislation makes no distinction and the terms are used interchangeably.

The DPA 2018 does not cover data that is truly **anonymous**. Data that is **pseudonymous** would be covered by the DPA 2018 where it is possible to re-establish the link to an individual. It is important to consider whether data could be truly anonymous. There are situations where enough items of data could be combined to make it possible to identify an individual.

There are some classes of data that are not covered by the UK GDPR. The first class is data used for domestic or household purposes (including recreation). The other two classes concern law enforcement and intelligence services; however, the DPA 2018 does have provisions regarding these two classes. In addition, there is the so-called **special purposes exemption**, which protects processing for the purposes of journalism, art and literature, and academic work in appropriate circumstances.

13.2.2 Terminology

Several terms are defined in the DPA 2018 and UK GDPR, in addition to personal data:

- **Data controller** means a person who determines why and how personal data is processed.

- **Data processor** means a person who processes personal data on behalf of the data controller and who is not an employee of the data controller. An example is an application service provider, such as a company that provides online hotel booking services.

- **Data subject** means a natural person who is the subject of the personal data.

- **Processing** means any action that is performed on the data, which the DPA 2018 states as encompassing 'obtaining, recording, holding, using, disclosing and erasing data'.

- **Special categories of personal data** is defined in the DPA 2018 as personal data 'revealing racial or ethnic origin, political opinions, religious or philosophical beliefs, or trade union membership, and the processing of genetic data, biometric data for the purpose of uniquely identifying a natural person, data concerning health or data concerning a natural person's sex life or sexual orientation'. Processing of this data is prohibited by default. There are exemptions that allow the data to be processed in certain situations (e.g. employment or health and social care). The DPA 1998 referred to this as 'sensitive personal data'.

For the data controller and the data processor, the UK GDPR states that the person may be a legal person, natural person, public entity, agency or other body.

13.2.3 Principles

UK GDPR has seven principles, contained in Article 5. Those in Article 5(1) correspond to six of the eight principles in the DPA 1998. The principles of Access and Overseas Transfer from the DPA 1998 are not listed as principles in the UK GDPR, but the issues are covered in its other articles. Article 5(2) also includes the principle of Accountability, which was not present in the DPA 1998. This section discusses the principles.

Lawfulness

Personal data shall be processed lawfully, fairly and in a transparent manner in relation to the data subject.[1]

The GDPR introduced six lawful bases for an organisation being able to process personal data and they are discussed in Section 13.2.4. The ideas of fairness and transparency are key ambitions of the data protection legislation. The aim is to have a framework for data processing that enables people to trust the way that organisations process their data.

Purpose

Personal data shall be collected for specified, explicit and legitimate purposes and not further processed in a manner that is incompatible with those purposes.[2]

---

1   UK GDPR, Article 5(1)(a).

2   UK GDPR, Article 5(1)(b).

Data controllers must carefully consider and document the intended purpose or purposes for processing a set of data. Linking to the first principle and the idea of transparency, these purposes must be made known to individuals through a privacy statement or similar method.

There may be times when an organisation processes a set of data that could help it to do something different. For example, an e-commerce organisation will typically have address data about its customers so that it can send them their orders. The intended purpose could also include sharing the address data with delivery companies (a data processor, in this example) that deliver on behalf of the e-commerce company. The e-commerce company then wants to use those addresses to send marketing information to its customers by post. The e-commerce company would need to check whether its documented purposes allow it to do this. For this example, it is a new purpose that is not covered by the original purpose of fulfilling an order. If the e-commerce organisation wanted to start sending its marketing information, it would need to seek consent from its customers in most cases. For some marketing activities, the 'soft opt-in' part of the Privacy and Electronic Communications (EC Directive) Regulations 2003 (PECR) may apply. See Section 14.7.1 for further discussion of PECR and the soft opt-in.

Data minimisation

> Personal data shall be adequate, relevant and limited to what is necessary in relation to the purposes for which they are processed.[3]

Many violations of this principle are due to ignorance rather than an intent to behave in a way contrary to the DPA 2018. Local government has a bad record of compliance with this principle, for example requiring people wanting to join a public library to state their marital status. Shops that demand to know customers' addresses when goods are not being delivered are also likely to be in breach of this principle.

Data controllers need procedures to assess planned data collection, checking what is requested and whether there is an adequate justification for each item of data.

Accuracy

> Personal data shall be accurate and, where necessary, kept up to date; every reasonable step must be taken to ensure that personal data that are inaccurate, having regard to the purposes for which they are processed, are erased or rectified without delay.[4]

Data controllers must work to comply with this principle, but it can be difficult to comply in all situations. In the UK, doctors have great difficulty in maintaining up-to-date data about their patients' addresses, particularly patients who are students, because students change their addresses frequently and rarely remember to tell their doctor. Universities have similar difficulties.

---

3   UK GDPR, Article 5(1)(c).

4   UK GDPR, Article 5(1)(d).

Storage

Personal data shall be kept in a form which permits identification of data subjects for no longer than is necessary for the purposes for which the personal data are processed; personal data may be stored for longer periods insofar as the personal data will be processed solely for archiving purposes in the public interest, scientific or historical research purposes or statistical purposes.[5]

This principle raises more difficulties than might be expected.

First, it is necessary to establish how long each item of personal data needs to be kept. Auditors will require that financial data is kept for at least seven years and sometimes longer. Tax investigations can be initiated in relation to periods up to 20 years in the past in the UK where the taxpayer has committed fraud. The limitation periods for civil law can vary depending on the type of action. For example, there is a limitation of six years in actions for breach of contract and twelve years in actions for deeds. So, it may be prudent to hold some data for lengthy periods of time. It is appropriate to keep some personal data indefinitely (e.g. university records of graduating students). In all cases, the purpose for which the data is kept must be included in the stated purposes for which it was collected.

Second, procedures are needed to ensure that all data is erased at the appropriate time. This must include erasure from back-up copies.

Security

Personal data shall be processed in a manner that ensures appropriate security of the personal data, including protection against unauthorised or unlawful processing and against accidental loss, destruction or damage, using appropriate technical or organisational measures.[6]

Data controllers and data processors must take steps to assess and apply appropriate security measures that take account of appropriate state-of-the-art techniques and issues such as the risk to a data subject if data is mishandled or lost. This is not a new idea for data protection, but it is now a legal requirement.

The principle highlights **technical measures**, which could include user accounts with passwords, two-factor authentication, encryption and management of who is authorised to access the different systems that hold the data. There are also **organisational measures**, such as training staff in data and information security and processes for staff to apply for permission to access some systems.

It is important to review these measures regularly and update them to improve security.

---

5   UK GDPR, Article 5(1)(e).

6   UK GDPR, Article 5(1)(f).

Access

The DPA 1998 contained the wording 'personal data shall be processed in accordance with the rights of data subjects'. Although the UK GDPR does not include this as a principle, it does specify the rights of data subjects in more detail. These rights are discussed in Section 13.2.5. Both the DPA 1998 and the current law give individuals a right of access to personal data held by an organisation about them in most cases, which is known as a **subject access right** (the individuals being known as **data subjects**).

Overseas transfer

There are restrictions on transferring data from the UK to other countries. This is to limit the transfer to other countries or international organisations unless there is a guarantee of adequate levels of data protection. Such protection may be at the country level (if the country's laws offer adequate protection) or at the level of the individual organisation (if a multinational organisation has its own adequate internal controls on personal data). In 2021 the EU approved the UK GDPR as providing adequate protection, which therefore permits exports of data from the EU or European Economic Area (EEA) to the UK.

The USA does not have data protection laws that currently satisfy the UK and EU requirements for international transfer. Over the years, there have been attempts to put in place framework agreements to facilitate transfer of data to the USA. There was the Safe Harbour arrangement, which was replaced by the EU–US Privacy Shield. In 2020, the Court of Justice of the EU gave a judgement in the Schrems II case that the EU–US Privacy Shield no longer provided adequate safeguards. In the absence of a general framework for transfer to the USA, the responsibility passes to the individual data controllers to assess whether transfers to US companies will guarantee adequate protection for the data.

The US issue is an example of **restricted transfers**. There are several ways that companies can make restricted transfers to countries that do not provide adequate protection; these are known as **safeguards** and **exceptions**. Safeguards involve some form of approved agreement; examples include **standard contractual clauses** and approved **binding corporate rules**. If a safeguard is not possible, there are a small set of restrictions that might enable the data transfer to take place. An example exception is explicit consent from an individual for the restricted transfer. The Information Commissioner's Office (ICO) provides guidance on these and other safeguards and exceptions.

It is important to realise that this principle means that if the personal data is being processed using the cloud, all the computers processing the data must be in countries that meet the data protection requirements. Cloud providers understand this issue and for some services they will be able to offer data controllers a choice of which geographical regions will store and process the data. It is the data controller's responsibility to ensure that it has made the relevant choices for the data that it manages in the cloud.

This principle can be viewed in two ways. It can be seen as protecting data subjects from having their personal data transferred to countries where there are no limitations on how it might be used. It can also be seen as specifically allowing businesses to transmit personal data across national borders provided there is adequate legislation in the destination country. In practice, of course, if a website is physically located in a country that does not have adequate data protection legislation, a visitor to that website from a country that does have such legislation has no protection.

The UK's restrictions on international transfer are currently aligned with the EU GDPR. The UK has the option to diverge in the future as it is no longer a member of the EU. In 2021, the EU issued new versions of standard contractual clauses. In 2022, the UK government introduced an **international data transfer agreement**. For organisations that might want to transfer data internationally, it is important to seek expert advice to assess whether this is possible and how it can be done in such a way as to meet UK GDPR requirements.

Accountability

The controller shall be responsible for, and be able to demonstrate, compliance with the principles.[7]

There was no corresponding principle in versions of the DPA before 2018. However, it has always been the case that the data controller is responsible for ensuring compliance with these principles in respect of all the personal data for which they are responsible.

It is important for data controllers to be able to demonstrate how they are compliant. Examples of ways this can be achieved include:

- being able to show that staff have been trained in data protection and information security;
- having records to show what data is gathered, how it is processed and who is responsible for that data.

Training staff before any data is collected will help data controllers to minimise the risks of not meeting their legal requirements.

13.2.4 Lawful basis

Data controllers must identify a valid lawful basis for processing personal data. The UK GDPR specifies six lawful bases.

- **Consent:** A data subject has given clear and deliberate consent for a data controller to process their personal data for a specified purpose. If consent is used as a lawful basis, it must be considered for the different items of data. For example, if a data controller wants to ask for consent to contact a person by email, phone and text message, then there should be individual consents for each item. A request that asks for consent to contact a person, but does not specify which form of communication, is not enough.

- **Contract:** A data controller needs to process personal data to fulfil a contract. For example, an e-commerce company processes name, address and payment details as part of fulfilling a customer's order. This basis may also be used for activities that require a data controller to process data before starting a contract. For example, a company may process data so that it can provide a quote.

---

7   UK GDPR, Article 5(2).

- **Legal obligation:** A data controller has a legal obligation to process specified personal data. For example, an organisation is legally required to report to Her Majesty's Revenue and Customs (HMRC) when an employee starts working for the organisation and when payments are made to the employee.

- **Legitimate interests:** A data controller has legitimate interests in processing the data as part of its regular activities. For example, a university processes marks for student assessments when running its courses. This is a legitimate part of the university's process, and it is also processing that students would expect to happen. Although this can seem to be a very useful basis, there are checks to prevent it from being used inappropriately. One check considers whether the data subject would reasonably expect the processing to happen or whether the processing would cause harm to the data subject. For example, it would not be reasonable for a university to use legitimate interests as the basis to publish information on its website showing the degree results for all students in a particular year. The students' right to privacy is likely to override any legitimate interests in this situation.

- **Public task:** A data controller needs to process personal data to perform a task in the public interest; that task requires a clear basis in law. For example, UK councils can process data to create the electoral register, which specifies who is registered to vote.

- **Vital interests:** A data controller can process data about a data subject if it is vital to protect someone's life. For example, a medical professional may need to process data about a person's health conditions if they are treating them for life-threatening injuries at the scene of an accident. This is a very limited lawful basis. It is not likely to be relevant for other situations where another lawful basis would be more appropriate. For example, this would not be relevant for processing data about a patient with a long-term illness who is receiving ongoing treatment from health professionals.

Except for consent, a key test for each lawful basis is whether it is necessary to process the data. If it is not necessary, the lawful basis cannot be used to support the processing.

Each situation needs to be considered carefully and the data controller needs to select the most appropriate lawful basis. It is important for the data controller to document what decisions it has taken about the basis and the justification for that basis.

For **special categories of personal data**, an organisation must have a valid lawful basis to process the data (UK GDPR Article 6) and a valid condition for processing this data (UK GDPR Article 9).

There are times when different parts of data processing will require different lawful bases. For example, when customers complete the checkout process for an e-commerce site, they will typically be asked for their name, delivery address, billing address and other details. This information could be covered by the contract lawful basis as it is necessary to sell the goods or services. The form may also ask if the e-commerce company can contact the customers in the future by email about product details and promotions. This is not necessary processing under the contract basis, so a different basis must be considered for that specific part of the form; the regulations known as

PECR must also be considered (see Section 14.7.1). For information used for marketing, the consent basis is the most appropriate.

Consent can appear to be a useful basis for data processing. In some situations, it is the most appropriate or the only option. If consent is used, then there must be a real choice for the data subject and they have the right to change that choice and withdraw their consent in the future. For this reason, it is not the preferred basis for employees' data as it is hard to prove they genuinely consented given the imbalance of power between employer and employee. More is said about consent in Chapter 14 regarding laws about web browser cookies and marketing information.

13.2.5 Rights of data subjects

The UK GDPR provides living individuals with the following rights:

- right to be informed;
- right of access;
- right to rectification;
- right to erasure, also known as the right to be forgotten;
- right to restrict processing;
- right to data portability;
- right to object;
- right regarding automated decision making and profiling.

These rights reflect the aims to have fair and transparent data processing that protects individuals. The rights to be informed, to have access to data and to correct mistakes seek to build trust in the way that data is handled.

There are conditions about when some of these rights apply. For example, the right to data portability only applies when the lawful basis for processing was consent or the performance of a contract, and the processing was performed automatically.

With more automated decision making taking place in society, the final right is interesting. If the data is processed automatically and is likely to be used as the sole basis for making a decision relating to data subjects – for example, deciding whether to grant them a loan – they have the right to be informed by the data controller of the logic involved in making that decision. They can also demand that a decision relating to them that has been made on a purely automatic basis be reviewed.

Data controllers need to have procedures in place so that they recognise when these rights apply and they can handle the requests within a month. The ICO provides guidance about when that starts and what to do about things like requests made on weekends or on public holidays or if a person needs to provide a form of ID before the request can proceed (see the Further Reading section).

13.2.6 Personal data breaches

A personal data breach occurs when there has been a breach of the security of personal data. This could refer to several issues regarding personal data, including unauthorised access or disclosure; accidental loss, destruction or modification; unauthorised or unlawful processing; or a negative impact on individuals caused by making the data available or unavailable.

The UK GDPR places a duty on organisations in a limited number of cases to report personal data breaches. This is where the breach could lead to a risk to people's rights and freedoms. This breach may be deliberate or accidental. Notifiable breaches must be reported to the relevant supervisory authority within 72 hours of discovering the breach. There is also a duty to notify individuals of data breaches but only where there is a high risk to their rights and freedoms.

That may mean an employee reporting a breach to the data protection officer in their organisation. Depending on the type of breach, it may need to be reported to the ICO and the affected individuals.

As a result of this duty, organisations need to design procedures so that they can detect when there is a personal data breach. There also need to be procedures on how to report breaches, who is responsible for handling those reports, how to decide whether a breach is notifiable to the ICO or not, and when it must be notified to the individuals concerned. As with most aspects of the current data protection legislation, organisations are expected to plan rather than wait until issues occur.

13.2.7 Operation of the UK GDPR

The ICO can impose monetary penalties when an organisation fails to comply with the data protection laws. The fines are designed to be proportionate to the infringement and they should discourage the issue being repeated.

There is a maximum monetary fine of £17.5 million or 4% of the annual worldwide turnover of the organisation, whichever is higher; this is the 'higher maximum'. For some categories of infringement, there is a lower 'standard maximum' of £8.7 million or 2% of the annual worldwide turnover, whichever is higher.[8] Many fines will be lower than these amounts. The maximums are designed so that senior executives take steps in their organisations to comply with the law to reduce the risk of incurring a fine.

The ICO's website lists enforcement actions that it has taken. Some of these actions have included monetary fines and other actions instruct organisations to correct problems to avoid fines in the future.

The following examples are based on reports from the ICO (see the Further Reading section):

- In 2020, the ICO fined Cathay Pacific Airways Ltd for failing to have adequate security to protect personal data from its loyalty scheme. This related to an

---

8   DPA 2018, Section 157.

issue between 2014 and 2018. The investigation found failings in the company's procedures and technical measures that had enabled a data breach to occur. The company was fined £500,000 under the older powers of the DPA 1998.

- In November 2020, the ICO fined Ticketmaster UK Ltd for failing to protect the payment details of several million data subjects in the UK and the EEA. The investigation identified that bank card details had been compromised for several thousand of these data subjects. The ICO issued a fine of £1.25 million.

- In January 2022, the ICO served an enforcement notice on the Ministry of Justice, which is part of the UK government. The ICO had determined that the ministry had failed to meet its legal obligations to provide data subjects with copies of their data. The enforcement notice instructed the ministry to take action to comply with its legal duties. The ICO has the right to impose a fine if it judges that the ministry has not adequately responded to the enforcement notice.

- In 2022, the ICO fined Clearview AI Inc more than £7.5 million. The company was found to be using images of people in the UK that it had obtained from public online sources. The data was collected without people's knowledge. The company used those images, together with images of people from outside the UK, to create a global database that can be used for facial recognition. The ICO also issued an enforcement notice that instructed the company to remove the images of people in the UK from its database and to cease collection of such data that is publicly available on the internet.

The DPA 2018, the UK GDPR and the EU GDPR are all published with guidance notes to help explain the context and implications of the laws. It will take time for organisations to understand the full implications, although that is not a defence if an organisation does not comply with the law. The ICO provides an excellent set of guidance on data protection (including examples of issues) to help organisations interpret the obligations. Even with this guidance, expert opinions will be needed for some situations.

The data protection laws are not there to prevent organisations from lawfully processing data. The laws are written so that organisations understand what is lawful and how to handle data safely. The law also helps data subjects to understand their rights and how to challenge organisations that fail in their legal obligations.

Nearly everyone in an organisation will be involved in some form of processing of personal data. It is everyone's responsibility to be aware of the general issues. Further, organisations must make sure that staff are trained in the issues that affect their roles.

Some organisations are required by law to have a data protection officer. These include public authorities and public bodies, organisations that undertake regular monitoring of individuals on a large scale, and organisations with core activities around processing special categories of personal data or criminal or offences data. Other organisations choose to have one, even though it is voluntary. The ICO recommends that organisations document any decisions about whether to have a data protection officer as part of the principle of accountability.

13.3 PRIVACY

The general issue of privacy and the law is far too large and complex to be considered here. We shall therefore consider only those specific issues that relate to the use of information systems and the internet. The starting point is the Investigatory Powers Act 2016, which replaced a number of areas of a similar Act of 2000, known as the Regulation of Investigatory Powers Act 2000 (RIPA). RIPA still applies in some situations, but it is mostly the 2016 Act that is discussed in this section.

The 2016 Act provides a framework for controlling the lawful interception of computer, telephone and postal communications. There are related regulations called the Investigatory Powers (Interception by Businesses etc. for Monitoring and Record-Keeping Purposes) Regulations 2018. The 2016 Act allows government security services, law enforcement authorities and some other public bodies to intercept, monitor and investigate electronic data only in certain specified situations, such as when preventing and detecting crime. Powers include being able to demand the disclosure of data encryption keys.

Under the 2016 Act and the 2018 regulations, organisations that provide computer and telephone services can monitor and, where appropriate, record communications without the consent of the users of the service, provided this is done for one of the following purposes:

- to establish facts – for example, on what date a specific order was placed;
- to ensure that the organisation's regulations and procedures are being complied with;
- to ascertain or demonstrate standards that are or ought to be achieved;
- to prevent or detect crime (whether computer related or not);
- to investigate or detect unauthorised use of telecommunications systems;
- to ensure the effective operation of the system – for example, by detecting viruses or denial-of-service attacks (see Sections 15.1 and 15.3 for details about the latter);
- to find out whether a communication is a business communication or a private one – for example, monitoring the emails of employees who are on holiday in order to deal with any that relate to the business;
- to monitor communications to confidential counselling services that are run free of charge, though users must be able to choose to remain anonymous.

The monitoring rules apply not only to telecommunications service providers but also to businesses. For the monitoring to be lawful, the telecommunications system must be provided by the controller of the system (e.g. a business) to enable people to undertake relevant business activities. Organisations intercepting communications in this way are under an obligation to make all reasonable efforts to inform users that such interception may take place.

The 2018 regulation includes the qualification of 'where appropriate' when mentioning the possibility of recording a communication. The regulation states that such monitoring and recording need to be relevant to the activities of the system controller (the business). However, it does not provide details about what would constitute an appropriate situation to enable a business to record information. Discussions of the regulation suggest that an appropriate recording might be made of phone conversations for training purposes, such as may happen at call centres.

The 2016 Act itself grants certain government agencies, including police and intelligence services and HMRC, the right to ask for interception warrants to allow them to monitor communications traffic to or from specific persons or organisations. Interception is the most intrusive activity, so it is restricted to a small set of organisations. Other parts of the Act apply to a wider set of organisations.

RIPA, the 2016 Act and its associated regulations were subject to criticism about issues such as the range of organisations that were permitted to conduct some form of monitoring or surveillance. The Home Secretary presented a drafted Communications Data Bill in the 2014–2015 parliamentary session that would have addressed some of the weaknesses of RIPA, but it was withdrawn as a result of Liberal Democrat opposition. In 2016 Parliament passed the Investigatory Powers Act 2016, which is the current legislation. The Act significantly tightened the controls over the surveillance powers of the police and the intelligence services, while giving them greater powers.

The Act was heavily criticised by security experts, some sectors of the telecommunications industry and Members of Parliament. There was concern about whether the Act contained sufficient safeguards to protect against abuses of power. There was also concern that provisions that allowed for the seizure of keys undermined the security of public key systems. This is likely to be an area of ongoing debate in the coming years concerning how to balance the needs for appropriate security measures and individual privacy.

We should emphasise that there are many other aspects of privacy that we cannot deal with here including rights under the Human Rights Act 1998 and the common law duty of confidentiality. These include, for example, the publication on the internet of photographs taken without the consent of the subject and the use of parabolic microphones to eavesdrop on private conversations at a distance. The right to privacy depends on the common law duty of confidentiality, the Human Rights Act 1998 and the DPA 2018, any or all of which may be relevant in a particular case.

13.4 FREEDOM OF INFORMATION

The primary purpose of the Freedom of Information Act 2000 (FOI Act) is to provide clear rights of access to information held by authorities in the public sector. Under the terms of the FOI Act, any member of the public can apply for access to such information from public authorities. The FOI Act also provides an enforcement mechanism if the information is not made available. There is no right to use the FOI Act to obtain information from anyone other than a public authority. The legislation applies to Parliament, government departments, local authorities, health trusts, doctors' surgeries, universities, state schools and many other organisations in the public sector.

The main features of the FOI Act are:

- There is a general right of access to information held by public authorities while carrying out their public functions, subject to certain conditions and exemptions.

- In most cases where information is exempted from disclosure there is a duty on public authorities to disclose where, in the view of the public authority, the public interest in disclosure outweighs the public interest in maintaining the exemption in question.

- The ICO is in charge of this area and an Information Rights Tribunal was created in 2000 under the FOI Act with wide powers to enforce the rights.

- A duty is imposed on public authorities to adopt a scheme for the publication of information. The scheme, which must be approved by the Commissioner, must specify the classes of information the authority intends to publish, the manner of publication, and whether the information is available to the public free of charge or on payment of a fee.

Information in this context has a rather wider meaning than in normal usage so that it includes the text of documents, such as minutes of meetings. The FOI Act does not apply to personal information: data protection legislation already gives individuals access to information held about themselves and prevents a member of the public having access to personal information held about anyone else. There is, however, a possible conflict with the UK GDPR in cases where documents include personal information, because the information that has to be released under the FOI Act may include personal data that must be kept confidential under the UK GDPR. There is case law and guidance on this and often it is a substantial task for those responding to FOI Act requests to remove (redact) personal data from vast quantities of documents that are required to be disclosed under the FOI Act.

The ICO provides guidance about situations where some personal data may be published. An example is salary and expenses information. Authorities covered by the FOI Act are expected to reveal the salaries of their senior staff (or, at least, the salary scale on which each senior member of staff is positioned) and any expenses that they claim. More recently, the salaries of senior civil servants have routinely been published on the government's website and salary information about senior staff in local authorities may be included in the authorities' accounts. Where the information is routinely published publicly, no separate FOI request is needed. FOI requests for salary information of other staff would need to be assessed separately and the ICO provides guidance on what may be acceptable.

Where FOI requests are made to obtain details of public contracts, such as those awarded to a company's competitor, the data supplied will first be checked and where necessary parts removed that are confidential. For example, curricula vitae can form part of such public sector contracts and they would need to be checked. It is common for commercial contracts with public sector bodies to include a clause stating that if the public body receives an FOI request relating to the contract, the authority will first notify the other contracting party before disclosing information. This will give the contracting party a chance to assess whether the data proposed to be disclosed is exempt from the FOI Act or not. The ICO guidance and legal advice may be needed to assess whether complex exemptions apply to a situation.

The USA also has a Freedom of Information Act. It was passed in 1967 and is thus much older than the UK Act. It is also fundamentally different from the UK Act. In particular, since 1975, the US Act has applied to personal data, including that held by the law enforcement agencies, and has, notoriously, been used by criminals to force those agencies to reveal the information they hold about the applicant's criminal activities. It has created a very substantial administrative burden for US government agencies; the FBI, for example, reported that it received an average of 15,000 requests per year between 2012 and 2021.[9]

Unlike the other legislation discussed in this chapter, the FOI Act creates a requirement for new information systems and for packages that can be used to develop them. Such systems are commonly known as record management systems and document management systems.

FURTHER READING

The website of the ICO contains useful information relating both to data protection and to freedom of information. There are guides that discuss the practical implications of the laws. Also, the site contains records of the enforcement notices that have been applied, including those mentioned in Section 13.2.7. The site can be found at:
    https://www.ico.org.uk

The text of the DPA 2018 is available from:
    https://www.legislation.gov.uk/ukpga/2018/12/contents

The UK GDPR does not have an obvious name, making it difficult to find on the UK government's website, https://www.legislation.gov.uk. Its full title is 'Regulation (EU) 2016/679 of the European Parliament and of the Council of 27 April 2016 on the protection of natural persons with regard to the processing of personal data and on the free movement of such data (United Kingdom General Data Protection Regulation) (Text with EEA relevance)'. The text can be found at:
    https://www.legislation.gov.uk/eur/2016/679/contents

Some readers may be interested in an amended version that shows changes to the UK GDPR that came into effect from 1 January 2021. This amended version is known as a Keeling Schedule. The schedule for the UK GDPR can be found at:
    General Data Protection Regulation: Keeling Schedule (2018). https://assets. publishing.service.gov.uk/government/uploads/system/uploads/attachment_ data/file/685632/2018-03-05_Keeling_Schedule.pdf.

---

9   'Create an Annual Report' (n.d.), FOIA.gov, https://www.foia.gov/data.html.

The guidance from the ICO on the timescales around handling requests from data subjects can be found at:

'Right to Data Portability' (n.d.) Information Commissioner's Office. https://ico.org.uk/for-organisations/guide-to-data-protection/guide-to-the-general-data-protection-regulation-gdpr/individual-rights/right-to-data-portability/#ib25.

The Investigatory Powers Act 2016 can be found at:
https://www.legislation.gov.uk/ukpga/2016/25/contents

The PECR can be found at:
https://www.legislation.gov.uk/uksi/2003/2426/contents

The Freedom of Information Act 2000 can be found at:
https://www.legislation.gov.uk/ukpga/2000/36/contents

The following books provide further discussion of data protection topics covered in this chapter:

Holt, J. and Newton, J. (ed.) (2020) *A Practical Guide to IT Law* (3rd edition). BCS, Swindon.

Room, S. (ed.) (2021) *Data Protection and Compliance* (2nd edition). BCS, Swindon.

14 INTERNET ISSUES

After studying this chapter, you should understand:

- *the reasons why misuse of the internet gives cause for concern;*
- *the scope and limitations of the legislation that governs the use of the internet at present;*
- *why it is difficult to enact legislation that will effectively regulate the use of the internet.*

14.1 THE EFFECTS OF THE INTERNET

The benefits that the internet has brought are almost universally recognised. It has made access to all sorts of information much easier. It has made it much easier for people to communicate with each other, on both an individual and a group basis. It has simplified and speeded up many types of commercial transaction. And, most importantly, these benefits have been made available to very many people, not just to a small and privileged group – although, of course, the internet is still far from being universally available, even in developed countries.

Inevitably, a development on this scale creates its own problems. In this chapter we shall be looking at topics that are a matter of concern to everyone professionally involved in the internet, as well as to many other people. Some of the topics cannot sensibly be discussed in technical terms alone. There are social, cultural and legal issues that must all be considered. Different countries approach these issues in very different ways but the internet itself knows no boundaries.

Every country has laws governing what can be published or publicly displayed. Typically, such laws address defamation – that is, material that makes untrue allegations about people or organisations – and pornography – that is, material with sexual content. They may also cover other areas such as political and religious comment, incitement to racial hatred, or the depiction of violence.

Although every country has such laws, they are very different from each other. Some countries, for example, consider that pictures with nudity are indecent and have laws that prevent them from appearing in publications and advertisements. In other countries, such pictures are perfectly acceptable. In some countries, publication of material criticising the government or the established religion is effectively forbidden, while in others it is a right guaranteed by the constitution and vigorously defended by the courts.

The internet and, to an extent, satellite television have made these differences much more apparent and important than they used to be. Since material in digital form flows across borders so easily, it is both much more likely that material that violates publication laws will come into a country and more difficult for the country to enforce its own laws.

As the World Wide Web attracted many more users to the internet, an early focus became the roles and responsibilities of internet service providers (ISPs). Legislation was created that defined some of the issues and it is still in place. The current debate is focused on the roles and responsibilities of services on the internet, including social media companies, but there is not much legislation that specifically addresses social media.

We start by discussing the legal framework under which ISPs operate. Then, we look at the ideas that are being discussed around other online provision, including social media outlets. Next, we look at the problems related to differences between legal systems. Only then can we address the specific issues of defamation, pornography, child sexual abuse materials, spam and cookies. Finally, we look at the issue of commerce over the internet and the protection of consumers.

14.2 INTERNET SERVICE PROVIDERS

The central issue we need to consider is how far an ISP can be held responsible for material generated by its customers.

In Europe, the position is governed by European Directive 2000/31/EC. In the UK this directive was implemented through the Electronic Commerce (EC Directive) Regulations 2002. Unlike some of the other European Union (EU) regulations, this regulation was not kept as part of UK law when the UK left the EU. Although it is not law in the UK, there are aspects of the liability protections of ISPs that the UK government has said will be upheld until new UK-specific legislation is introduced.[1]

The EC Directive defined three roles that an ISP may play: mere conduit, caching and hosting. These roles are part of the liability protections in the EC Directive.

The role of **mere conduit** is that in which the ISP does no more than transmit data; in particular, the ISP does not initiate transmissions, does not select the receivers of the transmissions, and does not select or modify the data transmitted. It is compatible with the role of mere conduit for an ISP to store information temporarily, provided this is only done as part of the transmission process. As long as it is acting as a mere conduit, the regulations provide that an ISP is not liable for damages or for any criminal sanction as a result of a transmission.

The **caching** role arises when the information is the subject of automatic, intermediate and temporary storage, for the sole purpose of increasing the efficiency of the

---

1 'The eCommerce Directive and the UK' (2021), Department for Digital, Culture, Media & Sport, https://www.gov.uk/guidance/the-ecommerce-directive-and-the-uk

transmission of the information to other recipients of the service upon their request. The EC Directive states that an ISP acting in the caching role is not liable for damages or for any criminal sanction as a result of a transmission, provided that it:

- does not modify the information;
- complies with conditions on access to the information;
- complies with any rules regarding the updating of the information;
- does not interfere with the lawful use of technology to obtain data on the use of the information; *and*
- acts expeditiously to remove or to disable access to the information it has stored, having obtained actual knowledge that the information at the initial source of the transmission has been removed or access has been disabled, possibly as a result of a legal order.

These apparently complicated conditions are simply designed to ensure that an ISP that claims to be playing a caching role is behaving in accordance with industry practice.

Where an ISP stores information provided by its customers, it is acting in a **hosting** role. In this case, the EC Directive states that the ISP is not liable for damage or criminal sanctions provided that:

- the customer was not acting under the authority or the control of the ISP; *and either*
- the ISP did not know that anything unlawful was going on and did not know anything that should have led it to think that something unlawful might be going on; *or*
- when the ISP found out that that something unlawful was going on, it acted expeditiously to remove the information or to prevent access to it.

In the USA, ISPs enjoy much broader immunity than in Europe. In effect, even when they are hosting, they enjoy the immunity that in Europe is only granted to ISPs acting as mere conduits.

It seems very reasonable that an ISP should cease to enjoy immunity if it fails to remove unlawful material once it has been informed about it. However, this places the ISP in the position of having to judge whether or not material is unlawful. ISPs are not qualified to make such judgements and if they are forced to make them they will play safe – that is, they will usually accept that the material complained about is unlawful and will remove it. The person who posted the material has no legal redress. This means, for example, that if a website is set up to collect and display comments about a major company – be it a supermarket chain, a car manufacturer or a fast food chain – the company can, in effect, censor the comments that appear by complaining to the ISP that the material is defamatory. The ISP, aware that the complainant can deploy an army of expensive lawyers, is likely to play safe by requiring that the material be removed, regardless of whether it is true and in the public interest. There is no easy legal remedy that the owners of the website can use. This is a difficult issue and there is no obvious solution.

A further issue regarding ISPs is the question of anonymous and pseudonymous postings. It is common for contributors to online communities and social media to use pseudonyms for their postings. Their ISP will be aware of their true identity. Is the ISP allowed to release, and can it be compelled to release, this information to someone wishing to take legal action against a contributor? In the UK, ISPs are allowed to release such information and can be compelled to do so by a court. In the USA, ISPs cannot in general be required to release such information, although they may be required to do so in the case of serious crimes.

14.3 MODERNISING THE LEGISLATION

At the time of writing, the EU is beginning discussions on a new Digital Services Act that would modernise European Directive 2000/31/EC. This proposed Act would address issues such as transparency in advertising, including targeted advertising, disinformation and illegal content.

As noted, the EC Directive is no longer law in the UK. The UK government is preparing new legislation, called the Online Safety Bill. The bill has some similar ambitions to the EU's proposed Digital Services Act. It identifies problems with the way that content is created and shared on social media networks. There are questions about the transparency of algorithms that direct content to users and whether these can present material that causes distress or leads users to harm. If passed, the bill will place a duty of care on social media providers and search engines to their users. It also proposes that it is not sufficient to deal with issues when there are complaints and that, instead, ISPs should be proactive in detecting harmful content and removing it. This would be a change to the existing situation where companies could say that they are a mere conduit or have a caching or hosting role.

It has been difficult legislation to draft and there will be much more debate before the EU and UK proposals can become law. As noted in the previous section, it could lead to companies being conservative (by removing content) and risk complaints of censorship. Yet, there are examples where the current situation leads to harm. In one case, a teenager was shown stories about self-harm and suicide based on content they had accessed (see the Further Reading section). The algorithms provided similar articles to what had been viewed, providing more stories. The teenager copied some of those stories and took her life. People defining such algorithms do not set out to cause harm, but there is work to do to improve how they function and to introduce safeguards to improve online safety.

In the UK, it is proposed that Ofcom will be given the responsibility of regulating this area. It will require investment in Ofcom to do this and investment in people in the social media and search engine providers to comply with the law.

If passed, the legislation is likely to target the largest social media companies and search engines. These are important topics for the health and wellbeing of society. Even if a company is not directly covered by the legislation, it is incumbent on IT professionals to look at the issues covered and how their businesses should work with data, advertising and their users.

14.4 THE LAW ACROSS NATIONAL BOUNDARIES

How the law operates across national boundaries is a difficult and intensely technical topic but one that is very important in the context of the internet. We can only give the most superficial description here.

14.4.1 Criminal law

Suppose a person, X, commits a criminal offence in Country A and then moves to Country B. Can Country A ask that X be arrested in Country B and sent back to Country A so that they can be put on trial? Or can X be prosecuted in Country B for the offence committed in Country A?

The answer to the first of these questions is that, provided there exists an agreement (usually called an **extradition treaty**) between the two countries, then in principle X can be extradited – that is, arrested and sent back to face trial in Country A. However, this can only be done under the very important proviso that the offence that X is alleged to have committed in Country A would also be an offence in Country B. What is more, extradition procedures are usually extremely complex, so that attempts at extradition often fail because of procedural weaknesses. Within the EU, the European arrest warrant obviates the need for extradition procedures. The case of Gary McKinnon, discussed in the next chapter, raised issues related to extradition in an acute form.

In general, the answer to the second question is that X cannot be prosecuted in Country B for an offence committed in Country A. However, in certain cases some countries, including the UK and the USA, claim **extraterritorial jurisdiction** – that is, the right to try citizens and other residents for most crimes committed in other countries. In particular, this right is used to allow the prosecution of people who, while abroad, commit sexual offences involving children. However, the issue of extraterritoriality is much wider than this and attempts to claim extraterritorial jurisdiction make countries very unpopular.

What does this mean in the context of the internet? Suppose that you live in Country A and on your website there you publish material that is perfectly legal and acceptable in Country A but that it is a criminal offence to publish in Country B. Then you cannot be prosecuted in Country A and it is very unlikely that you would be extradited to Country B. You might, however, be unwise to visit Country B voluntarily.

14.4.2 The Convention on Cybercrime

In 2001, the Council of Europe approved the Convention on Cybercrime. It deals with crimes committed on the internet and other networks, including criminal copyright infringement, computer-related fraud and hacking, and child sexual abuse imagery on the internet. There is an additional protocol relating to incitement to religious or racial hatred, to which signatories to the protocol may also sign up.

International conventions inevitably are slow to take effect. Governments sign the treaty showing that they approve of it. However, in many cases they will have to persuade their legislature to approve it and the laws necessary to implement it. This process, known as **ratification**, can take a long time and is often not at the top of a government's priorities.

Governments may be replaced and the incoming government may not feel committed to ratification.

The Council of Europe, which is quite separate from the EU, has 46 members and 6 observer states: Canada, Israel, the Holy See, Japan, Mexico and the USA. As of March 2022, 66 countries had signed and ratified the treaty while 11 had signed it but not yet ratified it. The USA is an example of a country that did not sign up to the protocol relating to hate material because it would be contrary to the First Amendment (see Section 14.5.2).

14.4.3 Civil law

There are some parts of the civil law where the position is reasonably clear cut. Any contract that involves parties from more than one country should, and usually will, state explicitly under which jurisdiction (i.e. which country's laws) it is to be interpreted. Where intellectual property law is concerned, there are international agreements to which most countries are signatories so that there is a common framework, even if it can be very difficult to enforce the rights in certain countries.

In many cases, the plaintiff will have some choice about where to take action. Very often the decision will be taken on practical grounds – there is little point in taking action in a country in which the defendant has no legal presence or few assets and it is probably unwise to take action in a country where the legal process is well known to be lengthy and expensive.

Consider the case of an ISP based in the USA with a European office in London. One of its customers is an Italian, resident in Italy, who posts an accusation about a French politician on his website (which is hosted by the ISP). The French politician complains but the ISP does nothing to remove the allegation. If the French politician wishes to take action, he can, in theory, do so in any of the four countries involved – England, France, Italy or the USA. His best hope of winning a court action may well be in France but there is little point in bringing an action in France unless the ISP has some sort of legal presence there. The same applies to Italy. The politician would probably opt for action in England on the grounds that, in such cases, English law is much more sympathetic to the person claiming to be wronged than is American law. It may still be necessary to persuade the English court that this is a matter that it can properly consider.

The Trans-Tasman Proceedings Act 2010 is an example of legislation where two countries have agreed to simplify how disputes are started against people or organisations in another country. The Act covers disputes in New Zealand and Australia. A person in either country can start a dispute against someone or an organisation in the other country. This replaced the earlier situation where a court would have to decide whether a New Zealander could take action against an Australian or vice versa.

14.5 DEFAMATION

Consider the following scenario. A university provides internet services for its students and allows them to write personal web pages. One student, who is a passionate fan of their local football club, believes the referee in their last game made a bad decision that caused them to lose the match. He believes that the decision was so obviously wrong that the referee must have been bribed. He puts a statement on his web page saying that the referee is corrupt. Someone draws the referee's attention to this allegation. The referee believes that his reputation has been badly damaged by the statement and he wants compensation.

This situation is covered by the law of defamation. Defamation means making statements that will damage someone's reputation, bring them into contempt, make them disliked and so on, but only if the statements are also untrue. In England and Wales, a distinction is made between **slander**, which is spoken, and **libel**, which is written or recorded in some other way (including by email).

There can be little doubt that, on the face of it, the statement in question constitutes libel unless the referee was indeed bribed. Prior to 2014, the UK law on defamation would have allowed the referee to start a case based on damage to reputation. However, the Defamation Act 2013 modified the situations where a case can be brought. It is now necessary to show that there is a case of 'serious harm', which means that there is, or is likely to be, serious financial loss. The referee would need to demonstrate that serious harm had been caused or would be caused as a result of people reading this fan's website.

For this scenario, let us assume that the claim is significant enough that it has led to financial loss for the referee. So, a case could be brought. The next question is who the referee should take action against. He could sue the student, but the student probably does not have enough money to pay any damages that might be awarded. Can he also sue the university, which presumably could pay damages?

14.5.1 Possible defences

The Defamation Act states that a person has a defence in several situations. Some of the situations are new compared to the previous Act. A simplified list of the possible defences is:

a. the defendant is not the author, editor or publisher of the statement complained of;

b. the statement complained of is substantially true;

c. the statement complained of was a statement of opinion and it was made clear in the statement what the basis was for the opinion;

d. the statement was published as a matter of public interest;

e. the statement was posted on a website and the operator of the website was not responsible for posting the statement;

f. the statement complained of was published in a peer-reviewed scientific or academic journal;

g. the statement was a report that is protected by privilege, such as a report of proceedings at court.

The author, the editor and the publisher of an instance of libel can all be held responsible. If the allegation had been published in a traditional student newspaper, printed on paper, and sold to students and others through newsagents or the Students' Union, the referee would have been able to sue the publisher of the newspaper (probably the Students' Union if it had a separate legal existence and, if not, the university) and the editor. This would be reasonable because everything published in the newspaper would be directly under the control of the editor, who is the agent of the publisher.

However, as the libel was published on a web page, on the university site, the university could reasonably argue that it cannot possibly vet everything that every one of its 10,000 students puts on their personal web pages. It is not, in fact, publishing the pages. It is only providing an infrastructure that allows students to publish their own web pages. Taking into account item (e) in the list of defences, the university could make the defence that it was not responsible for posting the article, provided that the student was not acting under its authority or control. For a defence to be possible, it must be possible for any claimant to identify the author of the statement, and the website operator (i.e. the university) must have responded in an appropriate length of time to any notice of complaint about the statement.

Although the Defamation Act does not specify a time limit, guidance notes explain that there are 48 hours (excluding non-working days) for the website operator to respond to a complaint (see the Further Reading section). The operator must contact the author of the statement and notify them of the complaint. There are then up to five days for the author to respond. If there is no response or an incomplete response from the author, then the operator must remove the statement. There are other timeframes described in the guidance about the interactions between the website operator, the author and the complainant. The important aspect is that the website operator needs to have a process that means it can receive and act on complaints within the necessary timeframes. Failure to have such a process may mean that the complainant begins legal action against the website operator.

The Defamation Act provides more details about defences and was an attempt to modernise how defamation is handled. The defences are described in the Act, but further guidance contains more information about how these defences will be applied (see the Further Reading section); an example is the application of the website defence. We have given a very simplified picture here.

14.5.2 International issues

Because so much material on the internet originates in the USA, it is appropriate here to say a little about the position there. US law relating to defamation is much more favourable towards authors and publishers than is the law in the UK. The First Amendment to the US Constitution guarantees the right to free speech and the US courts have always been eager to defend this right. The result is that many statements that might be considered defamatory in the UK would be protected as exercises of the right of free speech in the USA. This is particularly the case where the defamatory statement refers to a public figure. In this case, to succeed in a libel action, the public figure needs to show not only that the statement was factually incorrect but also that it was made maliciously or recklessly.

Suppose that an internet site in the USA, hosted by an American ISP, contains a statement about someone living in the UK that would be considered defamatory in the UK but not in the USA (a statement accusing a British politician of corruption, for example). The person who is the subject of the statement can reasonably say, 'I am British. I live in the UK. This statement can be read by anyone in the UK. Surely, I am entitled to the protection offered by UK law.' But the author of the statement and the ISP can both say, 'We live in the USA and we are governed by its laws. We understand those laws and we comply with them. We cannot be expected to know the law as it exists in all the other countries of the world and we cannot be expected to comply with those laws.' The complainant may be able to take action in the UK against the ISP, provided the ISP has a legal presence in the UK, but only in respect of the circulation of the defamatory statement in the UK. A court in the USA will not enforce UK law over such matters.

This is a case in which the global nature of the internet magnifies an issue. American newspapers and magazines do not contain much material about British politics, nor do they have a very wide circulation in the UK. If the statement had appeared in an American newspaper or magazine, it would not have achieved a wide circulation in the UK. But it is nowadays more likely that such a statement will be made on the internet and it is more likely that it will then be read in the UK.

All these considerations apply to defamatory information published on social media too, as two cases involving tweets show.

In 2010, Lalit Modi, a former chairman of the Indian Premier League (a cricket league), tweeted an allegation that the New Zealand cricket star Chris Cairns had a history of match fixing. Although the tweet initially went to only 65 people, it was picked up by the cricket website Cricinfo, where it was read by a further 1,000 or so readers. Cairns sued both Modi and Cricinfo for damages to his reputation. Cricinfo quickly acknowledged the libel and settled out of court, paying £7,000 in damages and around £8,000 in costs. Modi, however, refused to withdraw the libel and was ordered to pay Cairns £90,000 in damages. This was confirmed on appeal in October 2012. Note that the legal action took place in London rather than in India or New Zealand.

In 2020, the singer Justin Bieber began legal action against two users on Twitter who made statements that Bieber had sexually assaulted them in 2014. Bieber refuted the allegations and released information about his location and movements at the time when the assault was alleged to have happened. The legal action was started in the US state of California. There were delays in concluding the case, showing that these cases can take time to complete. Some of the delays related to slow responses from the defendants as they organised a legal defence. In 2022, Bieber announced that he had dropped the legal action.

14.6 PORNOGRAPHY

More or less every country has laws concerned with pornography. Beyond this simple statement, though, it is almost impossible to generalise. What is considered pornographic varies widely from country to country. What is accepted as normal by everyone in one country may be considered pornographic in another country. In some countries the possession of pornography may be a criminal offence; in others possession is not an offence but distribution and/or publication are. We are not concerned here with what should or should not be considered pornographic or what should or should not be prohibited. We are concerned simply with a country's ability to enforce the laws that it has chosen to enact.

Until the early 1980s, a country could expect to enforce its laws regarding pornography reasonably effectively. It was a comparatively simple matter for the police to stop the sale of material that was regarded as pornographic. It was easy to prevent cinemas showing films considered pornographic; again, this could be done by the police. And, apart from in a few areas near its borders, the only television broadcasts that could be received in the country would be ones that were broadcast from within the country and could therefore be controlled.

Three developments changed this. First, it became possible to broadcast television programmes via satellite, which meant that programmes could be broadcast from one country to be received in another. Second, the advent of the internet meant that individuals could receive pornographic material, in the form of images or text, in a way that was extremely difficult for the authorities to detect. In other words, pornography became available in an intangible form. And finally, the advent of the digital camera allowed photographs to be produced without the need for externally provided development services.

There is a second aspect to the problem of pornography. This is the problem of unsolicited pornography sent to people who find it offensive. This, however, is part of the wider problem of spam, which we deal with in Section 14.7. In this section, we are concerned with the problems that a country faces in enforcing its laws against pornography, in the face of internet users who are willing receivers of it.

There is one important difference between laws regarding defamation and laws regarding pornography. In most instances of defamation, any legal action will be under the civil law and will be initiated by the person or organisation who is the target of the defamation. In most cases concerning the publication of pornography, action will be under the criminal law and will be initiated by state prosecution services on the basis of information provided by the police.

14.6.1 The law in the UK

In England and Wales, the law relating to pornography is based on the Obscene Publications Acts of 1959 and 1964. The 1959 Act both repealed existing legislation and dispensed with the common law offences relating to obscene material. It created a criminal offence of publishing an obscene article, whether for profit or not, and the 1964 Act extended that offence to include possessing an obscene article with a view to publication for gain. It is not an offence simply to possess an obscene article. In the context of these Acts, 'article' is taken to mean any type of article 'containing or embodying matter to be read or looked at or both, any sound record, and any film or other record of a picture or pictures'. The definition of publishing was amended in the Criminal Justice and Public Order Act 1994 so that it explicitly includes the transmission of electronically stored data.

The 1959 Act states that 'an article shall be deemed to be obscene if its effect or the effect of any one of its items is, if taken as a whole, such as to tend to deprave and corrupt persons who are likely, having regard to all relevant circumstances, to read, see or hear the matter contained or embodied in it'. Although the Act has been modified by subsequent legislation, some intended to bring its provisions into line with the world of computers and the internet, the definition of obscenity has not been changed. However, its interpretation has changed considerably; much material that would almost certainly have been found by a court to be obscene at the time that the Act was passed would now be regarded as quite acceptable.

Two important features of this definition are that the effect is to be 'taken as a whole' and that it is the effect on 'persons who are likely ... to read, see or hear' the material that matters. The 'taken as a whole' provision means that a prosecution under the Act cannot be based simply on a short excerpt, possibly taken out of context. Thus a 400-page novel, five pages of which contain graphic and explicit descriptions of sexual activity, must be judged as a whole. The Act also specifically states that a defendant should not be found guilty of an offence if it is proved that publication is 'for the public good on the ground that it is in the interests of science, literature, art or learning, or of other objects of general concern'. Furthermore, it is specifically stated that 'the opinion of experts as to the literary, artistic, scientific or other merits' of the article can be taken into account. The effect of these provisions has been that, starting with the famous case of *Lady Chatterley's Lover*, attempts to prosecute works that have any literary or artistic merit at all have proved unsuccessful and have now been abandoned by the authorities.

The phrase 'tend to deprave and corrupt persons who are likely, having regard to all relevant circumstances, to read, see or hear the matter contained or embodied in it' is potentially of importance in relation to the internet. In the 1980s, pornographic material was usually purchased in printed form from newsagents, where it was kept in a less accessible position and not sold to under-18s. Thus, those who were likely to read or see the material were likely to be adults who were deliberately looking for it. It could be argued that when the same material is posted on the internet, younger people are much more likely to gain access to it, possibly unintentionally. This could mean that material that a court would not judge to be obscene when it is printed and sold in a newsagent becomes obscene when it is posted on the internet, because it is likely to be seen or read by a larger group of people.

The position regarding child sexual abuse imagery is very different. The Protection of Children Act 1978 and subsequent legislation make the simple possession of indecent – that is, sexually explicit – material involving children a serious criminal offence. It is much easier to prove in court that material is sexually explicit than that it tends to deprave or corrupt. And mere possession is an objective fact in a way that possession with a view to publish is not. For these reasons, prosecutions under the Protection of Children Act are much more straightforward than prosecutions under the Obscene Publications Acts.

Sections 63 to 67 of the Criminal Justice and Immigration Act 2008 introduced provisions making mere possession of certain other types of obscene material – so-called extreme pornography – an offence, thus simplifying prosecutions related to such material.

14.6.2 The regulation of pornography in other countries

The First Amendment to the US Constitution famously states that:

Congress shall make no law respecting an establishment of religion, or prohibiting the free exercise thereof; or abridging the freedom of speech, or of the press; or the right of the people peaceably to assemble, and to petition the government for a redress of grievances.

The clauses about freedom of speech and of the press have been enthusiastically defended by the courts since the 1950s. Attempts by individual states to enact provisions against pornography have been struck down as unconstitutional by the Supreme Courts of the states themselves. An Act of Congress that would have made the internet subject to much stricter control than other media was struck down by the federal Supreme Court. As a result, even though much of American society is very conservative in its attitude to sexual matters, there is little legal control over pornography.

Within Europe, the level of legal control over pornography covers a wide spectrum, with some countries, such as Denmark and Sweden, having very few controls while others are as restrictive as or, in some cases, more restrictive than the UK. Quite often, controls are limited to material that depicts violent, non-consensual sexual acts. Worldwide, the range is still broader, ranging from countries in which the depiction of a woman in a modest one-piece bathing costume would be unlawful to countries in which there are apparently no restrictions whatsoever.

Notwithstanding this wide variation in the control of pornography in general, there is wide (though not universal) international agreement that child sexual abuse imagery should be banned. Some ambiguity can arise because of differences in the age of consent from country to country – pictures involving 14-year-olds might be regarded as child sexual abuse imagery in one country but not in another. Despite this, there is generally a clear understanding of what constitutes child sexual abuse imagery.

14.6.3 The Internet Watch Foundation

In the UK, the Internet Watch Foundation (IWF) was set up in 1996 to monitor and, where desirable and possible, take action against illegal and offensive content on the UK internet. It has the support of the UK government, the police and the ISPs. It can act against material on the web that contains:

- images of child sexual abuse originating anywhere in the world;
- adult material that potentially breaches the Obscene Publications Acts in the UK;
- non-photographic child sexual abuse images (e.g. computer-generated images or drawings) hosted in the UK.

The restrictions to the UK context for adult obscene material and non-photographic material reflect the fact that there is no international agreement that such material should be banned.

The IWF operates a hotline through which members of the public can report any internet content that they believe may be illegal. The IWF will locate and assess the material. If the material is considered illegal and falls within the IWF's remit, the IWF will pass the information to the police and, if the material is hosted in the UK, inform the ISP that is hosting it. If the material is hosted abroad, the IWF will inform all its ISP members so that access from the UK can be blocked. If images of children originating in other countries are involved, it will also inform Interpol and the police in the countries concerned.

In 2021, the IWF received around 360,000 reports of potential issues, of which about 70% related to material that was assessed as being potentially illegal. These reports came from a mixture of investigation by the IWF, the public and agencies such as the police. In the first full year of the IWF's operation, 18% of the illegal material was traced to sources within the UK. By the end of 2021, this had been reduced to 0.15%. However, the IWF's 2021 annual report notes an increase in cases. In the UK there was a 112% increase in identified cases between 2020 and 2021 (see the Further Reading section).

Managing content

In 2013, several online book stores were surprised to find that they had books on sale that were 'abuse-themed'.[2] This affected several stores including Amazon, Barnes & Noble and, in the UK, WHSmith. The problem was that these companies accepted content from another site, Kobo, that produced electronic books; this included self-published books. There should have been checks on the content before it was shared by Kobo to other sites, but something failed. The books could be found in the search results on the affected sites.

Amazon and Barnes & Noble continued to trade but started the process to remove the books. WHSmith took a different strategy. It made its entire website unavailable and replaced it with a statement, as shown in Figure 14.1. The website content remained unavailable until the books were removed.

Figure 14.1 Screenshot of the WHSmith home page, October 2013

A statement from WHSmith:

Last week we were made aware that a number of unacceptable titles were appearing on our website through the Kobo website that has an automated feed to ours. This is an industry wide issue impacting retailers that sell self published eBooks due to the explosion of self publishing, which in the main is good as it gives new authors the opportunity to get their content published. However we are disgusted by these particular titles, find this unacceptable and we in no way whatsoever condone them.

It is our policy not to feature titles like those highlighted and we have processes in place to screen them out. We offer over one million titles through our eBooks partner Kobo, many of which are self-published titles. Due to the massive amount of self publishing a number of these titles have got through the screening process.

We are taking immediate steps to have them all removed. While we are doing this we have decided to take our website off-line to best protect our customers and the public. Our website will become live again once all self published eBooks have been removed and we are totally sure that there are no offending titles available. When our website goes back online it will not display any self published material until we are completely confident that inappropriate books can never be shown again.

We sincerely apologise for any offence caused.

In the mean time if you have any questions for our customer support team you can contact them here.

---

2 'WH Smith Takes Website Offline after Porn E-book Scandal' (2013), BBC News, https://www.bbc.co.uk/news/technology-24519179.

From an IT perspective, this example raises issues about protecting yourself from errors by content partners. It was surprising that WHSmith effectively closed its online store to rectify the process rather than restricting some content, such as the books section of its website.

When designing content that takes data from other locations, an important point is to consider what could go wrong and how to limit any problems. We might focus more on the technical issues, such as whether network access will fail, but it is also necessary to consider issues with content. Having a way to isolate some content quickly, rather than closing an entire site, would be an appropriate feature to consider when developing and maintaining systems.

14.6.4 Future developments

As we have seen, the IWF has been very effective in blocking child sexual abuse imagery. The effectiveness of the IWF's work is the result of several factors:

- There is general international agreement that this sort of material should be suppressed.

- Sites that supply the material are not attractive to advertisers. Thus, for such a site to be profitable, it must charge its customers. Since the payments will necessarily be electronic, the customers can be traced.

- Prosecution is comparatively straightforward in the UK and other countries with relevant legislation.

These factors, in particular the first, do not apply in relation to pornographic material and there is little likelihood of effective action being taken against such material in the same way. Countries will continue to have different views about what is regarded as pornographic and what that means in terms of legal restrictions.

The issue can also be caught up in politics. For example, one UK prime minister stated that it was wrong that material that would not be allowed in a newsagent's shop was available on the internet. While we may sympathise with this sentiment, we must recognise that the internet has made it almost impossible to stop this happening – prevention could only be achieved through censorship of cross-border internet traffic on a scale so massive as to be completely unacceptable to society as well as so demanding of resources as to be unaffordable. Ideally, IT professionals with relevant skills will work with politicians to formulate legislation that brings about acceptable changes that meet the concerns of society while still being workable.

14.7 SPAM

The Information Commissioner's Office (ICO) defines spam as 'emails sent to you without your knowledge or consent, which often contain marketing'.[3] It is likely that

---

3 'Spam Emails' (n.d.), Information Commissioner's Office, https://ico.org.uk/your-data-matters/online/spam-emails.

spam email is sent to a large number of recipients without qualifying whether they might be interested in the content. Any regular user of email will be familiar with spam. We find our mailboxes filled with emails offering Viagra, penis enlargement treatments, incitements to visit pornographic sites, advertisements for dubious financial investments and so on. Statista.com reports there was a fall in the estimated amount of global email traffic being spam in the period January 2014 to January 2021, from about 70% to 43%.[4]

Internet users find spam to be irritating and often offensive. If they respond to any of these invitations, they may also find themselves defrauded and their bank accounts raided. It is easy to miss important emails in the welter of spam. Some spam carries viruses. The effectiveness of the internet is much reduced by the load of spam that it carries. Not surprisingly, there has been considerable pressure on governments to legislate to eliminate or at least alleviate the problem and several organisations have been set up specifically to fight spam.

There are some technical means of fighting spam, for example:

- closing loopholes that enable spammers to use other people's computers to relay bulk messages;
- using machine learning and other techniques to identify suspicious features of message;
- using virus detection software to reject email carrying viruses;
- keeping **stop lists** of sites that are known to send spam;
- scanning URLs in received emails and warning users if the links contain potentially malicious content, such as viruses or malware.

Most of these methods require constant vigilance, however, and are more suitable for organisations than individual users. There is widely available support from technology to help all users, such as email applications that can detect spam. These techniques and features offer a useful defence against spam, but there is a real risk that genuine email will be mistaken for spam and rejected.

The problem of spam is perceived as being of the utmost importance by the industry. There is substantial effort to develop and enhance technical solutions, but these need to be backed up by effective legislation.

14.7.1 European legislation

The European Community Directive on Privacy and Electronic Communications (2002/58/EC) was issued in 2002 and required member nations to introduce regulations to implement it by December 2003. In the UK, the directive was implemented by the Privacy and Electronic Communications (EC Directive) Regulations 2003 (PECR), with further amendments up to 2018. The PECR have remained part of UK law following the UK's exit from the EU.

---

4   'Global Spam Volume as a Percentage of Total E-mail Traffic from January 2014 to December 2021, by Month' (2022), Statista, https://www.statista.com/statistics/420391/spam-email-traffic-share.

The PECR address some issues that are not relevant here but their essential features relating to unsolicited email are:

- Unsolicited email can only be sent to individuals (as opposed to companies) if they have previously given their consent.

- Sending unsolicited email that conceals the address of the sender or does not provide a valid address to which the recipient can send a request for such mailings to cease is unlawful.

- If an email address has been obtained in the course of the sale of goods or services, the seller may use the address for direct mailings, provided that the recipient is given the opportunity, easily and free of charge, with every message, to request that such mailings cease.

The definition of electronic email is considered to include other related electronic communications, including text messages and direct messages on social media platforms.

The PECR are aligned with the UK General Data Protection Regulation (GDPR) (see Chapter 13), introduced in 2018, which means there is updated guidance on the consent provided. It is necessary for individuals to have clearly consented to being contacted by the company. This is based on the idea of an **opt-in**, which is a change to how companies acted before the GDPR. Companies that want to obtain consent are now expected to make clear statements and allow an option (e.g. a checkbox) for an individual to provide that consent. Good practice would be to have a checkbox for each type of communication so that individuals have a clear choice about how a company may contact them in future. Forms that contain checkboxes that are pre-checked and require an individual to uncheck them will not be considered as acceptable practice by the ICO.

Soft opt-in

The PECR does have a **soft opt-in** provision. It allows a business to market goods and services similar to those that a customer has bought from that business. It can also apply if a customer requests a quote for a good or service (e.g. by completing a web form) – the business is subsequently allowed to contact the customer about related items. There are limitations on the soft opt-in provision:

- The business must be marketing its own goods and services.

- This must be commercial marketing about products and services. Organisations such as charities and political parties cannot use the provision to send out marketing about new campaigns.

- The business must have collected the data directly from customers. The option does not apply if the business has bought contact information from other organisations (e.g. through bought-in mail lists).

- There must be an opportunity to opt out of the marketing when the data is first obtained and in all future communications.

In the UK, the enforcement of the PECR is in the hands of the ICO. The maximum penalty is a fine of £500,000.

The regulations have been seen as a step in the right direction. One weakness, however, is that they can only be effective in relation to spam sent from within the EU.

Another weakness in the UK legislation is the difficulty of enforcing the PECR effectively. Since it is not an offence to send unsolicited email to companies, it falls to individuals to take action against UK spammers. Few individuals are prepared to make the effort that this involves, particularly as any damages awarded will inevitably be comparatively small. Furthermore, if the spammer is a company, it may frighten the individual off by threatening to fight the matter to the highest court. In one case, after judgement had been given in favour of the complainant, the company repeatedly delayed payment of the damages and costs until it suddenly disappeared (see the Further Reading section).

14.7.2 Legislation in the USA

A superficially similar Act to the PECR came into force in the USA at the start of 2004. This is the Controlling the Assault of Non-solicited Pornography and Marketing Act 2003, otherwise known as the CAN-SPAM Act. Unfortunately, the Act has fundamental weaknesses, the main one being that it is legal to send spam provided that:

- the person sending the spam has not been informed by the receiver that they do not wish to receive spam from that source; *and*
- the spam contains an address that the receiver can use to ask that no more spam be sent.

These provisions mean that email users would have to respond to every piece of spam they receive asking for no more to be sent. Dishonest spammers can use these messages to confirm the validity of the email addresses. In Europe, it is the responsibility of the spammer to get the recipient's permission before sending the spam; in the USA it is the responsibility of the recipient to inform the spammer that they don't want to receive the spam.

The law has some very good provisions, mostly the technical ones that require valid return addresses and make it illegal to forge other routing information that accompanies each message. Coupled with some changes in the architecture of internet mail handling and increased anti-spam vigilance by ISPs and network operators, these could, over time, have real impact on spam volumes.

The CAN-SPAM Act allows ISPs to sue for damages in certain cases and several ISPs have initiated successful court action against spammers. In 2005, Microsoft won a $7.8 million civil judgement against Robert Soloway for sending spam through MSN and Hotmail services and Robert Braver, a small ISP in Oklahoma, was awarded over $10 million in a judgement against Soloway. It is not clear whether either claimant actually received the money awarded. In 2008, Soloway was sentenced to 47 months' imprisonment and ordered to pay $700,000 on email fraud and related charges. Other large-scale spammers have also been successfully prosecuted, many of the cases involving both spamming and other criminal activities.

14.7.3 Registration

Both the UK and the USA operate successful schemes that allow individuals to register their telephone numbers as ones to which unsolicited direct marketing calls must not be made. On the face of it this should act as a model for preventing spam. Unfortunately, the technical differences between the internet and the telephone network mean that this model is unlikely to work with spam. To enforce the law, it is necessary to be able to reliably identify the source of the communication. Telephone operators keep records of calls showing the originator and the destination of the call; such records are needed for billing purposes. It is therefore easy, in most cases, to identify the source of any direct marketing call about which a consumer complains and then take the action necessary to enforce the law, although this is not effective when the direct marketing call originates from overseas.

In most cases, use of the internet is not charged on the basis of individual communications but on the basis of data transfer limits, so there is no recording of individual emails and it costs no more to send an email from Australia to the UK than it does to send an email to one's colleague in the next office. Furthermore, **spoofing** (forging the sender's address on an email) and **relaying** (using other people's mail servers to send your spam) are easily achieved. This means there are no reliable records that can be used to identify where spam really came from and the use of relaying may mean that it is impossible even to determine in which country it originated. In these circumstances, there is little possibility that a prohibition on sending unsolicited email to addresses on a register could be enforced effectively.

14.8 COOKIES AND USER TRACKING

Tracking user actions across the internet has become a focus of industry debate – in particular, using cookies in web browsers. Cookies are small items of data that can be stored in a browser when a user accesses a site. A cookie might be used by the site that the user is visiting (e.g. to handle login information or analytics information to monitor site usage). Some sites use third-party cookies, which can be used to track users across different sites. These cookies might be used to help identify products that a user has viewed and that can influence adverts that are shown to the user.

The PECR also cover the use of cookies. There are requirements to inform users that cookies are being used and to provide an option to decline cookies being stored in the browser. If a user declines the use of cookies, this may have an impact on what functionality is available to the user. For example, if cookies are used to remember the most recent search term that a user has entered, and the user has declined the use of cookies, the website might need to reset the search term each time they use the search functionality.

As a result of the PECR, websites that use cookies started to add statements to inform users of this fact, with an option to accept the use of cookies or decline the use of cookies. However, with the introduction of the GDPR in 2018, there was a notable change in the way that the information was provided. As discussed in Section 13.2.4, the GDPR introduced six legal bases under which data can be processed. For cookies on public websites, rather than internal corporate websites, the appropriate legal basis will be consent. Further, the GDPR expects there to be a legitimate choice about whether to provide that consent and an obvious action where a user provides the consent. This has led websites to introduce more obvious notices about cookies, with these notices often being the main item seen by a user when they first visit a site. Some sites, for example news sites in the USA, decline access to their content if the user is unwilling to accept the use of cookies.

It has become common to differentiate between types of cookie. These are typically:

- **Required** cookies are essential to the technologies used to run a site. For example, these might be cookies used by the web programming language to manage data entry in forms.
- **Functional** cookies are used to manage functionality on a website. If these are declined by a user, some functionality may not work.
- **Performance** cookies help a site's maintainers to understand how the site is used, by tracking which pages are accessed and in which order.
- **Advertising** cookies are used to track users and provide personalised advertising across different websites. These are typically set by third-party providers that the website uses and works with.

There is no choice about the required cookies if a user wants to access a site. If a user wants to decline those cookies, they need to leave the site. For the other types of cookies, users are given a choice about which to accept. The important aspect for GPDR is that there must be a valid choice and users must be able to choose to view the site without accepting all the cookies. A user may choose to accept functional cookies, for example, but decline performance and advertising cookies.

It is worth noting that if the only cookie used is to manage the authentication of a user on a website, that cookie does not need permission and does not need to be declared to users.

The sets of choices are changing, as companies react to the choices that users are making. When users decline certain types of cookies, it may have an impact on the activities of the website and, probably, the revenue the site gains from advertising. This typically means that users are being provided with more information. In principle this leads to more choice, but arguably it leads to users being overwhelmed and simply defaulting to choosing 'Accept All'.

It is unlikely that the average internet user understands what they are agreeing to when they click 'Accept All' when asked about cookies. If we look at the more detailed information that is provided, we can see that a single site may be asking for permission for a few hundred companies to be able to set cookies. The exact numbers will vary by website, but between 200 and 400 companies might be listed on these more detailed websites – typically ones that rely on advertising.

Recently, some of these dialogs have begun showing options for consent and legitimate interest – two of the legal bases in the GDPR. The introduction of an opt-in for legitimate interest is interesting. First, there are dialogs that have this pre-checked, so users would need to remove that consent. Second, if there is an option to opt in or opt out, is there really a legal basis for legitimate interest? If the legal basis is truly legitimate interest, then it would be because the user would typically expect the data processing as part of using the service. It is questionable whether a user may expect several hundred companies to track information about them. It will be for the ICO and the courts to decide if the legitimate interest claim is allowed to be used in this way, but only if someone brings a case on this topic. Any organisation that chooses to say that setting cookies is a matter of legitimate interest should clearly document why it holds that view.

The PECR have been in use for several years. It is the GDPR that has prompted the largest change regarding cookies and the information provided to users. It is likely that the financial penalties introduced by the GDPR have primarily motivated this change.

Cookies are not the only way to track users, but they are a common technique. This situation will continue to develop as companies look for ways to continue their business practices but comply with the legislation. While the GDPR is a law made in the EU, and the UK GDPR is derived from that, the legislation has implications more widely across the internet for any organisations that control and process data about UK or EU citizens.

14.9 CONSUMER CONTRACTS REGULATIONS

The basic law regarding selling over the internet is contained in the Consumer Contracts (Information, Cancellation and Additional Charges) Regulations 2013. These replaced the earlier Consumer Protection (Distance Selling) Regulations 2000 (and an associated EU directive). The 2013 regulations apply to goods and services ordered over the telephone or over the internet. The Explanatory Memorandum to the regulations notes that 'it will ensure that consumers and traders are clear about the bargain they are making in three main areas: information which traders should provide to consumers; cancellation rights and responsibilities; and measures to prevent hidden costs'. The regulations still apply in the UK despite its departure from the EU.

The regulations require suppliers to provide certain information before any contract is agreed. The detailed list is in Schedule 2 of the regulations. The list includes:

- the name of the supplier and an address;
- a description of the good or service that is being offered;
- the total cost, including tax;
- the delivery charge, if any, and the method of delivery;
- the method of payment;
- the customer's right of cancellation and, where applicable, the complaint-handling process;
- any communication costs for concluding the contract (e.g. the cost of a premium-rate telephone call);
- how long the offer is valid for;
- the duration of the contract, if it is not a one-off.

The information must be clear and understandable and it must be provided, along with all terms and conditions, either in physical form or in a digital form that the consumer can store. The supplier must fulfil the contract within 30 days of its being made unless an alternative date is agreed with the consumer.

The consumer has an automatic right to cancel the contract for up to 14 days after the goods are delivered or, in the case of contracts for the supply of services, for up to 14 days after the contract has been agreed. If the supplier has failed to provide all of the required information, however, the customer has an automatic right to cancel the contract up to 12 months after delivery of the goods or, in the case of services, up to 12 months after the date of the contract. The supplier must reimburse the customer within 14 days of the cancellation, with some conditions specified in the regulations about when the 14 days start.

The right to cancel does not apply in certain cases, such as customised products, newspapers and magazines. Also, cancellation does not apply to a digital download, such as an online movie rental, if the content is downloaded. To protect the consumer in this situation, they are asked to confirm that they understand that cancellations are not possible once the download starts.

As with other online protections, such as those for email marketing and cookies, there is a protection for pre-checked items. A consumer cannot be charged if an item is added to their purchase that they did not explicitly select. For example, if a customer is buying technical equipment, it is not permitted to automatically add insurance cover for the item. It is permitted to offer the insurance cover to the consumer as part of the process and they can choose to accept the offer, but it cannot be automatically added.

FURTHER READING

The various items of UK legislation, and explanatory notes about them, can be found at:
https://www.legislation.gov.uk

For an article that provides a starting point on the issue of young people being exposed to harmful information online, see:
'Tech Giants Targeted in Harmful Content Crackdown' (2022) BBC. https://www.bbc.co.uk/news/technology-60264178.

Guidance notes on how the Defamation Act 2013 applies to websites can be found at:
Defamation Act 2013: Guidance and FAQs on Section 5 Regulations (2014) Ministry of Justice. https://assets.publishing.service.gov.uk/government/uploads/system/uploads/attachment_data/file/269138/defamation-guidance.pdf.

The consumer site Which? provides a useful discussion of online selling:
'Consumer Contracts Regulations' (2021) Which? https://www.which.co.uk/consumer-rights/regulation/consumer-contracts-regulations.

The website of the Information Commissioner's Office can be consulted to see fines that have been levied for breaches of the regulations around spam:
https://ico.org.uk

The website also has a good discussion of the PECR:

'Guide to Privacy and Electronic Communications Regulations' (n.d.) Information Commissioner's Office. https://ico.org.uk/for-organisations/guide-to-pecr.

And it has guidance on direct marketing:

Information Commissioner's Office (2018) *Direct Marketing*. https://ico.org.uk/media/for-organisations/documents/1555/direct-marketing-guidance.pdf.

The IWF's website is:

https://www.iwf.org.uk

For details of issues dealt with by the IWF, see:

'2021 Trends and Data' (2021) Internet Watch Foundation. https://annualreport2021.iwf.org.uk/trends.

Although it dates from 1997, the following reference is a valuable and comprehensive source of information. It uses the old term 'child pornography' rather than the current term 'child sexual abuse materials':

Akdeniz, Y. (1997) 'Governance of Pornography and Child Pornography on the Global Internet: A Multi-layered Approach'. In Edwards, L. and Waelde, C. (eds), *Law and the Internet: Regulating Cyberspace*. Hart Publishing, Oxford. Available at https://www.cyber-rights.org/reports/governan.htm.

For details of Justin Bieber's lawsuit, see:

Spangler, T. (2022) 'Justin Bieber Files $20 Million Defamation Lawsuit Against Two Twitter Users Over Sexual Assault Allegations'. *Variety*. https://variety.com/2020/digital/news/justin-bieber-lawsuit-twitter-sexual-assault-defamation-1234691102.

A summary of the UK spam case referred to in Section 14.7.1 can be found at:

'Firm "Ordered to Pay Spam Costs"' (2007) BBC. http://news.bbc.co.uk/1/hi/technology/6423113.stm.

The Robert Soloway case mentioned in Section 14.7.2 is described in more detail online:

Gohring, N. (2008) 'Top Spammer Sentenced to Nearly Four Years'. PCWorld. https://www.pcworld.com/article/148780/spam.html.

15 COMPUTER MISUSE

After studying this short chapter, you should:

- *understand the legal position regarding the misuse of computers and how common offences are handled under the law;*
- *appreciate why the law has had only a limited effect on the extent of computer misuse.*

15.1 THE PROBLEM

In recent years, the public (or, at least, the media) has been much more concerned about the misuse of the internet than about the more general misuse of computers. Nevertheless, crimes committed using computers form a significant proportion of so-called white-collar crime and it has been necessary to introduce legislation specifically aimed at such activities. Until 1990, when the Computer Misuse Act (CMA) was passed, hacking – that is, gaining unauthorised access or attempting to gain unauthorised access to a computer – was not in itself an offence. Attempts were made to convict hackers of stealing electricity but the quantity of electricity involved was minute and impossible to measure precisely. Courts were reluctant to convict and, even if a conviction was obtained, the penalty was trivial.

As a result of the Court of Appeal decision in 1988 to uphold the appeal of two people who had hacked into private mailboxes, legislation to tackle computer crime was brought forward remarkably quickly, resulting in the CMA in 1990. The internet, although becoming widely used for email, was little known to the general public in 1990 and the CMA did not attempt to address issues arising from its misuse. The arrival of the World Wide Web and the enormous growth in the importance of the internet during the 1990s made it necessary to address some issues, such as denial-of-service attacks, that were not covered by the CMA, and this was done in the Police and Justice Act 2006 (PJA), which made several important amendments to the CMA.[1]

It is a good general principle that legislation should not be introduced to deal with special situations that already fall within the purview of more general laws. For this reason, the CMA does not address some topics, in particular computer fraud, that are better dealt with by more general legislation.

---

1 A denial-of-service attack is an attack on a website in which it is flooded with so many requests for service that either the links to the site or the site itself are no longer able to respond to legitimate requests. Such attacks have become extremely common.

15.2 THE COMPUTER MISUSE ACT 1990

The CMA created three offences that can briefly be described as:

- unauthorised access to a computer;
- unauthorised access to a computer with intention to commit a serious crime;
- unauthorised modification of the contents of a computer.

We shall look at each of these in more detail below. It is important to note that the offences are committed if either the computer in question or the offender (or both) are in the UK at the time of the offence. This means that someone who hacks into a computer in the UK or infects it with a virus from anywhere in the world is guilty of a criminal offence and can, in principle, be prosecuted in the UK.

Section 1 of the CMA states that:

a person is guilty of an offence if

1. he causes a computer to perform any function with intent to secure access to any program or data held in any computer; *and*
2. the access he intends to secure is unauthorised; *and*
3. he knows at the time when he causes the computer to perform the function that that is the case.

This is called the **unauthorised access** offence. It was originally punishable by a fine of up to £5,000 or up to six months' imprisonment but the PJA increased the possible prison sentence to two years.

There are several points that need to be emphasised:

- A person can only be guilty of the offence if they intend to gain unauthorised access and know, or should know, that the access is unauthorised. In other words, you cannot be guilty of the offence by accident.
- The wording of the Act makes it clear that a person who is authorised to access some programs or data on a computer is guilty of the offence if they attempt to gain access to other programs or data to which they are not authorised to have access.
- It is no defence to claim that no harm was done. The attempt to gain unauthorised access itself constitutes the offence.

Section 2 of the Act is concerned with gaining unauthorised access to a computer with the **intention of committing a more serious offence**. A blackmailer might attempt to gain unauthorised access to medical records, for example, in order to identify people in prominent positions who have been treated for sexually transmitted diseases, with a view to blackmailing them. A terrorist might try to get access to a computer system for air traffic control with a view to issuing false instructions to pilots in order to cause accidents to happen.

The need for this offence arises because, if a criminal were apprehended as a result of unauthorised access before committing the more serious offence, it would otherwise not be possible to prosecute them for the serious offence, even though there might be ample evidence to show what they intended to do. This offence carries a penalty of up to five years' imprisonment or an unlimited fine.

Section 3 of the Act relates to **unauthorised modification** of the contents of a computer. It states that:

a person is guilty of an offence if

1. he does any act which causes an unauthorised modification of the contents of any computer; *and*
2. at the time when he does the act, he has the requisite intent and the requisite knowledge.

The Act then goes on to explain that:

the requisite intent is an intent to cause a modification of the contents of any computer and by so doing

1. to impair the operation of any computer; *or*
2. to prevent or hinder access to any program or data held in any computer; *or*
3. to impair the operation of any such program or the reliability of any such data.

Furthermore, the Act goes on to make clear that it is not necessary to have any particular computer or any particular program or data in mind. Like the offence under Section 2, this offence originally carried a maximum penalty of five years' imprisonment and/or an unlimited fine, but again the PJA increased both.

It is the offence created by Section 3 that gives the Act its power. For example, it makes each of the following a criminal offence:

- intentionally spreading a virus, worm or other pest;
- encrypting a company's data files and demanding a ransom for revealing the key required to decrypt them;
- concealed redirection of browser home pages;
- implanting premium-rate diallers (i.e. programs that replace the normal dial-up code for a computer with the code for a premium-rate service).

15.3 AMENDMENTS TO THE COMPUTER MISUSE ACT

In 2004, the All-Party Parliamentary Internet Group (now part of the All-Party Parliamentary Group on Broadband and Digital Communication and previously the Communications Group), a group of British Members of Parliament and members of the House of Lords, carried out a review of the workings of the CMA (see the Further Reading section). It took evidence from a large number of individuals and organisations, including BCS and the Institution of Electrical Engineers (now the Institution of Engineering and Technology), many of whom urged the need to extend the Act to include many more specific offences.

The group concluded that the Act needed comparatively little modification. It recommended an additional offence of 'impairing access to data', which could be used to prosecute the perpetrators of denial-of-service attacks, which cannot always be prosecuted under Section 3 of the Act. It also recommended an increase from six months to two years in the maximum prison sentence for the unauthorised access offence. The recommendations of the group were largely accepted by the government and implemented in the PJA, which made a number of important amendments to the CMA.

First, the penalties for the basic offence of unauthorised access were increased. The maximum penalty on summary conviction (i.e. conviction in a magistrates' court) was increased to imprisonment for up to twelve months (six months in Scotland) and/or a fine of up to £5,000. Under the CMA, the basic offence could only be dealt with in a magistrates' court. The PJA allows for trial in a Crown Court (i.e. before a judge and jury), with a maximum prison sentence of two years. The main purpose of the change was to make it apparent that Parliament regarded the offence as a serious one. It also had the side-effect of making the offence an extraditable one – that is, a person in Britain charged with committing the offence in another country could be sent by a British court to stand trial in that country.

Second, the PJA amends the offence defined in Section 3 of the CMA so that it covers unauthorised acts with intent to impair, or with recklessness as to impairing (i.e. not caring that they might impair), the operation of any computer. The point of this change is that it removes the requirement that the hacker has modified something. Thus it covers denial-of-service attacks, where the operation of the targeted computer is impaired not by modifying its contents but by flooding it with messages or other requests. The maximum penalty for the new offence on summary conviction is the same as for unauthorised access but on indictment (i.e. in a Crown Court) it is raised to 10 years' imprisonment and/or an unlimited fine. The maximum penalty is intended to recognise the fact that such attacks may be intended to compromise a nation's security or to damage a large company permanently.

Third, the PJA introduces a new offence of 'making, supplying or obtaining articles for use in computer misuse offences'. This offence is designed to attack the growing market in hackers' toolkits – sets of software tools that facilitate the unauthorised penetration of computer systems. The penalties are the same as for unauthorised access.

Section 41 of the Serious Crime Act 2015 made a number of amendments to the CMA. By far the most important is the creation of a new criminal offence of carrying out 'unauthorised acts causing, or creating risk of, serious damage'. The maximum sentence is 14 years, unless the offence created a significant risk of serious damage to human welfare or national security, in which case the offender is liable to imprisonment for life. This is intended to cover activities that disrupt the functioning of such systems as air traffic control, water supply and health services.

In May 2021, the Home Secretary announced a formal consultation that would lead to a review of the CMA. At the time of writing, no report of the review has been released. A number of responses to the consultation expressed concern that the wording of the CMA inadvertently means that some legitimate activities carried out by cybersecurity, threat intelligence and counter-fraud professionals to prevent and detect cybercrime potentially fall within the scope of its offences.

15.4 OPERATION OF THE COMPUTER MISUSE ACT

The CMA has been used to prosecute a significant number of high-profile cases successfully. Some examples are:

- On 16 May 2013, at Southwark Crown Court, Ryan Cleary and three other men were sentenced for offences under the Act. During a three-month period in 2011, the group had hacked into the websites of Sony, News International, PBS and Fox, among others, and carried out denial-of-service attacks on the various sites, including those of the UK Serious Organised Crime Agency and the CIA. Cleary was sentenced to 32 months, and two other men to 30 months and 24 months respectively. The fourth, who at the age of 18 was the youngest member of the group, was sentenced to 20 months in a young offenders' institution.

- James Jeffery hacked into the website of the British Pregnancy Advisory Service and acquired the records of some 10,000 women who had had pregnancies terminated. In April 2012, he was sentenced to 32 months in prison. He had been threatening to publish the information on the web.

- In January 2021, Kim Doyle, a former RAC employee, and William Shaw, a director of TMS (a claims management company), pleaded guilty at Manchester Crown Court to charges of conspiracy to secure unauthorised access to a computer. Doyle had accessed road accident data such as names, telephone numbers and registration numbers, which she was not authorised to access, and had passed the data to Shaw, whose company then used the data to make nuisance sales calls. They were each sentenced to eight months' imprisonment, suspended for two years, and ordered to carry out 100 hours' unpaid work and contribute £1,000 to costs. Confiscation orders – that is, orders to pay back profits made from their criminal activities – were also made against them. Doyle was required to pay £25,000 and Shaw £15,000. This case was brought by the Information Commissioner's Office, which would normally bring cases of this nature under the Data Protection Act 2018 (see Chapter 13). The decision to proceed under the CMA is thought to have been because it makes a wider range of penalties available to the court.

Notwithstanding a few such high-profile cases, there is a general feeling that given the extent of hacking and the number of viruses and other malware in circulation, these figures are extraordinarily low. In the years from 2008 to 2018 inclusive, only 488 defendants were proceeded against in England and Wales for offences under the Act, an average of just over 44 per year.[2] The number of prosecutions brought in the Crown Court would be much lower.

2   G. Corfield, 'Guilty of Hacking in the UK? Worry Not: Stats Show Prison is Unlikely', *The Register* (2019), https://www.theregister.com/2019/05/29/computer_misuse_act_prosecutions_analysis.

There are a number of reasons for this low number of prosecutions:

- A company that has suffered an attack that constitutes an offence under the CMA will often prefer to avoid the adverse publicity that could result from a trial, particularly since the rules of the court might prevent it rebutting such publicity. A bank, for example, might be reluctant to see an apparent security weakness publicised because this might cause it to lose customers or expose it to the risk of further attacks. In other words, by prosecuting a company risks further losses and there is little likelihood of any significant gain.

- Since the police do not have the resources or the expertise to investigate more than a tiny fraction of the cases, the decision to prosecute would almost certainly mean devoting much management time to the case and calling in external experts, whose fees would be high.

- Many prosecutions under the Act have failed because of legal technicalities.

- In many cases, the perpetrators of offences outlawed by the Act come from outside the UK, from countries that do not have the resources or, on occasion, the will to take action against the offenders – or indeed, in some cases, encourage and support them.

- Where convictions have been obtained, the sentences imposed have been at the lower end of those that the Act provides for and have not reflected the seriousness of the offences.

- Far more publicity has been given to cases in which the defendant was acquitted or received a very light penalty than to those in which the defendant was convicted and sentenced appropriately. Thus, for example, in 1993 at Southwark Crown Court, Paul Bedworth, then 18, who had hacked into and made changes to the *Financial Times* database that cost the newspaper £25,000 and had also hacked into systems at the European Organisation for Research and Treatment of Cancer that resulted in it receiving a £10,000 telephone bill, was acquitted on the grounds that he was addicted to hacking. This verdict received a great deal of publicity but much less publicity was given to the fact that two men arrested with Bedworth were each sentenced to six months' imprisonment. (The acquittal of Bedworth was widely held to be perverse – the jury seems to have ignored the judge's instructions.)

The well-publicised case of Gary McKinnon served further to muddy the waters. McKinnon admitted gaining unauthorised access to US defence computers from the UK and causing them to become temporarily inoperable, although he denied malicious intent. He claimed that his motivation was to reveal information about 'free energy' and UFOs that was being deliberately suppressed by the USA. Following indictment in 2002, the USA sought his extradition. He fought against this, asking to be tried in the UK and claiming that, because he had Asperger's syndrome, it would be a violation of his rights under the European Convention on Human Rights to extradite him to the USA. Every court hearing ruled against him but a massive popular campaign, founded on anti-American feeling and opposition to the 2003 extradition treaty between the UK and the USA, led the Home Secretary to withdraw the extradition order in 2012, and it was subsequently announced that McKinnon would not be prosecuted in the UK. Thus, a confessed law-breaker, who had committed serious damage to computer systems in a friendly foreign country, was allowed to avoid trial.

15.5 COMPUTER FRAUD

Computer fraud involves manipulating a computer dishonestly in order to obtain money, property or services, or to cause loss. Most of the techniques that are used are much older than computers. Such tricks as placing fictitious employees on a payroll or setting up false supplier accounts and creating spurious invoices are still the commonest type of fraud, as they were before computers appeared. The introduction of computers has made it possible to carry out more spectacular frauds and, because of the reluctance that many people have to question a computer's output, has perhaps made it less likely that these will be uncovered. Nevertheless, the offences are the same as before.

The law relating to fraud in England, Wales and Northern Ireland is largely contained in the Fraud Act 2006, which substantially clarified what had been a complicated and confused area of the law. It also removed several technical problems related to cases of fraud where a computer was involved. There is thus nothing special about fraud cases in which a computer has been involved. That having been said, it is important to realise that the collection and preservation of evidence generated by, or arising from, computer systems requires specialised expertise. The risks of naively relying on computer-generated evidence are clearly exposed by the Horizon case (see the Further Reading section). The Horizon system, developed by Fujitsu, was introduced by the Post Office in 1999 to handle the finances of the sub-Post Office network. Over the following 14 years, the Post Office prosecuted 736 sub-postmasters and sub-postmistresses based on information from the system that appeared to show substantial sums of money going missing from the post offices concerned. Seven hundred people were given criminal convictions and some jailed. Starting in 2019, the Criminal Cases Review Commission has been reviewing these convictions, which in almost all cases so far considered have been quashed, as the individuals were innocent and the computer system was at fault. Immense damage was suffered by the individuals concerned and the compensation that the Post Office must pay is enormous.

In Scotland, there is and always has been a single common law offence of fraud. It has not been felt necessary to introduce a statutory offence.

FURTHER READING

The text of the CMA, including subsequent amendments, is available from:
https://www.legislation.gov.uk/ukpga/1990/18/contents

The first five sections (1, 2, 3, 3ZA and 3A) are fairly easy to read but the succeeding sections, while necessary, are highly technical (in the legal sense) and relate to questions of jurisdiction and mechanisms for enforcing the Act.

The Crown Prosecution Service has published guidance for prosecutors considering prosecutions under the CMA. This can be found at:

'Computer Misuse Act' (2020) Crown Prosecution Service. https://www.cps.gov.uk/legal-guidance/computer-misuse-act.

The All-Party Parliamentary Internet Group's review of the CMA can be found at:

All-Party Internet Group (2004) *Revision of the Computer Misuse Act: Report of an Inquiry by the All Party Internet Group.* https://www.cl.cam.ac.uk/~rnc1/APIG-report-cma.pdf.

The Home Office's call for responses to the 2021 consultation on the CMA can be found at:

'Computer Misuse Act 1990: Call for Information' (2021) Gov.uk. https://www.gov.uk/government/consultations/computer-misuse-act-1990-call-for-information.

The following article, although now somewhat dated, gives a thoughtful analysis of the CMA in more depth than has been possible in this chapter:

MacEwan, N. (2008) 'The Computer Misuse Act 1990: Lessons from Its Past and Predictions for Its Future'. *Criminal Law Review,* Vol. 12, 955–967. Available at http://usir.salford.ac.uk/15815/7/MacEwan_Crim_LR.pdf.

Cases brought under the CMA rarely involve legal subtleties and are therefore usually only reported in newspapers rather than in law journals. The resulting reports are usually rather superficial. Newspaper reports about the cases mentioned in Section 15.4 can readily be found by typing the name of the accused into a search engine. In the case of Gary McKinnon, however, there is a huge amount of material on the internet, most of it biased in one direction or another. Two court judgements that are readily available and that give some idea of the issues can be found at:

McKinnon v Government of the United States of America and Another [2008] UKHL 59. https://www.publications.parliament.uk/pa/ld200708/ldjudgmt/jd080730/mckinn-1.htm.
The Queen on the Application of Gary McKinnon v Secretary of State for Home Affairs [2009] EWHC 2021. https://www.bailii.org/ew/cases/EWHC/Admin/2009/2021.html.

There is a great deal of material available about the Horizon case. The following article is a good introduction:

'Marshall Spells It Out: Speech to University of Law' (2021) Post Office Trial. https://www.postofficetrial.com/2021/06/marshall-spells-it-out-speech-to.html.

APPENDIX
SAMPLE CONTRACT OF EMPLOYMENT

In what follows, angle brackets (< >) indicate text that is specific to an individual contract (e.g. the employee's name) while square brackets ([ ]) indicate commentary that does not form part of the contract.

CAMBRIAN CONSULTANTS LIMITED

Contract of Employment for Permanent Professional Employees below the Rank of Director

This contract of employment is made between *<employee name>* ('the Employee') and Cambrian Consultants Limited of *<address>* ('the Company').

1. This contract shall become effective on *<start date of the employment>* and shall subsist until it is terminated by the other party as provided below. No earlier period of employment counts for such purposes.

2. This contract supersedes all other contracts or agreements between the parties, whether oral or written.

   [As usual, the contract needs to make sure that things that may have been said during negotiations have no legal weight. This contract fulfils the requirements for the compulsory principal statement (see Section 9.9) of employment terms required for all employees by employment law.]

3. The Employee shall be employed as a *<job title>* (grade *<A to F>*) at an initial salary of *<starting salary>* pounds per annum, which shall be paid monthly in arrears, no later than the last day of the month. This grade and salary will be reviewed after the first six months of employment and annually thereafter.

4. The Employee's normal place of work shall be the Company's premises located at *<full address of place of work>*. The Employee may be required from time to time to work elsewhere; in such cases travel and subsistence expenses shall be payable in accordance with the Company's usual rates and procedures.

5. Normal office hours shall be from *<start time>* to *<end time>*, on *<start day>* to *<end day>*, with *<duration>* break for lunch. The Employee shall normally work these hours, or such other hours as may be agreed with the Company, and may from time to time be required to work longer hours.

6. The Employee shall be entitled to 24 days' annual paid holiday per calendar year, in addition to statutory and bank holidays. Holiday entitlement can only be carried over from one calendar year to the next with the written permission of a director or authorised manager. For employees starting or terminating their employment during the year, holiday entitlement is accrued at the rate of two days per complete calendar month; employees who have holiday entitlement outstanding when their employment terminates shall be entitled to a payment in lieu of one 1/240th of their annual salary for each complete day of holiday outstanding. The Company also provides the statutory minimum leave for maternity and paternity and other similar such rights.

7. The duties of the Employee shall be such as are from time to time assigned to <Employee's pronoun> by the Board of Directors or by authorised management. No collective arrangements, including those negotiated by a trade union, are part of the employment. Where the Company considers training to be necessary, it will make arrangements for, and pay for, such training.

8. After the Employee's first month of completed service, the contract of employment may be terminated by either party giving one week's notice in writing to the other for each year of the Employee's completed years of service, subject to a minimum of four weeks and a maximum of twelve weeks.

   [There are lots of other ways that notice conditions may be specified but the above is the legal minimum. It is quite common for all employees above a certain grade or with more than one year's service to be on three months' notice. Some contracts also start with a probationary period.]

9. The Company does not operate any pension scheme other than auto-enrolment and its provider is <name of pension provider>.

   [It is a legal requirement that all employers offer auto-enrolment pensions although employees may choose to opt out.]

10. In the event of the Employee being unable to work due to sickness or injury, the Company will pay the Employee's full basic salary for a period of eight weeks. Thereafter the Employee will be entitled to statutory sick pay in accordance with the statutory sick pay scheme, up to the expiry of 28 weeks from the first notification of the incapacity.

    [Sick pay can be an expensive business.]

11. All intellectual property developed by the Employee as part of <Employee's pronoun> employment shall be the property of the Company and the Employee shall, at the request of the Company and at its expense, undertake any actions necessary to confirm such ownership, including but not limited to the filing of patent applications.

12. Unless otherwise agreed by the Company, the Employee shall treat as confidential all information <Employee's pronoun> acquires as a result of the employment, unless and until that information enters the public domain. In particular, the Employee shall obtain the permission of the Company before publishing any material arising from the employment, such permission not to be unreasonably withheld. The obligation of confidentiality shall continue for a period of five years following the termination of the employment.

13. The Employee shall at all times act in good faith and in such a way as to promote the best interests of the Company.

14. The Employee shall abide by all the rules and procedures promulgated within the Company.

15. The Employee shall not make any financial commitment on behalf of the Company except as duly authorised.

16. The Employee shall not, for a period of twelve months following the termination of the employment, solicit business from, or otherwise approach, any client of the Company, except with the prior agreement in writing of the Company.

17. The Employee shall not, for a period of twelve months following the termination of the employment, entice or seek to entice any employee of the Company to leave its employment, except with the prior agreement in writing of the Company.

18. The Employee shall abide by any additional conditions that may from time to time be imposed as a result of the Company's contracts with its clients.

19. At the request of the Company, the Employee shall apply for, and maintain, professional registration and corporate membership of an appropriate professional body.

20. The Employee shall ensure that *<Employee's pronoun>* dress and personal appearance are appropriate to the environment in which *<Employee's pronoun>* is working.

21. The Employee accepts that *<Employee's pronoun>* has a responsibility for the health and safety of all employees and shall abide by all health and safety regulations promulgated by the Company and its clients.

22. An Employee who believes that *<Employee's pronoun>* has a grievance against the Company shall, in the first instance, raise the matter in writing with the Managing Director, who will endeavour to settle the matter to the Employee's and the Company's satisfaction. If the matter cannot be satisfactorily resolved in this way, the Employee and the Managing Director shall each submit to the Chair of the Board of Directors a written statement of the grievance and the efforts made to resolve it. The decision of the Chair shall be final.

23. Full details of the Company's disciplinary procedures are provided in the staff handbook.

Signed .... (Director)
for and on behalf of Cambrian Consultants Limited
Date ....

Signed .... (the Employee)
Date ....

INDEX

www.ingramcontent.com/pod-product-compliance
Lightning Source LLC
Chambersburg PA
CBHW082032230326
41599CB00056B/6270